T3-BNI-878

WITHDRAWN

COMMUNIST REFORMATION

Edited by G. R. Urban

COMMUNIST REFORMATION

Nationalism, internationalism and change in the world Communist movement

St. Martin's Press
New York

This symposium, with the exception of the chapter by Manuel Azcárate, consists of dialogues broadcast in 1978 and 1979 by the Radio Free Europe Division of RFE/RL Inc., with whose kind cooperation it is here published.
The chapter by Manuel Azcárate is reproduced by permission of *Encounter*.

The use of diacritical marks in this volume is restricted to words and names occurring in French, German, Italian and Spanish.

© RFE/RL Inc. 1979
All rights reserved. For information, write:
St. Martin's Press, Inc., 175 Fifth Avenue, New York, N.Y. 10010
Printed in Great Britain
First published in the United States of America in 1979
Library of Congress Catalog Card Number 79–5326
ISBN 0–312–15280–9

Contents

The editor wishes to express his gratitude to J. F. Brown for scholarly advice generously given in designing and carrying out the work contained in this symposium.

INTRODUCTION

The 1968 Prague Reform Movement may be profitably looked at from at least four angles of vision. Each offers the chronicler of history a self-contained microcosm, yet only in conjunction can they satisfy the curiosity of a metahistorically inclined observer: What, if anything, does it tell us about the human condition?

If our observation post were on a hill not far above the Hradcany Castle in Prague, we would be conscious of every detail of a welter of Communist-inspired reforms and Communist reformers, each claiming our attention momentarily before the next heaved into sight, and each offering some spontaneous remedy for the ills and abuses of Czechoslovak society. From a slightly more distant vantage point, we would see a deliberate attempt by a number of highly intelligent, responsible Marxists to work out an alternative model to 'existing socialism' and regain the sovereignty of the Czechoslovak state. From a greater distance still the conflict of Soviet and American geopolitical interests alone would remain visible, with more and more of the economic and ideological/cultural detail becoming blurred and rendered meaningless. Finally, we might claim that the Prague Spring was about the liberation of man from a self-imposed bondage of a particularly treacherous kind and its replacement by a new moral and social order. The Reform Movement ended, and was almost destined to end, in Russian occupation because these clusters of assumptions, though rational enough within themselves, were in profound conflict or were simply irrelevant to one another.

There was, in the spring of 1968 (and indeed a great deal

earlier) general agreement in Prague that Czechoslovak 'socialism' stood in urgent need of de-Russification and de-Stalinisation. For a variety of reasons which the following pages attempt to make clear, neither had been set in train even to the extent to which it had in Poland, to say nothing of Hungary. In Prague in 1968 one could make out a case for reforms arguing from the young Marx, the desperate state of the economy, or the liberal-democratic traditions of the Czech lands (Slovakia being a very different matter)—but, in one way or another, the need to reclaim 'socialism' from Soviet mismanagement was widely recognised.

The Prague reforms—if the initial jumble of half-baked ideas may be graced with that name—were not meant to run against the existing system. Nor was it expected, least of all by Dubcek, that they would jeopardise Soviet goodwill, still less that they would be deliberately given, or allowed to acquire, an anti-Soviet edge. On the contrary: labouring under the false, but—within the perimeters of their thinking—entirely reasonable assumption that their Party was a truly independent, fraternal Party wholly unlike those of defeated Hungary or East Germany, many of the reform Communists believed that Moscow would tolerate their ideas—concurring with them at best, at worst condoning them.

Some, indeed, tacitly set out to save Soviet Communism from itself. They felt that by returning Marxism to its Western and (as they believed) libertarian origins and cleansing it of the accretions of a totalitarian Leninism and a counter-revolutionary Stalinism, they were rendering a service to world 'socialism' as a whole, including its unregenerate Soviet offshoot. In 1956 the Hungarians had been punished—so the Prague reformers argued—because they had renounced the Warsaw Pact and attempted to revive a social order which had been 'overtaken' by history. Prague would commit no such error: the continuity of 'socialism', the leading role of the Communist Party, and Czechoslavakia's membership of the Warsaw Pact were not to be put in question.

And they were not. Such indeed was the good or bad (as the case may be) faith of the reformers that on the sensitive issue of political pluralism many of them, while protesting their permissiveness, quietly welcomed the inhibitions imposed by 'existing socialism', because these provided an assurance that the reforms would be held within the confines of the single-party system. Any loose talk about a multi-party democracy was variously dismissed as an invitation to chaos, regression to an inferior social order, or simply too risky, abrupt and premature.

One need say little about the Soviet perception of the 1968 Reform Movement. It is hardly surprising that a coercive, totalitarian regime should be apprehensive about any initiative which might, no matter how remotely, spell internal disintegration. Nor could it be expected that the Soviet leaders would meekly assent to a geopolitical change which seemed to them to be grossly to their disadvantage, since the domestic penalties of the suppression of the Czechs were small, of their non-suppression large, and there was no real danger that the American-Soviet relationship would lastingly suffer if suppression were decided on. The rationale of Soviet hegemony demanded maintenance of the domestic *status quo* just as much as it demanded the non-surrender of territory conquered during the Second World War and the *putsch*-like proceedings which followed in its aftermath. Retreat from Lenin amounted to a retreat from Bohemia, and vice versa. Both were revolutionary ('counter-revolutionary') because, the Prague reformers' protestations notwithstanding, they represented in Russian eyes a frontal challenge to Soviet power.

'The fundamental challenge of a revolution is this: certainly wise governments forestall revolutions by making timely concessions. . . . However, once a revolution is in train it cannot then be moderated by concessions. Once a revolution has occurred, the preeminent requirement is the restoration of authority. . . . *After* authority is restored there is another opportunity to make concessions.'

This justification of the Soviet invasion of Czechoslovakia (and of Hungary in 1956) was written not by Brezhnev, or Suslov, or Ponomarev. It comes from the pen of Henry Kissinger and is part of his indictment of the Carter Administration for the loss of Iran in 1979 (*The Economist*, 10 February 1979). If we accept the rationale of Soviet thinking in 1968, it is hard to accuse the Soviet leaders of having done anything which the United States would not have done in their place under Dr Kissinger.

Indeed, the Johnson Administration, in so far as it was conscious of the geopolitical potential of the Prague upheavals, reacted to them in consonance with the Soviet (and Kissingerian) rationale. To the extent that the Prague Spring was a domestic squabble among Communists, the US was not interested. To the extent that it was liable to upset the results of the Yalta agreement, the US was especially not interested. To the extent that it threatened to interfere with the first round of the SALT I discussions and President Johnson's visit to Moscow, the Prague events represented an embarrassing distraction from the main stream of American preoccupations.

In other words, the Soviet and American perceptions of the Reform Movement were in remarkable harmony, and even though Brezhnev's boast to the (involuntary) Dubcek delegation that on 18 August 1968 he had obtained Johnson's assurance that the US would do nothing to interfere with the Soviet invasion is most probably a fabrication, it is nevertheless true that the US behaved *as though* such an assurance had been hinted at or given.

Even in their display of *non possumus* the two powers had a good deal in common: the Russians in their unwillingness—or inability—to perceive a middle course between military occupation and the full acceptance of the Prague reform programme, and the Americans in their unwillingness—or inability—to see that there were several diplomatic, economic and psychological options open to them whereby they might support the Prague reformers without any danger of provoking a world war.

Among these rival perceptions—each right (and self-righteous) in its own way—the Prague Spring was lost. But was it lost entirely? Eurocommunism, it has been said, may be conveniently traced back to the Prague Reform Movement. While this is a gross simplification—some of the early Bolsheviks were, in theory at least, 'Eurocommunists' (for example, Lenin and Trotsky considered allocating territories to the Anarchists for their social experiment)—it is certainly true that the Prague reforms gave a powerful boost to those West European Communists who had long hoped to see the

Soviet type of Communism reformed from within. Realising that their own access to power was impeded by the image of the Soviet state as a savage totalitarian despotism, they had a legitimate interest in seeing this crippling disablement removed.

The invasion of Czechoslovakia put paid to these hopes but not to the need for an alternative to the Soviet model. Indeed it underlined the contrast between the counter-revolutionary fascistoid character of the Soviet system and that other kind of 'socialism' which Communists of the Western persuasion hoped, and still hope, to install as one more appropriate to Western conditions. Whether Eurocommunism can ever become a viable branch of the Communist movement without turning itself into Social Democracy—in which case it would cease to be even a twig on the family tree—is very much open to doubt.[1] But Prague will at the very least go down in history as consummate evidence that many of those Western Communists, including the Czechs, who had already been retreating from the promise of a millenarian 'socialism' were, in the summer of 1968, irreversibly forced into opposition to the Soviet state, the Soviet Party and the men who led them.

One may, of course, ask whether all this means very much for the cohesion and peace of Western society. The answer cannot be reassuring. The Eurocommunists are small in number, and their roots in their parties and electorates uncertain. Moreover, nothing has happened to challenge the truth of Max Eastman's observation that Western intellectuals who remained cool and sceptical to the (as he thought) progressive efforts of the Bolsheviks under Lenin and Trotsky, rallied with extreme emotion to the USSR under *Stalin*. It is still true that for every Santiago Carrillo, Manuel Azcárate, Jean Elleinstein and Rudolf Bahro there are scores of Romain Rollands, Harold Laskis, Sidney and Beatrice Webbs and Jean Paul Sartres waiting to have their delusions about Soviet society confirmed. One of the great intellectual errors of our century has been to imagine that Soviet 'socialism' attracts because it is free. On the contrary, much

[1] Cf. *Eurocommunism*, ed. G. R. Urban (Maurice Temple Smith, London; Universe Books, New York; 1978).

of its appeal rests precisely on the assumption that Soviet society is purposeful, rigorously ordered and *unfree*. The magnetism of unfreedom for free men appears to be second only to the magnetism of freedom for those who have been denied it. It is, therefore, well to remember that while the suppression of the Czech Reform Movement may have brought many latent Eurocommunists out into the open, it may also have added to the number of those who find satisfaction in the imposition of a 'clean', undisputatious and monolithic order and the power which imposes it.

The Prague Spring is nevertheless a landmark in the history of the world Communist movement. Its significance, however, lies not in its short-lived success, but in its suppression. For while a liberalised Czech Communist society would soon have run into all the mundane difficulties which revolutionary regimes have a habit of encountering the morning after heads have rolled, the 'reform-movement-*suppressed*' will enter Communist mythology with the full force of a promise which has not yet been attained but *is* attainable and waiting to be fought for. On such hopes have Communists built their past successes—on such delusions they have marched, and marched others, to destruction.

There is yet another element, perhaps the most important, which merits discussion. Prague has again taught us something about the limits beyond which coercion, even self-coercion, cannot be pushed. Men who supported Stalinism with enthusiasm and were frequently mired in its worst sins nevertheless reached a point of disillusion where Stalinism, then Leninism, and in many cases Marxism itself had to be renounced and denounced as a dangerous irrelevance. Fathers who delivered their sons and sons their fathers to the NKVD under Stalin now warn us that they were dupes of a murderous tyranny and cry for its destruction. Can so great an evil be washed away by a simple repudiation of faith? Perhaps not. Yet, having wrestled with their consciences for twenty or thirty years, these men have earned the right to be heard. Their story is the psychological ground on which the Prague Spring was raised.

In the end we are left with the question: Is the

Reformation of Communism possible, and if so, is it feasible? But for that to be meaningfully answered we have first to ask: Is *Communism* possible, and if so, is it feasible? Writing in 1844, Marx believed that 'Communism is the riddle of history solved'—the riddle being alienation and history what Marx was writing about. One hundred and twenty-seven years and several wars and revolutions later, one of Marx's most famous, if heretical, disciples, Milovan Djilas, squarely asserted, not only that Communism in the Marxist sense was unfeasible, but that *no* Communism was 'capable of evolving into democracy'.

The history of the 1968 Czechoslovak Reform Movement, spanning as it does the whole distance from Marx to Djilas, offers a rare opportunity for testing Marx in his original, Russified, and re-Europeanised versions against the realities of life in the last quarter of the twentieth century. On the conclusions we draw from it depends our answer to the question whether piecemeal reforms of Communism can in fact lead to a genuine Communist Reformation.

G. R. Urban

Eduard Goldstücker

Kafka Returns to Prague

Prague winter

Urban The conception, birth and first faltering steps of some new departure in human affairs—such, more than the 'finished' facts of history, are the notions that exercise the historian's imagination in questioning an elusive and silent past. Fortunately for the historical record, the preliminaries to the 1968 Czechoslovak upheavals are not consigned to the silence of history. Indeed, speaking as we are near the tenth anniversary of the occupation of Czechoslovakia, of few modern events can it be said with less justification that history is the victor's propaganda. The Prague events are well documented—some would indeed say (bearing in mind *Vom Nutzen und Nachtheil der Historie fuer das Leben*[1]) that they are too well documented for their message clearly to enhance Czechoslovak national self-confidence. Let me, then, suggest that we begin this conversation by looking at the winter which preceded the Prague Spring and more particularly at the intellectual beginnings of the Reform Movement in which you yourself played so conspicuous a part.

I am conscious of the fact that the hopes and frustrations of the Czechoslovak reform Communists are metaphorically encapsulated in your experience of Communism in Czechoslovakia. I am especially curious to know how the profoundly humanistic culture of a scholar of your distinction could, for many years, coexist with the cult and culture of Stalin, even though the two never coalesced.

[1] Friedrich Nietzsche's essay *Of the Uses and Disadvantages of History for Life.*

Goldstücker To start a long story with a telegraphic summary—the intellectual background to the Prague events may be compressed into one sentence: the quick and thorough disillusionment, after February 1948, of a large number of Czech and Slovak intellectuals who, in the wake of the war, had enthusiastically embraced socialism as the promise of a free and democratic way of life.

As you know, the Novotny leadership saw to it that the spirit of the 20th Soviet Party Congress did not immediately reach our country. It therefore fell to the second Czechoslovak writers' congress (held immediately after the 20th Party Congress) to raise the first critical voices against the continuing enslavement of Czechoslovakia as a country and of every Czech and Slovak as a citizen.

The small flame lit at this congress was short-lived and brutally extinguished, but the bitterness of the sentiments which had been voiced there was a warning that a profound disappointment had set in which would not be easily stilled. Here and there, especially in the pages of *Literarni Noviny*, critical opinions continued to be heard, but these too were silenced. For example, Karel Kosik, the Marxist philosopher (still in Prague), was deprived of his academic post and humiliated by a grossly inferior appointment, and Ivan Svitak was expelled from the Party and had a very difficult time of it.

Despite all this, however, and despite Novotny's ability to resist and to suppress demands which were being raised for the regime's de-Stalinisation—including one for the immediate convocation of a special Party Congress to discuss the implications of the 20th Congress of the Soviet Communist Party—disaffection in the country continued to grow. Every section of society had its own reasons for feeling deprived or disappointed, and it was not difficult to see why.

Reading Trotsky the other day I came upon a pertinent quotation from Marx which had slipped my memory. Marx says that the mark of the viability of any economy is society's ability to economise with *time*, and the whole task of socialism, as Trotsky later developed this idea in exile, is so to organise the life of society that less time is spent on the mechanics of living than under non-socialist rule.

Well, the people of Czechoslovakia were made to experience the opposite: every citizen, and especially every housewife, was forced to spend *more* time and *more* energy on acquiring ordinary goods and services than under capitalist society. In other words, we had, historically speaking, moved *backwards,* and we had done so because we had come under the domination of a social order—the Soviet type of socialism—which was in many respects historically backward. That was our problem before 1968, and that is still our problem today.

What we had, therefore, in Czechoslovakia in the early 1960s was the coincidence of a sinking economy and, partly as a result of that, a general unease, anomie, and disappointment in all sections of society. I will not go into explaining why the economy landed us in trouble, for it has been done again and again. Suffice it to say that our economy suddenly began to show what was politely termed a 'minus growth'. We had the distinction of being the first so-called socialist country ever to experience this. It meant that the five-year plan, which had been promulgated only in 1960, had to be scrapped, and, under the impact of the economic collapse, the minds of our leaders were, for the first time, made accessible to the idea of economic reform. Under the dual impact, then, of the crisis of the economy and the 22nd Soviet Party Congress—which had, in 1961, deepened and sharpened the criticism of Stalin—it became possible to circulate fresh ideas with some measure of freedom. Novotny was now compelled to do something about the economy and about de-Stalinisation, so that in December 1962 the Party Congress passed a number of resolutions which created modest elbow-room for reform.

Urban December 1962 was, then—for a convenient date—the beginning of the ferment which eventually culminated in 1968?

Goldstücker No, the intellectual ferment had been in action for some time, but it was given an extra boost when Jean-Paul Sartre, speaking at the Moscow world 'peace' conference in July 1962, made an impassioned plea for the termination of the Cold War. The Cold War, he said, must be de-fused; culture must be demilitarised, and he quoted Franz Kafka as a case in point. It was high time, he noted, that Kafka was judged on his merits and not treated as a weapon in the East–West contest—

Urban —and soon after Sartre's speech you wrote in *Literarni Noviny* (16 February 1963) with remarkable foresight:

> But before this [Kafka's 'demilitarisation'] can happen we must fulfil one very important condition: to see to it that even the weirdest imagination could not apply any of Kafka's visions of bureaucratic chicaneries and cruelties to our public affairs. If the history of our time has proved anything beyond a shadow of a doubt, it is that it was fatally wrong to believe that a new and higher social order could be created without the benefit of humanism and justice, and that great human achievements in any field could be indefinitely loudly advocated in theory, while being trampled upon in fact.

Goldstücker Well, Sartre's speech could not at first be published in Czechoslovakia, but, under our pressure, and with several months' delay, it was finally printed in our papers. I was at the time head of the department of Germanic studies at the Charles University in Prague, and I decided to call a meeting of a specially formed committee of Czechoslovak Germanists to examine the problem of Kafka. I was led by the consideration that while the whole world was reading and commenting on Kafka, and foreign visitors were streaming to Prague to honour his shrines, it was absurd that the country of his birth should not be allowed to take note of his existence. In 1948 a Prague publisher had planned to bring out the complete works of Kafka in Czech translation, and the first volume, *America*, had been printed. But then came February 1948: the print was shredded and the whole plan had to be scrapped—

Urban —a Kafkaesque fate to befall Kafka. But you seem to be referring to February 1948 as though you disapproved of the Communist Party's rise to power—

Goldstücker No, I regarded it as inevitable. What I decidedly rejected, and reject, are the *consequences* of February 1948, more particularly the one-party state and the Stalinist despotism which were partly forced on us by Moscow, but partly willingly installed by the Czech Party leadership under Gottwald.

Urban You are not, I take it, saying this with the benefit of hindsight?

Goldstücker Not at all. I wasn't at home at the time; I was serving with the Czechoslovak Embassy in London, and I returned for my first visit only sixteen months after the take-over, in June 1949. It was then that doubts began to form in my mind. What disquieted me most was not that February 1948 had happened—it had been on the cards that it would—but the blatant imposition of an Asiatic tyranny on a country where, quite apart from the rights and wrongs of imposing tyranny on any country at any time, it was wholly *unnecessary*. For the second time in my life I saw a massive bloodletting of the best brains of my country and, since 1968, I have now been witnessing a third. By what right can a regime call itself socialist which systematically decimates the ranks of its most precious productive forces—its brain power? These were my thoughts in 1949, and these are my thoughts today.

Urban Why do you say that February 1948 was 'on the cards'—that it was inevitable? In 1946 and 1947 Gottwald went about uttering such impeccably democratic, parliamentary sentiments that no Eurocommunist could improve on them in *1978*!

Goldstücker Because between 1945 and 1948 the character of Czechoslovak society as a whole, and more particularly the internal political balance, were reflections of the wartime alliance between the West and the Soviet Union. The moment that ended—and it did end by 1948—the days of the coalition government were numbered. From then on the East–West rift cut across Czechoslovakia, and the collapse of the pre-February coalition was a foregone conclusion.

Of course, illusions of various kinds were being fostered to the effect that Czechoslovakia could stay out of the contest, or could indeed be manoeuvred in a Westerly direction; but after Yalta and the dissolution of the anti-Nazi alliance these were dangerous as well as futile hopes.

Urban Who, to be precise, entertained such illusions—the non-Communist parties, Benes?

Goldstücker Not Benes—he took stock of the international situation back in 1943 and decided to mend his fences with Moscow. After Yalta it was even clearer to him that Czechoslovakia could never belong to the Western sphere of influence. But certain politicians, encouraged by the West, were under the misapprehension that government could be maintained without or even against the Communists. The role of the US Ambassador, Lawrence A. Steinhardt, in keeping such ideas afloat is unquestionably established.

Urban You are not implying that the non-Communist parties—and the Americans—somehow deserve to be faulted for having tried to support the legitimate democratic order against the machinations of Stalin?

Goldstücker Not at all; they were guilty of naivety, but that, mind you, is a cardinal sin in politics. When the twelve non-socialist ministers of the coalition government resigned, they thought they could for all practical purposes force Gottwald and the Communists out of power. Why did they think that? Because they were led by the memory of a manoeuvre which had been successfully practised by governments before the war: when government is paralysed it tenders its resignation to the President of the Republic who thereupon appoints a caretaker government composed of civil servants. This takes all the unpopular decisions which the politicians didn't want to take, and is eventually replaced by another political government. It was with this scenario in mind that the non-socialist twelve resigned in February 1948. The only trouble was that they miscalculated the time and the place, and the character of the Communist Party. I was always astounded by the massive simple-mindedness of the twelve ministers. I knew most of them to be highly intelligent people with extensive political experience. The greater was my surprise to see that they were totally innocent of the fact that for any Communist Party worth its salt the combination of parliamentary *and* extra-parliamentary methods was an article of faith and practice. To have imagined, in Czechoslovakia in 1948, that the simple act of resignation would induce Gottwald to think that he had no option but to resign himself on behalf of the *whole* government was a fantastic piece of political unworldliness! Gottwald lost no time in turning to the streets and the factory brigades, and took power.

Urban Isn't your emphasis on the inevitability of the Communist take-over in February 1948 a rationalisation of your tacit approval of it, even though you are strongly opposed to its consequences? By saying that the February events were the by-product of the disintegration of the wartime alliance, aren't you in fact implying that it is hardly worth our while to examine the circumstances surrounding the February take-over?

Goldstücker No, the disintegration of the coalition in Prague was a direct result of the disintegration of the anti-Nazi coalition between the US and the Soviet Union. Neither Benes's wartime courtship of Moscow, nor the Czechoslovak people's genuine friendship for the Russians was allowed to affect the pursuit of Soviet power.

Urban If, as you say, the February coup was a reflection of the Cold War then emerging, why were Rumania, Bulgaria and Hungary also taken—much before the Cold War got into its stride?

Goldstücker The legitimation of Soviet policy towards these countries was derived from the fact that they were enemy states. We, on the other hand, were allies.

Urban But wasn't Poland an ally, too, and yet she was not spared?

Goldstücker But a very problematic ally. In the middle of the war there was Katyn, the disruption of diplomatic relations between Moscow and the London government—and so on. But *we* were *the* most loyal allies right from the beginning—and indeed a few months after their arrival, by October 1945, to be precise, the Soviet troops left Czechoslovak territory.

Urban Didn't, then, this withdrawal of Soviet troops, and the liberal democracy which was allowed to flourish between 1945 and February 1948, offer rather convincing proof that your twelve non-socialist politicians were perhaps not completely naive in thinking that Czechoslovakia could go on functioning as a democratic republic—friendly to the Soviet Union but independent?

Goldstücker Anything can be adduced as convincing proof if you insist on being guided by wishful thinking, but the state of the real world warranted no such assumption.

Kafka

Urban You have brought me to a point in your story where the debate surrounding the rehabilitation of Kafka became an important factor in preparing the intellectual climate of 1968.

Goldstücker Yes—the small chink opened in the Stalinist armour by the combined effects of our economic bankruptcy and the 22nd Soviet Party Congress was used by some of us for calling, in May 1963, a conference on Kafka. We decided to invite certain Marxist scholars who had either written on Kafka or were preparing to do so. Our purpose was to examine whether there was truth in the stereotyped Soviet allegation that Kafka was a decadent bourgeois pessimist who had nothing to say to socialist society.

Urban My guess would be that east of the post-war divide you must have had some difficulty in finding scholars who had more than a nodding acquaintance with Kafka—

Goldstücker —nodding is the word. When Victor Nekrassov, a Russian writer I respect, was asked, during a tour he was making of Italy, what he thought of Kafka, he was honest enough to admit that he had no idea who Kafka was. But, to do him justice, upon his return to Russia, and feeling rather ashamed of his ignorance, he proceeded to write on Kafka. What sort of a cultural milieu is it in which a finely-tuned and generally well-read man like Nekrasov can spend a lifetime without having so much as heard of one of the world's principal intellectual influences?

Urban It is as though Marx had never heard of Proudhon or Lenin of Chernyshevsky. My own experience of certain distinguished Soviet writers now in the West (I will not name them) bears out what you say. In an age when radio and television are supposed to have made all the world's frontiers highly porous, the success of Soviet cultural isolationism is astounding.

What were the results of your Kafka conference?

Goldstücker The conference made it impossible for the so-called socialist regimes to sustain their rejection of Kafka—they could no longer not publish him. The Poles and Hungarians, who *had* published Kafka selectively, were now prepared to publish him without censorship, and indeed, in Hungary *The Trial* appeared shortly after the conference. Even in the Soviet Union the ban was lifted. East Germany was the last of the dependent countries to follow suit, even though the East Germans required no translation. Throughout Central and Eastern Europe the effect of Kafka was instantaneous. In Russia, people who managed to obtain copies of the limited editions in which Kafka was printed made hand-written copies and had them surreptitiously circulated.

Urban One can see many reasons why Kafka must have seemed sensitive or subversive—'Never mention rope in a hanged man's house', one is warned by an old Hungarian and Czech proverb. But what was Kafka's central offence in the Stalinist argument?

Goldstücker The problem for the so-called socialist guardians of our culture was that Kafka creates a world in which the real and the unreal are inextricably mixed; in which the protagonist never knows whether he has his feet planted on firm soil or whether he is on some sandy substance that shifts to suit the convenience of his masters. In other words, people experiencing the illogicalities and horrors of Stalinism found in Kafka a symbolic expression of their own fears and sufferings.

Urban As one noted victim of the Stalinist show-trials, you had, I should imagine, more reason than most to be intensely conscious of the relevance of Kafka's symbolism.

Goldstücker I don't think one had to go through my kind of experience to do so. Kafka speaks of the condition of man under Stalinism in all its aspects. The moment you open his novel, *The Trial*, you are in the midst of the spine-chilling milieu of totalitarianism: 'Someone must have been telling lies about Joseph K., for without having done anything wrong he was arrested one fine morning. . . .' You are ushered into a world where the accused is never allowed to discover under what law and in the name of what authority he is being indicted; where it is never even clearly stated whether he is, in fact, charged with an offence—except for the minor inconvenience that he is under arrest. It is a world in which the Court is impervious to proof, and a man's innocence only serves to conjure up enormous fabrics of guilt. But neither innocence nor guilt can be proven or disproven, because the Law is secret, the Court never sits, the files are locked away, and the verdicts of the Judges are never recorded. I will not go on, for the story is well known.

In Kafka's nightmare world the guardians of Soviet culture recognised their own, albeit perhaps only subconsciously. Hence their hostility to Kafka, and hence the *imposition* of their hostility on the cultural policies of their Central and East European dependencies.

Only a few weeks ago I attended at the Sorbonne an international conference on Kafka. Efim Etkind gave a paper on 'Kafka in the Soviet Union', and his conclusion was that Kafka for the Soviet citizen is not a piece of fiction but the ground on which he walks and the air he breathes.

He told us by way of a splendid illustration that, well before Kafka was published in the Soviet Union, translations had been secretly prepared and circulated of some of his work without giving the name of the author. A great many readers thought that these clandestine books were not fiction at all but accurate descriptions of Soviet reality!

Urban Whatever psychological reasons may account for the Soviet establishment's hostility to Kafka, those publicly marshalled for his continued suppression were formulated under the ideological slogans of 'alienation' and 'decadence'. What were the issues?

Goldstücker Well, of course, Kafka's Stalinist critics could not say that Kafka had presciently written about Stalinist Russia, much less that there was anything wrong with the Stalinist system. He was, therefore, pilloried as an incarnation of the decadence and pessimism of a declining bourgeoisie. Kafka, it was alleged, was spreading gloom and cynicism—he was not enhancing but retarding the formation of the mind of the socialist citizen. His mordant critique, it was argued, of a depersonalised and dehumanised society was the self-reflection of capitalism entering the terminal stage of its disease. It had nothing to teach socialist society, because the latter was, as everybody knew, marching forward, forever optimistic, and in sole possession of the secret of the future!

Urban No doubt you knew how to explode such sophistry?

Goldstücker We didn't quite explode it but we eventually rendered it ineffective all the same. Kafka's critics, among whom the East Germans predominated (Anna Seghers, incidentally, also attended our meetings, but she was brought there by her love of Kafka and did not participate in the proceedings), were brought to admit that Kafka was a great writer; but they immediately added that as he lived in a capitalist society his work could only be interpreted as a mirror held up to capitalist society. Hence, it was said, he had nothing to impart to socialism, and his work, with all its literary merit, must be looked upon as a relic of history. This was a cleverly evasive formula—a polite way of saying: 'Just keep him out of our hair'.

But that was exactly what we could not do, for, quite apart from the notion of decadence, the more formidable question of alienation had still to be tackled. The alienation of the individual under *capitalism* was, of course, enthusiastically affirmed, but those of us speaking from a more critical point of view insisted that alienation also occurred in a society such as ours—one on the 'march' towards socialism. In my own contribution to the discussion I argued—and after 1968 this argument was frequently quoted against me as proof of my counter-revolutionary tendencies—that a society in transition from capitalism to socialism was especially vulnerable. The conquest of power, I said, created merely the right *conditions* for the resolution of the manifold ills of society, but it did not bring about the resolution *itself*. Indeed, I went on, in the transitional period the individual may well be even more severely affected by alienation than under capitalism, and in my written summing up of the discussion, in May 1963, I re-emphasised that alienation in that period had to be seriously reckoned with.

Urban Given the acoustics of the early 1960s, these were pretty scandalous claims, and I well remember the stir they created.

Goldstücker Yes, almost at once a philosophers' conference was called in East Germany, where some of the polemics against our really laughably commonplace claim that a socialist society was no guarantee against alienation, reached hysterical proportions.

Urban Soviet/Communist sensitivities on this point of alienation always struck me as very Russian and perhaps all too human. In Russian history it has always been regarded as an act of treason not to want to live in Mother Russia (even in the United States it is bad form for a resident alien not to want to become an American citizen). Doesn't, then, the Stalinists' passionate rejection of any idea that the individual can be unhappy under socialism stem from Russian roots, rather than Marxist theory?

Goldstücker A bit of both, I would think. If you are ideologically committed you can admit to no flaw in your system. Let me add that 'counter-revolutionary' was not the only label my critics pinned on me as a result of my work on Kafka. In 1974, on the fiftieth anniversary of Kafka's death, there appeared in East Germany an article by an East German journalist (of unsavoury reputation) in which it was blandly stated that Kafka had always been held in high esteem in the German Democratic Republic. We accept Kafka, the article said, but we reject 'Kafka-revisionists' of the stamp of Garaudy and Goldstücker. (Ernst Fischer, too, used to be included in this list of heretics, but Fischer had died in the meantime, so his name was spared.)

'Kafka-revisionism' is a fine invention which I cherish!

Urban Did the Soviet edition of Kafka make good headway?

Goldstücker A funny thing happened to the Soviet edition on its way from the publisher to the reader. By 1965 a one-volume selection of Kafka's works *was* published. We could never find out the print-order, but it has been estimated that about 125,000 copies were printed, which was, for a population of 240 million, not an excessive figure. Yet there were surprisingly large quantities of this one-volume edition of Kafka in the Russian language to be had at the Soviet bookshop in *Prague*, which made us think.

Well, in the autumn of 1965 Ilya Ehrenburg attended a 'peace' conference in Sofia, and on his way back he stopped over in Prague (he loved the city, and used every opportunity to spend a few days there). We of the Czechoslovak Writers' Union gave him dinner, where I presided. In the course of our conversation we came to talk of Kafka whom Ehrenburg had long considered the most famous son of Prague. The Soviet edition of Kafka was brought up, and I observed to Ehrenburg that it was certainly gratifying to see that Kafka was at long last being made available to the Soviet public. Ehrenburg smiled ironically: 'I have seen a great many copies of the Soviet edition of Kafka in the bookshops in *Sofia*,' he said; 'it seems to me we have published Kafka for the Bulgarians!'

Urban In what respect, to be precise, did your rehabilitation of Kafka prepare the ground for the 1968 Reform Movement?

Goldstücker It deprived of any validity one important pillar of cultural policy—and thereby acted as a curtain-raiser to a wider questioning—namely, the notion that 'decadent' art and literature were of no relevance to socialist society.

Shortly after the Kafka conference we had Sartre in Prague, and we organised with his participation a discussion (later published and translated into several languages) on the whole problem of decadence in literature. I had already argued at the Kafka conference, and I again argued now, that the hazy notion of decadence was being bandied about too freely. We had, I said, to look at it historically and recognise that those great writers and artists who did, for one reason or another, adopt a certain style of expression which conservative critics labelled as decadent were often the creators of new forms of articulation from which later generations, including socialists, would benefit—

Urban —an application of the Marxist notion that new social forms are always born within the womb of the old?

Goldstücker Subconsciously, perhaps. In my summing up of the discussion, I quoted Baudelaire as an example, making clear my conviction that the so-called decadent traditions in literature and art had a valid and important role to play in the culture of socialism.

The publication of Kafka and the debate surrounding his rehabilitation were decisive. They allowed us to advance a few paces and prepare the ground for those who came after us. It now became possible to retrieve the works of the Czech *avant-garde* of the 1920s and 1930s which had been suppressed under Stalin; to reopen the discussion of structuralism in literary history; to rehabilitate the Prague linguistic circle of the 1930s, and so on. And, in the wash of these changes, it also became easier to raise some of those fundamental questions about the character and purpose of socialism which were to find their most vivid expression in the spring of 1968.

Urban You found a way of escaping from the Kafkaesque 'burrow' of Stalinism—using Kafka?

Goldstücker I would put it more modestly—we *began* to see light at the end of the rabbit warren.

War of national liberation

Urban Let me side-track you again for a moment. You spoke of the twelve non-socialist ministers' illusions which led them, in February 1948, to resign from the coalition government in the (as you thought) futile hope of reducing Communist power in the cabinet. You also spoke of the Communist intellectuals' disillusionment with the Gottwald regime after the February take-over. It would appear that all protagonists in your story were political innocents—the Communists no less than their opponents. Was this really so?

For disillusion to be possible there had to be illusions first. But one could, by 1946 or 1947, only sustain illusions about Stalinist Russia if one refused to be influenced by the real world; and this blindness to the real world was the error for which you have just chided the non-socialist ministers in the pre-February coalition. Am I right in thinking that post-war Communist hopes rested on a combination of wishful thinking and a misanalysis of the character of the Soviet system?

Goldstücker You have made the problem sound a little too clear-cut. The young generation, Communists and non-Communists alike, which was emerging from a decade of Nazi rule *was* (in retrospect perhaps unreasonably) hopeful and optimistic, but one has to understand these hopes in the context in which they had arisen. A devastating war was over; barbarism had been defeated—but you were alive, and it was again possible to plan for the future. The architect of victory was the Soviet Union under Stalin—it was predominantly under *its* leadership that the Hitlerian nightmare had lifted. You had, therefore, no reason to question Soviet credentials—indeed you had every reason to trust them.

With the 1949–1952 show-trials, the doctors' plot and the rest, the goodwill was, as I've said, rapidly dissipated. Russification and an oriental tyranny were imposed, and a mockery was being made of socialism. By the time I came out of prison at the end of 1955 disenchantment had reached such virulence that I found my Communist friends infinitely *more* bitter about the regime than I was with four years of imprisonment just behind me.

Urban But it is, is it not, a little astonishing that future leaders of the 1968 Reform Movement—Vaculik, Kohout, Svitak, Hübl, Klima and many others—were at this time faithful supporters of the Stalinist system (I say 'a little' because my surprise is tempered by what the history of heresies tells us about the rise of heretics)?

Goldstücker They were, but the show trials gradually brought it home to them that there was something gravely amiss with the whole system—that splendid words were being used to cover up beastly realities. And it is this discrepancy between words and deeds from which the spirit of rebellion classically arises. Moreover, the bloodletting concentrated, as I've said, on the intellectual brainpower which was being savagely deplete The most fervent dedication to the ideals of socialism could not withstand the onslaught of *these* facts.

Urban I don't want to sound cynical or disrespectful of the sufferings of the men who were victimised, but wasn't it to be expected that the despots' first concern would be to remove any threat to their rule? And that surely meant eliminating two centres of likely infection: people who had shown their courage by resisting other forms of oppression (Katyn and the Warsaw uprising come to mind as examples), and others who were, by virtue of their education and intelligence, almost destined to question, irritate and eventually subvert any kind of tyranny. In Czechoslovakia these two elements largely coincided, which probably explains the Czech intellectuals' special bitterness. But what *does* any dictatorship worth its salt first do when it sets up house against the will of the people if not eradicate the intellectually active elements?

Goldstücker But then it should not claim recognition as the liberator of mankind and demand to be revered accordingly, but show itself in its true colours—as a *colonial* oppressor!

Urban You regard the Soviet Union as a colonial oppressor?

Goldstücker Of course I do!

Urban In 1978 as much as in the 1960s?

Goldstücker One can establish point by point, without special pleading, that since August 1968 the intellectual life of Czechoslovakia has been systematically reduced to that of a colony.

We have to do here with a system which comprises two irreconcilable elements: on the one hand it possesses the prerequisites of a socialist economy (*prerequisites*, I stress, no more); on the other hand, it is also a primitive pre-industrial kind of political system. The two don't go together; they can only be *held* together by a very powerful apparatus of oppression. The single most important force which drives and guides all modern society—brainpower—is, therefore, stultified. It is surrounded by and subordinated to dogma which first renders it impotent and then kills it.

Mind you, this kind of situation was foreseen by Marx. He spoke of the conflict between the *forces* of production and the *relations* of production, and he was entirely right in saying that the productive forces always come out on top, and the obstacles to production are always removed—

Urban —meaning?

Goldstücker —meaning that the Stalinist and neo-Stalinist system is sentenced to be destroyed by its own internal contradictions.

Urban External pressure would play no role?

Goldstücker That may, of course, *help*, but the seeds of destruction are inside the system.

Urban But don't you think the longevity of the system—it has survived for sixty years now despite breakneck modernisation—should temper our expectations? Tsarism, too, was anachronistic after, say, the 1870s, yet it took two revolutions and two lost wars to bring it to its knees.

Goldstücker Tsarist Russia could maintain itself because it was only after the turn of the century that it began to be *fully* exposed to modern technology and large-scale industrialisation. When these did arrive and reached the masses, Tsarism collapsed—

Urban —and I would infer from your reasoning that, as the impact of Western technology and the spread-effect of Western social mores have been infinitely more rapid in the 1970s than they were under the Romanovs, the Soviet Union in our time is on a much shorter fuse than Tsarist Russia was at the turn of the century?

Goldstücker This may well be so.

Talking of oppressive governments before the First World War puts me in mind of a melancholy comparison. Under Austro-Hungarian rule we used to complain bitterly that our two nations were being denied the opportunity to unfold their potential—that we were being patronised, chaperoned, treated as cultural inferiors, and generally kept in a state of national oppression. Well, it is ironic to reflect that the sort of hardship we suffered under the Habsburgs pales into insignificance when compared with Czechoslovakia's current state of colonial unfreedom.

Urban The Soviet leaders appear to have managed to unite against them two formidable elements: the intelligentsia and nationalism. This has taken some doing, for neither the Czechoslovak intelligentsia nor Czechoslovak nationalism was anti-Soviet or anti-Russian—on the contrary.

Goldstücker Oh, our intelligentsia was traditionally very *friendly* both to the Russians and to Russian interests. But let me take this question on wider ground.

What happened in Czechoslovakia after 1938, after 1948 and after 1968 was the imposition on the people, and especially on the Czechs, of a way of life which was totally alien and inapplicable. The overwhelming majority was deadly opposed to it; it could only be enforced by repression. The occupation in August 1968 and what has been done in Czechoslovakia since place a very special burden of responsibility on the Soviet leaders. Not only did they ruthlessly squash a *socialist* reform movement under the transparently false slogan that it was a prelude to counter-revolution, but they then proceeded to hold up to the world 'normalised' Czechoslovakia as a model of socialism. Nothing *less* normal has been seen in history; no greater *disservice* has yet been done to socialism, nor has the meaning of words been more flagrantly corrupted.

Czechoslovakia has been pulled back by a whole historical epoch. Everything we have gained since the end of the eighteenth century has been put in question. While under the Habsburgs it was the language of the nation that was threatened, now there is no hindrance to the free use of the *language*, but what is being *said* in that language has become the instrument of oppression. We are being forced to re-start the whole process of our national emancipation.

Urban It is interesting that you should link the suppression of the Prague Spring with Czechoslovakia's national emancipation. Am I right in detecting in your words a tacit approval of Czechoslovak nationalism?

Goldstücker People in the West tend to pooh-pooh nationalism no matter what it represents, forgetting that the nationalism of an oppressed people is something totally different from the kind of nationalism great powers on the road to imperialism habitually employ as ideological camouflage. Lenin observed that the nationalism of a subject nation contains elements of democracy—hence its struggle for liberation has to be supported.

Urban Are you saying that Czechoslovakia in 1978 is engaged in a struggle for national liberation?

Goldstücker Yes, the people of Czechoslovakia are engaged in a struggle for national liberation of a new kind. The Soviet leaders understand this well enough. My hope is that the Western world, too, will come to understand it.

Urban You told Antonin Liehm in an interview (in *The Politics of Culture*) that Czechoslovakia has had neither the time nor the opportunity to *transcend* the phase of nationalism because at any rate Slovak national emancipation has never been fully attained. 'It goes without saying,' you observed, 'that before nationalism can be transcended it must first be fully realised, and this is an inevitable stage which cannot be skipped.' You said this in Prague in the summer of 1967, little, as I suppose, suspecting that within ten years you would be able to see, and would welcome, Czechoslovakia embracing this missing phase in its history—with an anti-Soviet edge.

Goldstücker I did not foresee it, and I would not have welcomed the prospect if I *had* foreseen it—but now that Soviet action has provoked a nationalistic response, we must see it for what it is in the Leninist sense, and support it.

Let's be clear on one point: the Soviet attitude to struggles of national liberation is one of thorough hypocrisy. Moscow supports them whenever and wherever it thinks it can gain advantage in its global tug-of-war with the United States and its allies, but inside their own empire the Russians are forcing nations which have already fought, and won, their struggle for national emancipation to repeat it all over again. This is my reason for saying that Soviet Russian rule is pulling these nations back by a whole historical epoch. The Russian leaders are *creating* a situation in which opposition to the imposed regime *must*, because it has no other choice, take on the character of a national struggle for liberation. And if you are unenlightened enough to invite upon yourself the hatred of the whole of Central and Eastern Europe, you must expect upheavals. I am, incidentally, as certain as can be that future upheavals will not be limited to one country—

Urban —why do you say that?

Goldstücker —because people learn from experience—especially bitter experience.

Urban Might the impact of Eurocommunism have something to do with your forecast?

Goldstücker Nobody knows what precise conditions will bring about a change, but all the basic prerequisites for it are there. If and when it does come, the Russians will have no one to blame but themselves. *They* are the destabilisers of European security.

Siege society

Urban We seem to be coming back, as one inevitably does in talking of the East and Central European countries' attempts to have a certain détente with the Soviet Union, to the nature of Russian rule and the circumstances in which it was, and is, exercised. Soviet society has been variously described as a 'siege society', 'mobilisation society', 'command society' (and economy)—all stressing different aspects of the same thing. Do these labels correctly sum up the Czechoslovak experience of Soviet rule?

Goldstücker They do—I would personally emphasise the notion of the militarisation of society. The Soviet Union as a whole is governed as though it were a vast army in permanent battle order. A siege of the country is assumed to be either in progress or about to burst upon it—everyone is, therefore, manning battle stations. Soviet terminology expresses this to a fine degree: all the talk is about 'fronts', 'brigades', 'advance guards', 'rear guards', 'struggles', 'battlements', 'gaps' in various defences, 'campaigns'—'there are no fortresses the Bolsheviks cannot take!' and so on. The kind of rigid hierarchy—the 'Yes Sir!' mentality—which governs military life governs the whole of society. Orders coming from above are never questioned—they are executed. Subordinates are there to be subordinated—and they are. In other words, the ordinary Soviet citizen is treated like a conscript—with massive duties but no rights. His role is to obey, and the men whose orders he obeys are the General Staff in the Kremlin. I need not tell you how well this model of society has gone down in Czechoslovakia!

To get the feel of the combined art of militarisation and Russification, imagine a country in which every theatre, every orchestra, every publishing house, every newspaper, the radio and television have annual quotas of Russian works imposed on them which they must print or perform. From top to bottom Czechoslovak life is an enforced imitation of Soviet exemplars.

Urban The Soviet Union is a vast country with a varied population and rich cultural traditions—isn't there some good to be derived from Soviet models? I do realise that when, for example, Nazism was in full flood it was, at the popular level, difficult to appreciate the achievements of German culture, and even the language was looked upon with aversion. But this is an attitude one would not want to support either in its anti-German or anti-Russian variety. Personally, I strongly disapprove of both.

Goldstücker Of course, every nation, every society has something to offer to every other nation and society, and I will yield to no one in my admiration for the monuments of Russian culture. But the Russians *have* made it extraordinarily difficult for us to admire their achievements by *imposing* admiration. And even though you and I would know how not to allow hurt national sentiment to overlap into blanket condemnation, to the majority of people it will not be immediately obvious how Russian tanks and occupation forces contribute to universal brotherhood or the enhancement of culture.

In 1968 Brezhnev made the mistake of thinking, and saying, that in a single generation the Czechs would have forgotten the 1968 invasion, and their friendly sentiments to the Soviet Union would be restored. Not so. Brezhnev may have come to believe his own propaganda—which is always an invitation to disaster.

Urban But didn't he have some historically sound reasons for believing that facts would eventually prove him right, seeing that the Czech people learned to live quite happily and, from the cultural point of view, fruitfully, with Austro-German culture under the Habsburgs and, a generation after 1938, appear to be highly appreciative of current German culture—an interest which is returned by the Federal Republic?

Goldstücker Well, Czechoslovakia in its nexus with the Soviet Union provides us with an example of a situation which is rare in history—a country coming under the domination of one more backward than itself. All the great stable empires—I do not mean meteoric empires such as Genghis Khan's—were built on the fact that the dominating partner, the metropolitan country, was superior and had something to offer to the countries dominated: economic sophistication, cultural development or just peace and security. There were, of course, exceptions, the most famous being the conquest of Greece by Rome; but the Greeks through their superior culture eventually imprinted their learning and values on Rome and, in a sense, reversed the conquest.

The Soviet Union has nothing to offer—economically or culturally—and what it *can* provide in the sphere of security is a Pax Sovietica which no one wants. Initially, while socialism in Czechoslovakia was in its adolescence, we were grateful to the Soviet Union for shielding us. But this protection has changed into ruthless domination which annuls the benefits of past protection.

Urban The Romans, as you have said, were enlightened enough to import Greek men of learning and art to refine their culture and bring it closer to Greek standards which they knew to be superior. Has there been any tendency in the Czech-Soviet relationship either on the part of the Czechs tacitly to export, or on the part of the Russians tacitly to import, 'Greek' teachers from Czechoslovakia?

Goldstücker Oh no, no, no! Deep down in their souls the Russians are nursing a terrible inferiority complex which prevents them from doing any such thing. This, for heaven's sake, would be an admission of inferiority, which would never do!

Urban But it was done—true, in the teeth of great resistance—under Peter the Great and, by fits and starts, after—

Goldstücker —ah, but the 'true' Russians—including, incidentally, Solzhenitsyn—still consider Peter's import of Western ways and Western culture as an egregious sin against Mother Russia: a violation of the organic growth and quintessential identity of the Russian nation!

Urban —even though Peter's reforms constituted, up to 1917, the most significant single attempt to reduce Russia's technological lag *vis-à-vis* the West?

Goldstücker Oh, yes—from the point of view of Russian nationalism, which is, behind the façade of 'socialism', paramount in the counsels of the Soviet Union, Westernisation is a cardinal offence. Don't we both remember that outbreak of Russian chauvinism which engulfed all of East and Central Europe after 1948—nothing being of any value in technology and science that had not been invented by a Russian? The exaltation of Popov as the inventor of the radio and the parallel fall of Marconi; the elevation of Yablochkin and the demise of Edison; the craze surrounding Michurin and Lysenko with their faked genetics?

Urban Indeed one remembers the introduction in Hungary of the Soviet practice of using the abacus as the sole *arrivé* method of accounting, and the simultaneous fall of sophisticated accounting machines which were kept under lock and key, until after Stalin's death, as 'unsocialist' means of technology.

Goldstücker Yes, whether the issue is small or large, the model has to be followed. Of the macro-abuses of recent vintage the federalisation of Czechoslovakia offers a good example. One point in the programme of the 1968 Reform Movement was the federalisation of the country both at the state and the party levels. There were heated discussions as to how this should be done—whether there should be two elements, made up of the Czech lands and Slovakia, or three: Bohemia, Moravia/Silesia and Slovakia. Eventually it was decided by the State Committee for Federalisation, of which Husak was the president (and I happened to be a member), that the Federation should be a dual state consisting of the Czech lands and Slovakia, with the proviso that Moravia and Silesia would be given due recognition in the Czech part of the federation. The date by which the appropriate legislation was to be completed was set: 28 October 1968 to mark the fiftieth anniversary of the foundation of the Czechoslovak state. This target was duly met, and on 1 January 1969 two sovereign socialist republics were created with certain parts of their sovereignty surrendered to the federal government.

It would have logically followed, and indeed it was so planned in 1968, that the federalisation of the Communist Party of Czechoslovakia would be simultaneously set in train. It was essential that the new political balance created by the division of the state should be matched by the federalisation of the Party.

Now—as you know—a unified Communist Party of Czechoslovakia had existed since 1921. After the Second World War the Communist Party of Slovakia was created with its own Central Committee and Politburo, and although this Party was subordinated to the one in Prague, a situation was, in fact, brought about in which Slovakia now had its *own* Communist Party while the Czech lands did not. This is what the 1968 Reform Movement was trying to put right, and the attempt was not immediately squashed by the occupation. Indeed it was after the occupation that a bureau to prepare for the foundation of a Communist Party of the Czech lands was established under the federalisation programme—but the attempt never got off the ground.

Urban Why?

Goldstücker Because—and this is a grotesque story—a separate Communist Party for the Czechs would have diverged from the Soviet model. In the Soviet Union there is one Communist Party for the whole Union, and there are Communist Parties for the Ukraine, Georgia, Uzbekistan and so on, under Moscow's control. But there is no separate Communist Party for the Russian population for the logical though, of course, unstated, reason that the Communist Party of the Soviet Union is under ethnically Russian control, so that the CPSU *is*, in a very important sense, the *Russian* Communist Party.

The establishment of a separate Communist Party for the Czech lands would have fallen foul of the Soviet model, and this could never be allowed. Whether out of a sense of nationalism, political sclerosis or plain immobilism, the Soviet leaders insist that their models must be followed down to the last detail. For a nation rooted in the democratic and libertarian traditions of Western Europe, this heavy-handed exercise of the worst traditions of Byzantium is repulsive and wholly unacceptable.

The need to believe

Urban I am a little hesitant to confront you with a question which has been rendered trite by over-use—but let me ask it all the same because it is germane to our theme. How is it to be explained that men of high intelligence and learning such as yourself and many of your colleagues in the Czech Communist intelligentsia, did not, from the beginning, apply to the Soviet practice of 'socialism', the same searching scrutiny that you apply, and teach your students to apply, to your daily activities as scholars, writers and scientists? Shelves have been written about the intellectual's proclivity to succumb to the lure of power and, especially, to the temptation of totalitarianism (the historian's ambition to *make* history, having *written* it all his life, is apparently particularly hard to resist). The literature surrounding the Moscow show-trials of the 1930s is especially rich in every kind of theory—I don't think we need rehearse the details—yet every time I am faced with a live human being who *did* believe but then crossed the credibility-barrier and believes no longer, I have to ask myself: how *could* he? And the more I respect him for his non-political qualities, the greater my puzzlement.

Goldstücker I grew up between the two world wars—at a time when the Soviet Union was the only country which had successfully completed a socialist revolution and was, in comparison with other countries, weak and threatened. We Communists naturally considered it to be our prime duty to shield this state, and our solidarity with it was so unquestioning that we managed to keep out of our minds everything that was critical of it. And when I say 'keep out of our minds', I mean it literally: our minds were simply not attuned to receiving things we did not want to hear. As I said in another context, the Soviet example endowed us with a tremendous fund of confidence, deep as the oceans, on which we sailed. For example, when André Gide, erstwhile admirer of the Soviet Union, returned from Russia and published, in 1936, his *Retour de l'URSS* in which he expressed his grave disappointment, I, together with other Communists, refused so much as to read it simply because we knew that it did not agree with our views. *Ipso facto* Gide and his book were placed among our enemies. We *wanted* to believe, therefore we did.

Urban Were you after 'religious' certainty?

Goldstücker After *certainty*, though not religion in the ordinary sense. I have recently read an American scholar's book on Huss and the rebellion against the authority of Rome. In explaining why the Reformation *had* to come about, he says in a memorable sentence: 'faith changed into creed'. This is precisely what happened to our critical faculties. Creed is a dangerous quality: clearly, without an ingredient of faith you cannot mobilise masses into action, but excess of faith is liable to degenerate into creed and carry you where you did not want to go. The great human problem is always one of balance: how do you sustain the right degree of dedication—one that is strong enough to inspire but not strong enough to overpower your critical faculties? Smaller problems have broken greater men.

Urban Did you believe the official accounts of the Moscow show-trials?

Goldstücker Oh, yes, I believed them intrinsically. I was convinced that Lenin's Party could do no wrong and say nothing that was untrue. And, of course, to trust the official accounts was made easy for us by highly respectable Western witnesses who had come back from Moscow testifying that—yes, it was all true and correct.

Urban You didn't pay much attention to Western critical opinions which were also much in evidence?

Goldstücker No, no—expressing doubt, or even listening to doubt, was, for us, automatically a sign of being on the side of the enemy; we took absolutely nothing from the enemy.

Urban But surely some of you must have known men like Bukharin personally, or if you didn't know *him*, some of you must have known Boris Souvarine and his early, 1935, critique of Stalin—and one can think of any number of cases where the discrepancy between the abject confessions in the Moscow court-room and the internal evidence you must have had of the personal character, record and ideas of the accused should have aroused your suspicion, even if the poor scenarios didn't?

Goldstücker Our dilemma was *horrible*. But if you believe in your Party as the vanguard of progress and the embodiment of a scientific world outlook, then, faced with a situation where you have to choose between the Party and an individual human being, you will always try to believe and opt for the Party, no matter how close that individual human being may be to you even as a friend or relative. That's the kind of ideological framework we had created for ourselves.

Urban The individual is expendable?

Goldstücker —not expendable, but you are convinced that the individual can *err*, whereas the Party cannot, because it is led by the collective wisdom of the working class—or so we used to think.

Urban The church is always right?

Goldstücker Of course it is! Your reason is switched

off—your faith is riveted to the institution. Our mistake was to project our really *subjective* microcosm onto our perception of human affairs as a whole—to believe that the key we thought we had to the world was scientific and therefore of universal application. The mental reassurance to be derived from this was great—the penalties to be paid for it were even greater.

Urban You have said that the certainty you were looking for was intellectual rather than religious even though you attained and sustained it with all the dedication of faith. But I notice that elsewhere you have used the word 'religion' in another sense, too—not connoting belief in some supra-human deity or order but, going back to the word's Latin origins, as *re-ligio,* that is, indebtedness to our ancestors, our past and, more generally, the idea of continuity in civilisation. To safeguard this 'religion', you have written, is the sole guarantee against our relapse into barbarism.

Why should a man who has dedicated all his life to revolution now stress the indispensability of maintaining our links with the 'chain of generations'?

Goldstücker If you look at the two outstanding manifestations of barbarism in our time—Nazism and Stalinism—you will find that the carriers of both were convinced that they were breaking every bond between themselves and what had gone before them—a past they came to regard as unworthy of them. The Nazis did away with the whole heritage of Christianity and went back to the mythical traditions of an unproven Germanic past: they were *new* men, a *new* species—supermen.

The carriers of Stalinism—the men of the secret police whom I had the misfortune to get to know only too well—also believed that they represented a new type of man—'Soviet man', Stalin's 'special people', a new breed of exalted human beings. I maintain that only people who have cut themselves off from the humanist legacy of mankind are capable of the inhumanities and horrors which we have witnessed in the last half-century. Bestiality arises whenever people shrug off the past as irrelevant, as overtaken by an ever 'new' present which has allegedly nothing to do with the hard-earned experience of earlier generations. There is an Indian proverb which says that every human being should realise at all times in his life that he is standing on the shoulders of his forefathers, and should feel the 'small feet' of future generations already resting on *his* shoulders. The great beauty of scholarship and the teaching profession is that you can try to do justice to this obligation.

Urban Don't American attitudes to history exhibit an analogous assumption—that the past has nothing to teach us? My impression is that the unsettling effect which the United States has on Europeans, and many sensitive Americans too, springs from this lack of a sense of rootedness (Henry Ford I's dismissal of history as 'bunk' is, I suppose, a back-handed compliment to something even Ford's wealth could not buy), and those Americans who suffer from it suffer from it exceptionally badly. 'Footlooseness' and 'future-shock', it has been observed, are preconditions of hypertension and nervous disorder.

In an earlier contribution to this series of discussions (later published in *Can we Survive our Future*?) an American sociologist, Philip Rieff, said:

> America has been a place to which people have come to escape the past; in this sense American culture is the cemetery of many pasts. . . . Barbarians are people without a constraining sense of the past, the mistakes of the past, the follies of the past, who are thus able with fewer inhibitions to attack the potentialities of the present. Therefore what characterises barbarism is an absence of historical memory.

Goldstücker I would not contradict Rieff. The myth that the United States is a 'new' world is still strong in America, and the idea of American 'exceptionalism'—that neither the rules of the past nor the experiences of other countries apply to the United States—was equally strong until the American defeat in Vietnam. Of course, in the United States this sense of owing no debt to the past has never been asserted as a state ideology, much less forced on the citizen with the thuggish methods of the Nazis and Stalinists. One could, and can, freely argue against it.

Urban The American Bicentenary was, to my mind, a

good demonstration that the American people, too, see themselves, and want increasingly to see themselves, as standing on the shoulders of their forefathers.

Goldstücker At the same time, historical amnesia in the United States is still powerful, and I incline to think that some of the American potential for hysteria, which is never far under the surface, is due to this lack of an assured and reassuring place in the continuity of civilisation. Hence also the compensatory braggadocio that what is good for America is good for the world.

Urban 'With God's help, we will lift Shanghai up and up, ever up, until it is just like Kansas city', Senator Kenneth Wherry, an undertaker turned statesman from Nebraska (as George Ball has described him) told a cheering audience in 1940—

Goldstücker —I would wish Shanghai a better fate.

Urban But, coming back to 'Soviet man'—and I'm now flying in the face of one of my earlier questions—let me ask you whether it does not strike you as surprising that the Marxist movement, with its profoundly historical rationale, should have been perverted to the point where the rejection of the past is elevated to the status of dogma? I think we need not go into the controversial question whether there is a conflict in Marx between the concept of revolution and the concept of gradualism in order to answer the narrower question: how did the barbarism surrounding the concept of 'Soviet man' come out of Marx?

Goldstücker The answer is simple: the myth of a higher, Bolshevik species of man was a Stalinist construct which had nothing to do with Marx or Lenin.

Urban But even though the construct itself may be alien to Marx, it has been argued by a great many respectable scholars that Stalinism grew out of Leninism as surely as Leninism derived from Marxism.

Goldstücker Both were the results of the interplay of concrete historical conditions—but there was nothing inevitable about them. They were not the *only* possible development. Bear in mind that the desirability of creating a truly democratic socialism was never lost sight of—not even under Stalin. For sixty years, openly or covertly, Communists have spoken about it and worked for it, but every time it looked as though it might come close to realisation it was nipped in the bud.

What we felt about Stalinism in the 1960s, after the traumatic experiences of the 1950s, was that Stalin had simply eliminated from Marxism its humanistic content, and the crux of our efforts in 1968 was to restore it to socialism. This explains Dubcek's use of the phrase 'socialism with a human face'; and the programme presented to the 14th Extraordinary Party Congress, one day after the invasion, sketched out in detail how this was going to be done.

Stalinism, to tell the truth, was not a deformation of socialism but its downright corruption. Stalin's misuse of language was the grossest confidence trick yet practised on the citizen by any modern political system. You had a democratic Constitution which had never been put into practice; you had government which was no government; you had parliament which was no parliament; trade unions which were no trade unions; 'soviets' from which every semblance of power had been removed. One could go down the whole list of Soviet institutions without finding *one* that did what it was supposed to be doing. What *we* tried to do in Czechoslovakia in 1968 was to inject genuinely democratic content into these atrophied and defunct institutions, starting with the democratisation of the nerve centre of it all: the Communist Party.

Urban Your comments are radical. You come close to saying that the entire socialist system as it was before 1968 was ripe for destruction. Would you, in fact, agree with certain observations Jean-Paul Sartre makes of the same period in his introduction to *The Politics of Culture*, in which he also discusses your own analysis of the shortcomings of the pre-1968 system? Sartre writes:

> The trials, the confessions, the paucity of thought, the institutionalised lie, universal mistrust—these were not abuses; they were the inescapable consequences of prefabricated socialism; no repair work, no patching could make them disappear, and regardless of what team was in power it, too, would be petrified and crushed, despite its good will, unless both Czechs and Slovaks fell upon

> the machine with hammers and pounded like deaf men until it fell to pieces and was ruined beyond repair.

Coming from a man who prepared the ground for your rehabilitation of Kafka and is himself a famous Marxist and socialist, these words carry a good deal of weight.

Goldstücker With all due respect to Sartre, I don't agree with his reading. I was observing the system from much closer quarters than he was, and I don't think he is right in saying that the system was beyond repair. *Much* of the system had to be tossed overboard, of course, and I have never minced words on this topic, but the groundwork was sound enough to make reform a worthwhile undertaking. It was entirely on the cards that a new and much improved regime could be erected on the foundations of the old, and the ideas of socialism could be given a fresh relevance. All preconditions for this existed in Czechoslovakia in 1968.

Urban A system based on pluralism and individual freedom?

Goldstücker Yes.

Urban Pluralism including the possibility of a multi-party system?

Goldstücker It would have tended to develop in the direction of a multi-party system. We certainly weighed it as a possibility, but our immediate concern was to avoid a power struggle and secure the continuity of the leading role of the Communist Party—but a Party reformed from within and responsive to a multiplicity of interests. There was general agreement that this was, under the circumstances, the only realistic way out. Any other alternative would have led to chaos.

Urban When you say that 'the groundwork' for socialism did exist on which a genuine socialism might have been, and perhaps might, in your view, still be built—what precisely have you in mind? Clearly the abolition of capitalism and the nationalisation of private property were big steps forward on the road to 'socialism'.

Goldstücker Marx distinguishes between the nationalisation (*Verstaatlichung*) of property and the socialisation (*Vergesellschaftlichung*) of property. The Soviet system did not develop beyond nationalisation. It is an etatist regime pure and simple, aggravated by a strong admixture of Asiatic despotism.

Urban Lombardo Radice rejects the Soviet model on a similar argument, calling it 'state socialism'.

Goldstücker It is not even that—it is simply a regime that has taken the means of production into state custody and directs the economy and society with command methods. The supposed beneficiaries and participants of the system—the people—are abused and manipulated.

Engels, you will recall, derided those comrades who believed that wherever a public pissoir was nationalised, socialism had been created. Bismarck, he said, nationalised the Prussian railways and created the world's first, and exemplary, social security and health system—but none of this made Bismarck, or Prussia, socialist! The Soviet Union has reached the *preliminary* stage of socialism, and got stuck there. The Prague reforms were an attempt to democratise the Soviet model in the sense of Marx's notion of 'socialisation'.

Urban Do you still believe that a 'socialism' other than the existing Soviet variety is a practical possibility—that it does not entirely belong to the realm of Utopia?

Goldstücker Oh, I still believe it, but only in Aristotelian fashion: as an idea that has as yet never been realised—as 'potential existence'.

A question of legitimacy

Urban Your reference to Aristotle is appropriate: you stress the notion that potential socialism may yet pass into real socialism—which is what you are saying when you refuse to endorse Sartre's claim that the system is past redemption. Your real problems start when socialism becomes institutionalised. The brunt of my talk with Jean Elleinstein[1] centred on this point: there is as yet no example of an acceptable form of socialism. The inhumanities of socialism are said to be due to the peculiarities of the Russian heritage—but what

[1] *Eurocommunism*, pp. 73–96.

is claimed to be good in socialism has yet to be shown to exist.

Goldstücker Oh, yes—the equation is even more involved than that. You will recall that the Swedish Communist Party was one of those that protested most against the occupation of Czechoslovakia. Shortly after the occupation general elections were held in Sweden, and the Party lost votes. I was at the time a visiting professor in Stockholm. One day I had an opportunity of having a long talk with the then Chairman of the Party, Hermansson, and we looked at the election results.

Hermansson told me that his Party had met with a great deal of sympathy during the election campaign, not least because of its support of the Czechoslovak Reform Movement and its condemnation of Soviet intervention. 'People went out of their way to tell us that they would *like* to vote for us, *but*, they added, "we have learned from the unhappy experience of Czechoslovakia that the stronger you are, the greater the danger of Soviet intervention. So, on balance, we will vote for the Social Democrats." '

Urban Not an illogical attitude, but it does mean that the European Communists can do no good—they are damned if they do, and damned if they don't: *support* of the Soviet invasion of Czechoslovakia would have invited the charge that the Swedish Communists were Soviet agents; *opposition* to it threatened to make them electorally so strong as to invite Soviet interest in their fortunes and make them unsafe to vote for. How do the Eurocommunists break out of this Nibelungen-like curse of a guilty past?

Goldstücker By showing that their attachment to democratic methods is absolutely genuine.

Urban But for that to be possible *one* country would somehow have to advance confidence to its Communist Party, and this is the risk no society has yet been willing to take.

Goldstücker True—and that is why it would be of world historical importance for a party such as the Italian to become part of a democratic coalition government, for then it could be shown that Communists of the Western persuasion are genuine, libertarian socialists. This is what the Kissingers of this world do not understand. All they can see is that the Communists have always supported the foreign policy aims of the Soviet Union and not those of the United States. Undoubtedly this has been so in the past, but it need not be so in the future.

Urban But aren't you assuming a little too readily that the Eurocommunist approach to 'socialism' is a well-established and popular trend in the West European Communist parties—whereas I'm not sure that it is? Richard Gardner, the US Ambassador to Italy, made it his business recently to talk to Italian Communists at grass-roots level in various parts of the country, and he discovered to his dismay that most grass-roots Communists were Leninists if indeed not Stalinists. Santiago Carrillo and his Eurocommunist colleagues had a somewhat similar experience with *their* conservative forces at the 1978 Congress of the Spanish Communist Party.

Goldstücker The process of re-educating Communists takes time. The message has to take root and sink in. Large numbers of people do not change their minds overnight. It has always been true, and by now it has become very obvious, that every Communist party suffers from a more or less latent internal split precisely on the kind of issue we have been discussing. The party leaderships, therefore, have to move slowly and with great circumspection for fear of making the hardened Stalinists impossible to reclaim and pushing those undecided about Stalinism into the arms of the Stalinists.

We had experience of this in 1968. After a long series of discussions in the Central Committee between October 1967 and 5 January 1968, Novotny was voted out of office and Dubcek elected. A communiqué had to be issued to tell the public what had happened, but when it came to the point of putting the changes into writing, members of the Central Committee somehow lost their nerve and decided to insist that nothing of any importance had really taken place: an evasive communiqué was drafted which merely said that 'certain measures' had been taken to secure a 'better realisation' of the resolutions of the 13th Party Congress of 1966. Not only that, but members of the Central Committee were given a special warning not to go beyond the words of the communiqué in their public or private statements.

Why was this done? Because the reformers realised that there was, among the Party rank and file, a good deal of 'conservatism'; that announcements of a drastic change might not find immediate support at grass-roots level; and that it was, therefore, best to change ingrained attitudes slowly, protesting all the way that nothing in fact had changed.

When Smrkovsky finally took courage and revealed the facts in our trade union paper, he was severely taken to task for his indiscipline; and when I made a somewhat similar statement in my first television interview as the newly elected chairman of the Writers' Union, a campaign was promptly organised against me in one of the largest Prague factories—ostensibly, and perhaps in part genuinely, by the 'workers'—but led by the factory's Stalinist Director General who was later deposed by his own work force (and is now, incidentally, a member of the Politburo). My point is that the re-education of the Communist Parties is a step-by-step process.

Urban You have, so far, left me with the overwhelming impression that your reforms in 1968, and your and your colleagues' thinking in 1978, contained and contain nothing remotely 'un-socialist', much less 'anti-socialist'—nothing that you could not have raised in the Soviet Union for routine discussion in the early 1920s with complete impunity. Why is it that five decades after the October Revolution and fifteen years after the death of Stalin, the world's strongest or second-strongest power was mortally alarmed at the sight of Communist writers, media men and film producers uttering mildly unorthodox sentiments in a country of contemptible size—one, moreover, which was friendly to the Soviet Union, firmly committed to 'socialism', and willingly incorporated in the Warsaw Pact? There must be some terrible skeletons in the Soviet cupboard.

Goldstücker There are; but before answering your last question let me at once squash the domino-theory type of apologia for the invasion of Czechoslovakia. This is, of course, a much favoured (though seldom clearly stated) Soviet argument which has, alas, been taken over intact by the Western governments—partly, I suspect, as justification for their inaction. It is just not true that, as a consequence of the reform of socialism, Czechoslovakia was going to leave or be eased out of the Warsaw Pact, opening up a chink in the Soviet defences. Our reforms never threatened the power-position of the Soviet Union, because we never threatened to welsh on the alliance. Your talks, in this series of discussions, with Dean Rusk,[1] Eugene Rostow and Senator Pell bear testimony to the fact that we never sought, never received, and were never offered outside assistance. Moscow's reaction to our reforms was the reaction of men in a state of panic. It betrayed, rather typically, the anxiety of a leadership which trusts nothing except the bayonets of Russian soldiers. Here, again, was a demonstration of the militaristic type of mentality at the level, one is ashamed to say, of the regimental sergeant-major rather than the staff officer.

Urban But don't you agree that if Czechoslovakia had been allowed to get away with a liberalised, Westernised type of socialism, the other East and Central European countries would have irresistibly followed suit, and the integrity of the Soviet Union itself might have come under strain as a result of internal pressures?

Goldstücker No, I don't. The Soviet leaders had all the paraphernalia of power in their hands to control the repercussions, if there were to be any, of our reforms. The apparatus of control and repression is an enormous, well-endowed and much perfected instrument in the Soviet state. It would have been more than adequate to allow or not to allow the influence of the Prague events to spread, in whatever form and measure the Soviet leaders decided.

Urban Why, then, this inexplicable fear?

Goldstücker On the military side, the Russians are still trying to fight off a deep-seated sense of inferiority *vis-à-vis* the West and especially the Germans, but their general sense of insecurity—and this is what you are hinting at when you speak of skeletons in the Soviet cupboard—has different sources. It has to do with the legitimacy of the regime.

What happened in Russia after the October Revolution was that, at the decisive moment, Lenin succeeded in

[1] *Détente* (Maurice Temple Smith, London, Universe Books, New York, 1976), pp. 243–261.

finding support among Russia's war-weary peasant masses by promising them two things: peace and land. Lenin alone was capable of making good that promise because the Bolsheviks alone were prepared to touch what to all other parties seemed sacrosanct: private property. But, for the reasons we know, peasant support was quickly dissipated: the Soviet Union came under the red terror, which has been more or less continuous ever since. *How do you govern a country where you know perfectly well that the majority of the people are against you?*

Urban This is the nut no Soviet leadership has yet managed to crack, and one which no regime *can* crack. What it can do is to terrorise the people with all means at its disposal.

Goldstücker Yes, and that is why the Russian people is such an enigmatic and dangerous dragon: it is in *chains*, it *has* been in chains for centuries, and when it breaks its chains it threatens to spread chaos and disaster. In 1968 we discovered to our shock and dismay (because our own contacts with the people have always been extremely close) that the Soviet leaders were *afraid* of the Russian people, but—more shocking still—we also found that, despite their fine theories, some Soviet *dissidents* also lived in fear of the Russian people. Their image of the people was (and is) that of some dark, anarchic, uncontrollable mass—*tyomni narod*—a kind of lava that engulfs and drowns you if you don't put up barriers against it.

Urban This picture is well attested in Russian literature—Gorky has much to say about it. 'We Russians are anarchists by nature', he wrote on 1 May 1918, 'we are cruel beasts; in our veins there still flows the dark and evil blood of slaves, the poisonous inheritance of the Tatars and of serfdom.' The question then is: should one approve of a regime which puts fetters on this predatory beast? H. G. Wells, after his visit to Lenin in 1918, wrote upon his return that one should. The Soviet regime, he argued, left much to be desired, but if the Soviet experiment broke down, the whole of Europe would be sucked into the Russian vortex. Hence: support the Bolsheviks as the smaller evil (*Russia in the Shadows*).

Goldstücker No—one should not support the system.

The Soviet Union has had *sixty years* to educate the people, to change darkness into light, to instil some measure of democracy and decency into the crude Russian masses—but it has done none of these things! It stands convicted in the eyes of socialists and the world. No only did the Soviet system *not* help the emancipation of the people even though it has materially improved their standard of living, but it has continued to use the citizen as an object of military subordination. Not only has the system *not* brought the people freedom, but it refuses to discuss with the people its own, *Soviet*, legislation. No regime can last in such circumstances—and I believe that sooner or later the system will, because it must, change from within.

Urban You don't think liberalisation would release an even worse evil than the one we are familiar with—for example, an extreme right-wing nationalism parading under socialist slogans, which really *would* win enthusiastic public support?

Goldstücker Ah, but that is already there, *in* the system as well as outside it! The Soviet generals, whose influence is visibly on the increase and who had a great deal to do with the invasion of Czechoslovakia, represent in their majority traditional Russian nationalism. Whatever the slogans they use, these men are hard-headed chauvinists with their eyes on the main chance. The dissident movement, too, contains a powerful wing of nationalists. They first started innocuously enough preserving ancient Russian monuments and reviving folklore, but by now they have blossomed into an openly chauvinistic enterprise which must enjoy protection in the highest places or else it could not function. They have their own newspaper, and their propaganda is blatantly obvious.

Urban Even Solzhenitsyn has been attacked in one of their publications as a 'hater of Russians' and 'lover of Jews'—these being the consequences of his advocacy of Orthodox Christian values. Elsewhere, nationalists predict in *samizdat* literature that by the year 2000 the Indo-European races, led by the Russians, will be engaged in a deadly struggle with 'NATO-Zionists'.

Are we witnessing an incipient 'Left-fascism', with the

Black Hundreds threatening to return in the colours of the 'Red Hundreds'?

Goldstücker I would not entirely exclude the possibility because, as I say, much of the nationalistic, antisemitic, obscurantist extremism is already part and parcel of the system or waiting to come into its own outside the system.

Urban Nationalism dressed up as socialism and international brotherhood—could there be a better formula for the pursuit of Russian national interest?

Goldstücker If one looks deep enough into the Soviet application of Marxism and Leninism it is clear that this perverted ideology is an infinitely more useful instrument for the pursuit of old-fashioned Russian imperialism than the Slavophile ideas of the nineteenth century. The Slavophiles' Russian nationalism was clearly stated and had, and could have, no international appeal. But now, one by one, the Slavophiles' targets are being achieved in the name of proletarian internationalism.

Urban It may indeed be said that there exists today in the Soviet Union a *Marxist* Slavophilism. It has been argued that the current variety of Russian nationalism stems from Stalin's slogan 'Socialism in one country': when the international working class refused to behave as Marx had predicted, the mantle of succession fell on the working class of the first country that embraced socialism; and when socialism in that country was sufficiently advanced for Khrushchev to declare the end of the class struggle and the arrival of the all-people's state, the mantle of succession fell on the Soviet people as a whole, and, first and foremost, on the Russian people. The chosen people, then, is the Russian nation by Stalinist as well as Slavophile reasoning, and particularly so by the combination of the two.[1]

But where does all this leave Czechoslovakia? In the light of what you have said, isn't any attempt on the part of Poles, Czechs or Hungarians to wriggle or break out of the Soviet embrace again and again doomed to failure?

Goldstücker As long as the mockery of socialism continues in the Soviet Union, direct oppression is the only means

[1] This point has been forcefully argued by Professor D. Pospielovsky in a lecture at Columbia University (May 1978, unpublished).

the Russians possess of enforcing compliance—their society, their economy, their culture have nothing to offer. But after Brezhnev—who knows? No due process has been devised to regulate succession in the Soviet leadership; every change in the Soviet leadership is, therefore, basically a *coup d'état*. When Brezhnev's successor discovers, as Khrushchev did when he took power, how much is wrong with the Soviet Union, perhaps he will feel that something has to be done to sweep away the dead wood and *re-energise* society. It will then be his turn, as Khrushchev's was after the death of Stalin, to put the blame for everything that has gone wrong on the dead leader and—perhaps—initiate a new and more hopeful departure.

Urban You don't think that the system has lost legitimacy to such an extent that this re-energising of society would prove impossible?

Goldstücker It *would* under Brezhnev—but it might prove possible under an enlightened successor.

Urban Wouldn't the whole system have to undergo *institutional* change to detach the reforms from the whims of the reformers?

Goldstücker It would and I am as confident as can be (which is not very much, of course) that institutional change would be part of the process.

Urban But we are, are we not, now talking of a highly hypothetical contingency—our immediate problems being those impressed on us by an expansionist and militaristic system?

Goldstücker They are. Soviet colonialism is a reality; everything else is a hope—no more.

Intellectual leadership

Urban What truth is there in the accusation, frequently made by critics of the Prague Spring, that the Reform Movement was the property of a fairly small group of intellectuals with whom, almost up to the invasion, the working class would have no truck? Personally I would find nothing objectionable in it if the accusation *were* true—intellectuals, after all, are there to use their intellect and offer leadership, and that seldom makes for popular acclaim.

But even from a 'socialist' point of view, the leadership of the 1968 Prague intelligentsia would seem difficult to fault. One is reminded of Lenin's famous, though not very original statement (in *What is to be Done*?) that the consciousness of the class struggle does not come automatically to the workers but has to be brought to them by an educated minority from outside the working class. One is, on another level, also reminded of Gramsci's view that in highly developed societies ('post-industrial' would be the word for it today) the socialist transformation of society ceases to be a predominantly working-class concern and becomes more and more the responsibility of the opinion-making intellectual section of society—which is, again, stating the obvious but has, nevertheless, filled some Marxists with revulsion and struck others with the force of revelation.

It would, then, seem to me that the leadership of the Czech intelligentsia in 1968 may be justified both in terms of the Leninist canon of Marx and, if one is a Eurocommunist, in terms of Gramsci's revision of all his ideological forebears. We may for our present purposes leave aside the Eurocommunist side of the argument, for the Eurocommunists stood and stand four-square behind the Prague reforms. But does the orthodox indictment hold water? And if it does, does it tell us anything important about working-class attitudes to the liberalisation of 'socialism'?

Goldstücker Marx's prediction of the inevitability of socialism is coupled with a warning that the working class must be fully conscious of its historical role and act on it. Both Marx and Lenin realised that the working class perceives the world and reacts to the world in terms of its narrow material interests—through its belly, to put it quite bluntly—and that it is, therefore, the intellectuals' role to articulate the interests of the working class and 'import', as Lenin put it, into this amorphous mass the consciousness of the class struggle. Now your argument is that we took Lenin's formula rather too literally and put ourselves as intellectuals at the head of the working-class movement—

Urban —but *reversing* the signs of Lenin's formula in that you were—or so a conservative Muscovite would argue—leading the working class towards *gradualism* and *evolution* and not, as Lenin wanted, towards *revolution*. Worse, you were, on this showing, doing so against the interests and without the support of the working class.

Goldstücker Ah, but this is not true. Let me first deal with Lenin's formula. The idea of injecting revolutionary consciousness into an otherwise lethargic, sluggish and narrow-minded proletariat is a very Russian notion which springs directly from the circumstances in which Lenin had to work when he wrote *What is to be Done*?

In Russia power has always been concentrated in the hands of a relatively small circle of people, and consequently the struggle for power has always been a matter for a small number of power-holders. The people were not only *not* consulted but were constrained to live in an entirely different social and cultural universe. This attitude of keeping the people at arm's length, of not considering them as part of the nation but, rather, as pawns in a game which is open to licensed players only, has survived to this day. I see Lenin's thesis as a typical survival of this Russian perception. And, as I have said, Russian dissidents are in no way emancipated from a similar distrust of the *narod*. They regard the people as wards incapable of understanding what is good for them or of summoning the will to take action when they *do* understand it.

But, of course, none of this applied in Czechoslovakia. It is true that, initially and superficially, it seemed as though the 1968 Reform Movement had been the work of the Czech intelligentsia alone. But this was a mere surface phenomenon. Let me remind you, lest we should forget, that the Prague Spring was initiated and led by the Central Committee of a ruling Communist Party.

Urban Didn't you, though, meet a good deal of resistance in the factories?

Goldstücker Not resistance—I would say there was an attitude of wait-and-see which one could well understand. Think of a man in his mid-forties: he has been through Nazi occupation, the post-war coalition, Stalinism, the show-trials, Novotny—the lot. The fortunes and misfortunes he has experienced, the changes he has seen around him, have made him wary. He is not anxious to stick his neck out—he prefers to mark time. The cautious words written into the Party Communiqué after Dubcek's election in January 1968 were drafted, as I said earlier, with this kind of man in mind.

But when the scope of the democratisation programme became fully visible, the active support of the workers was quickly won and eventually increased to such an extent that, after the occupation, it was the newly freed trade unions that defended the achievements of the Prague Spring to the very last.

Urban Wouldn't you say that the wariness of the typical Czech citizen you have described was really an expression of *indifference* not only to the clever things cultured people were cerebrating in Prague, but to the whole business of 'socialism' and the Communist Party in particular?

Goldstücker Well, I remember being told about a revealing speech made at the same Central Committee meeting in October 1967 at which the opposition to Novotny first took organised shape. The speaker was a representative from the highly industrialised area of Ostrava, and he said something along the following lines: 'I ventured to run a private poll in the Party organisations of my region, and I discovered that in 26 per cent of our basic Party groups there was not a single Party member under the age of twenty-five, and in another 18 per cent there was only *one*. If we carry on like this, comrades, the Party will die out.' Now this was a clear indication that in the broad non-intellectual masses there was an aversion against the Party. As far as the intellectually inclined *young* people were concerned, I was present at Party meetings where students who had been put forward for Party membership (they had first to serve two years as candidate members before they could be accepted as full members) declined to take up their candidature and were writing tearful letters *imploring* the Party not to accept them because they considered time spent at Party meetings as time wasted. They would be, they said, much better employed if they were allowed to carry on with their studies undisturbed.

We must concede—and I would be skinned alive if I said this in another place and another context—that the majority of the working class is basically conservative. In all manifestations of working-class life there is a tremendous emphasis on conservatism. Marx devised his socialism for workers in the highly developed capitalist countries using the most up-to-date means of production. But these are always and everywhere a small minority, which is one guarantee of their protectionist, conservative inclinations. Another, of more recent vintage, is technical innovation, automation and the like which destroy jobs and induce working men to stand up for the *status quo*—that too makes for conservatism. Moreover, the numerical strength of the working class is diminishing and their earning power is on the increase, whereas the expectation of Marx was that the numbers of working-class people would rapidly expand, and their earning power diminish. In America and some West European countries the 'workers' are now in a clear minority.

Urban Isn't it also true that the secret (and not so secret) ambition of almost every working-class man and woman is *not* to be working-class but to join the bourgeoisie—first in dress, manners and life-style, but later in substance, too? In most Western countries it is already difficult to corner authentic specimens of the 'working class'—everyone wants to be known as a 'service adviser', 'technical operator', 'house-keeping assistant', 'production controller', 'hair style creator' and the like, and I cannot see why socialists should quarrel with this slightly infantile but nonetheless real manifestation of social mobility. If the aim of socialism is a classless society, does it matter very much whether classlessness takes on the characteristics of bourgeois life (which is only another word for a higher living standard) rather than the life-style and language of the latter-day elect—the proletariat? The jump from the conservatism of your skilled worker to the bourgeois order is a very small one.

Goldstücker I don't think *embourgeoisement* need follow. It is, of course, true that every social class aspires to the condition of the class immediately above it, and that adds to the conservatism I have described. But your point is well taken—Marxist sociology has great difficulty in defining what exactly *is* 'working-class'. Is an engineer 'working-class', is a draughtsman, is an 'intellectual' employed on the factory floor? A great deal of uncertainty and even hypocrisy surrounds the discussion.

Urban I don't think the problem is as new as you make out. When H. G. Wells, to quote him again, came back from Moscow where he had seen Lenin, Zinoviev, Kamenev, Gorky and many others high up in the Party he was firmly convinced that no one in the Soviet Union knew what 'working-class' was or how to sight live working-class men and women. He pooh-poohed the class struggle and insisted that there was no mysterious body of wicked men called capitalists but only a 'scrambling disorder of mean-spirited and short-sighted individuals'.

Goldstücker Well, I do think there *are* capitalists, but that does not mean to say that the definition of what is working-class isn't getting more and more difficult. In Czechoslovakia, during the Novotny era, a grotesque situation arose when Novotny decided on a course of action which was in itself laudable but impossible to carry out: he wanted to stop the proliferation of bureaucratic jobs and beef up the working class. Twice he selected large numbers of administrative people—70,000 at one stage—for dismissal and had them forcibly transferred to the factories to turn them into 'workers'. He was stupid enough to believe that lawyers, book-keepers, economists and the like would thus automatically become members of the proletariat and improve the class-composition of society! And when the children of these people applied for university admission, the selection boards had the unenviable task of having to decide whether these young people were or were not of 'working-class' origin. Were they, or were they not? Here was a Kafkaesque situation!

Urban Throughout the nineteenth century, indeed up to the First World War, the significance of intellectual leadership was well recognised in the whole of Europe and the United States. In the Communist movement we saw it expressed by (and through the personal examples of) Marx, Engels, Lenin and many others. Outside the Communist movement, intellectual achievement, intellectual magazines and discussion were regarded as signs of the seriousness of society and accorded high respect.

The weakening and slow disappearance in our time of intellectual content from public argument and the erosion of the prestige of intellectuals is a phenomenon deplored by some, applauded by others. One typically West European and even more typically British argument holds that the leadership of the intellectuals is a sign of the backwardness of the whole of society, because it is a substitute for an under-developed or non-existent middle class: where the middle class is strong (as in twentieth-century Britain, France, Germany and the US) *it*, rather than the intelligentsia, tends to be the authentic repository of national consciousness, and the cases of Central and East European libertarian rebellions both in the nineteenth century and in our own are quoted as the most telling examples.

If this argument is true, Czechoslovakia does not fit the pattern. In 1968 Czechoslovak society rested (and it still rests) on two main pillars: a solid working class and an equally well-established middle class. Why, then, did the intelligentsia play so outstanding a role? Was it because the country was culturally still embedded in the nineteenth century (Marxist or non-Marxist) tradition, with its attendant belief that intellectual argument deeply matters; or was it because the middle class was so thoroughly discouraged and spiritually disenfranchised that it was incapable of recovering its role as the backbone and spokesman of national consciousness?

Goldstücker A bit of both. Remember that Czechoslovak national consciousness, indeed the rediscovery of a Czech and Slovak culture, were the work of intellectuals such as Dobrowsky, Palacky and Stur and later Neruda and Masaryk himself—all men of the academy, writers and scholars. The prestige of intellectual discussion was, therefore, well established in Czechoslovakia. You may regard this as a sign of the relative immaturity of the nation, or a survival of the moral seriousness of the nineteenth century, the disappearance of which, in the West, I personally profoundly deplore. At the same time it is true that, by 1968, our 'middle class' ('people' would be my word for it) had been so depressed and debilitated that its ability to make its weight felt was limited to those among its ranks who *could* speak up with relative impunity—and that meant the intellectuals within the Communist Party. In a one-party state opposition and reform could come from no other quarter.

I would, therefore, conclude that in 1968 the Czech and

Slovak intelligentsia performed the role of leadership both in the sense in which Marx, Engels and Lenin foresaw it, and in that of being the spokesmen—the only possible spokesmen—of what you have, wrongly as I see it, identified as the Czechoslovak middle class. The movement now grouped around 'Charter 77' is yet another sign that, under Soviet rule, intellectual leadership and national leadership are one and the same thing.

The trial

Urban We began this conversation with Kafka. We might usefully conclude it with the story of your own 'trial', for I suspect that your imprisonment and the circumstances surrounding it offer us an authentic *aperçu* of the mood of those twenty years of Czechoslovak history which began with February 1948 and ended with 21 August 1968. I will myself try to proceed in Kafkaesque fashion and not ask you *why* you were imprisoned, but simply take your involvement with the Slansky trial as read and invite you to tell me about prison as a place of Communist education.

Goldstücker I was arrested in December 1951, but well before my arrest I was conscious of a sharp deterioration in the country's situation: the economy was spiralling downwards, food was scarce, and a propaganda campaign was being waged to put the blame on imperialist infiltration, foreign spies and the like. This was the time when Colorado beetles were said to have been found on our territory, dropped, as it was claimed, by American aircraft to destroy the country's potato harvest—

Urban —and the joke which was current in London in those days was that the Americans took care to drop in some potatoes first because there was, under Czechoslovak 'socialism', nothing for the beetles to destroy.

Goldstücker The Colorado beetle propaganda was, of course, the crudest Stalinist fabrication. Later, in prison, an agricultural textbook was given to me to read (we had, naturally, no choice in the selection of our reading matter) which unwittingly answered the lie about the beetles. The book, published under the Protectorate in 1943, complained that the pest was spreading eastwards from Western Europe at so many miles per year, and that *by 1943* it had reached Bavaria. By 1949, therefore, on the simplest calculation, it *must* have reached Czechoslovakia without American help!

Urban Were you able to keep up with the outside world?

Goldstücker Not at all. I was completely isolated in a concrete cell measuring 4 metres by 2 metres. I was kept in a modern block near Ruzyne, built shortly before the war and later taken over by the secret police as a prison and interrogation centre. I spent eighteen months there, stretching over two winters, in solitary confinement.

Urban In solitary confinement for eighteen months?

Goldstücker Yes—I saw absolutely no one during that time except the secret police. Such was my isolation that when I was brought to trial in May 1953 I didn't realise that both Stalin and Gottwald were dead. It was only after I had been sentenced and pushed into another cell in the top-security wing of the prison that I discovered from two fellow prisoners that Stalin and Gottwald had died. I didn't at first want to believe them.

Urban Who were these two men?

Goldstücker One was a former trade union officer of the Benes party—an elderly man who had been sentenced to death and spent eleven months waiting for his execution. Our cell was, incidentally, right opposite the cell where people were being kept before their execution, and we could see them through the 'Judas hole' in our door.

Well, after eleven months in the death-cell, this man's sentence was commuted to life imprisonment, and he was taken across the corridor from the death-cell to where I met him. The interminable wait for the hangman's call had disturbed his mental balance a little. I deeply pitied this man and developed quite a sentimental attachment to him. He was a simple and very good man who had tried to serve his country and party to the best of his ability. I was convinced of his complete innocence.

Urban What had been the charge against him?

Goldstücker He had been accused of having maintained illegal contact with emigrés of his former party. That was enough in those days to earn you a death sentence.

The second man in my cell was a man younger than

myself—I was forty at the time—with only one eye in his head. He had been arrested on a charge of smuggling to East Germany, was given fifteen years, and sent to the uranium mines in the region of Joachimsthal near the West German border from where he attempted to escape. Now, according to Czechoslovak law, escape from the labour camps in the uranium mine area comes under espionage even if it is unsuccessful, so that this young man knew he was taking a great risk. He took it all the same. He was on the run for two days, and when he thought he had walked long enough and was on West German soil, lay down in a haystack and fell asleep. He was woken by the noise made by an approaching border patrol, took to his heels, but the patrol shot him down, caught him in the eye and recaptured him. He was sentenced again, given an additional sixteen years, so that he was down for a total of thirty-one years in prison! These were my two companions.

Some weeks after I had been sentenced I was transported to Leopoldov—a fortress designed under the Emperor Leopold against the Turks in the seventeenth century; but by the time the fortress was finished the Turks had been pushed back, so that Leopoldov never had any function other than serving as a prison—and a most horrible prison it was. I hesitate to talk about it.

I was brought there in chains, and as our bus stopped in front of the entrance, which was inside a tunnel, I could see inscribed on the wall 'Built in 1667'—words which reminded me of those greeting new arrivals in Dante's *Inferno*. . . .

Urban Chains on an old Communist?

Goldstücker Oh, yes—a political prisoner was considered to be the vilest criminal.

Urban Once they had settled you down to life imprisonment, did the treatment you were given improve?

Goldstücker Oh, no; what I experienced in Leopoldov was the beastliest nightmare you can imagine—except that it was reality. It was horrible—just *horrible*!

Urban How did you react to all this? Here was a man who had fought for Communism all his life, ending up for life in the dungeons of a Habsburg fortress on orders of the Communist government he had supported and helped to bring to power! If a Communist government had put *me* away, opposed as I was to any form of Communism, I would have regarded it as an act of tyranny, but I would not have been surprised or felt cheated out of my inheritance. But your position must surely have been different.

Goldstücker Yes—the first sentence I said to my interrogators after my arrest was precisely along the lines you've suggested. 'You have me at a great disadvantage,' I said, 'because had I been arrested by the enemy, I would resist—but here is my own Party doing it to me. *This* breaks my resolve.'

Urban And did it?

Goldstücker Of course. But it wasn't my Party alone that did it. When Communist convicts were brought into prison they were thrown in with a mass of common criminals as well as former Fascists, ex-Nazi officers, thugs from the Hlinka Guard, Tiso's men and so on. As former Communists we had the additional disadvantage of being under the constant threat of being *lynched*. I saw people savagely beaten up and kicked with the guards turning a blind eye.

Urban Were the confessions extracted on the Koestler/Bukharin principle—'you can do a last service to Communism and the Party by signing this false testimony and save your wife's, children's etc. lives'?

This explanation, brilliantly put in *Darkness at Noon*, found much favour with Western intellectuals because it offered a rationale for what seemed otherwise quite inexplicable. For what other reason, it was asked, would old Bolsheviks indict themselves and beg to be shot?

Goldstücker I read Koestler's book in Oxford in 1941—and I was horrified; but when I was put through the real thing, Koestler's version struck me as exceedingly mild.

Urban The procedure was less intellectual than Koestler imagined?

Goldstücker *Less* intellectual is the word! There was *no* discussion of principles *à la* Rubashov: you are a *criminal*, you are *treated* as a criminal, and you are treated as a criminal as long as you are prepared to confess that you *are* a criminal! And even if you don't make a confession, you are *convicted* as a criminal.

Urban Were you prepared to believe that you *were* a criminal?

Goldstücker Well, you have a split mind by the time they have finished with you: you have devoted practically the whole of your adult life to the Party; you have regarded it as the embodiment of historical truth—and here is the self-same Party revealing itself as a lie, but needing *you* to make it stick.

Urban Wouldn't this have struck a man under profound physical and psychological duress as a back-handed compliment—'even now, the Party needs me'?

Jean-Paul Sartre has the following to say about an earlier account you have given of your imprisonment:

> Goldstücker recounts how after being let out of prison he read the work of an analyst who saw in confession an 'identification with the aggressor', and he adds that to judge from his own experience this interpretation is not very far from the truth. The aggressor is the party, his reason for living, which excludes him and looms up before him like a wall that cannot be scaled and that makes him answer each denial with the voice of a policeman: 'There is only one truth—yours.' When the truth wants to be taken for the Great Wall of China, how can a mere man oppose it with fragile subjective convictions ('I wasn't in Prague that day; I've never seen Slansky')? It is better for the poor victim secretly to join the party once again, by identifying with it and with the cops that represent it, by embracing the scorn and the hatred they show toward him in the name of the party. . .Guilty! How dizzy this makes him! He will know peace, torpor, death.

This interpretation does not seem to me to be all *that* distant from Koestler's theory.

Goldstücker Being a good and imaginative writer, Sartre has made it sound a little too neat and convincing. The reality was different and a great deal simpler.

Urban But do you think the Koestlerian approach, 'you may perform a last service to your party', was used in the

Czech show-trials? We know from W. G. Krivitsky and others that it was used in Moscow in the late 1930s.

Goldstücker It might have been used. We know that some of the principal accused were approached by very highly placed people and told what the Party expected of them. For example, Rajk was seen in his prison cell by Kadar; and Slansky, shortly before his trial, by the half-wit Bacilek, who was then Minister of National Security, and some of these men were promised their lives if they signed the scenarios written for them—which they all did but were sent to the gallows all the same.

Urban Did it ever seriously occur to you to think that you might, after all, be guilty 'objectively speaking' (as party jargon would have it)—that 'rejoining' the Party through a confession might, as Sartre suggested, lighten your burden and re-align you with Lenin's Party?

Goldstücker No. When I was accused of crimes I knew I had never committed, when I saw the whole fabric of lies being prepared in front of my eyes for the final deposition, it was clear to me that neither the Party nor the Stalinist secret police had the slightest interest in establishing the truth, but only in making sacrificial animals of us for everything that had gone wrong under the Gottwald regime. I was asked to bear witness to lies—straightforward, hair-raising and often infantile lies—and I just couldn't do that.

One *could*, of course, for one reason—to put the horrors behind you. There comes a point where you can stand the interrogations and the torture no longer, and you say to yourself: 'I want everything to come to an end even at the price of my life. *Better* death than to go on like this'—and this was basically the secret of all 'confessions'. Your interrogators were determined to drive you to a state where death seemed a highly desirable alternative.

Urban Was Slansky, too, treated in this manner? Wasn't *he* subjected to the Koestlerian technique?

Goldstücker Not at all. He was repeatedly beaten, physically tortured—at least twice he tried to take his life. He, of course, must have known from the moment he was arrested that for a man in his position there could be no way out but execution. No—Koestler's picture is much too intelligent; it is a black-humour comedy. In reality you were treated as a criminal—cynically, brutally, without mercy.

Interrogators

Urban Who were the men involved in your interrogation?

Goldstücker Fascists! The mentality of the security police in Czechoslovakia and the other Central and East European countries is the mentality of fascism. Their personal behaviour and the methods used are those of fascism. These men could swap sides again at the drop of a hat. The colour of their shirts alone has changed—nothing else.

Urban One knows this to have been true of Rumania, Hungary, Bulgaria, Croatia and Slovakia where fascist types of parties existed, but surely in the Czech lands there were few fascists to change sides?

Goldstücker Very few—most of our thugs were ordinary toughs brought over from the Army if they had shown sufficient ruthlessness and disrespect for human dignity. But they were, in a broader sense, fascists all the same. They were first seconded to the police force, then selected for special training courses and assigned to the secret police. The more senior officers were sent to Moscow for additional training. One of my interrogators was a well-turned-out middle-aged man who had been a gendarmerie officer in pre-Munich Czechoslovakia and had led several gendarmerie charges against striking workers at the time of the depression. Under Nazi occupation he was put through a course with the Gestapo, and after the war he won further distinction at the Czechoslovak security police academy—whereupon he was thought fit to be let loose on Communists such as myself. His name was Kohoutek—'little cock'; my other tormentor was Doubek—'little oak tree'—and I always thought that 'little cock' ought to be hanged by the neck from 'little oak tree'. But he wasn't.

After my release I found Kohoutek himself in prison. Both he and his immediate commander had been thrown to the wolves for being responsible for the 'mistakes' surrounding the purge trials, including my own—and I was one of the witnesses when *his* trial came up. Kafka, you see, isn't a patch on reality!

Imagine that after the maltreatment I had received at the hands of this man, and having daily had to humiliate myself before this representative of God on earth (for such, of course, was his position in prison), I now saw *him* in the dock accused of the misuse of official power. Well, he and his companion were sent to prison, but when, a few months later, Zapotocky died and Novotny was elected, they were released under a presidential amnesty.

One day I ran into Kohoutek in the street. He came up to me without any embarrassment and told me what a grave injustice had been done to him because *he* had been put into prison while the men above him, who had given him his orders, were sitting in their official positions unscathed. So ensued between us a long Dostoyevskian conversation on guilt and punishment. . . .

Urban What did you feel when you came face to face with your tormentor?

Goldstücker I had mixed feelings. I first tried to look the other way, but he came up to me with an ingratiating smile—so, I thought, 'all right, I'll talk to him', because I felt the encounter was extraordinary. (Incidentally, Arthur London, to whom I had told this story, made use of it in his book and the scenario of the French film which was later made on the basis of it.)

Urban What was Kohoutek's attitude to you? Was he guilt-ridden? Contrite?

Goldstücker Oh, no. 'What could I have done?', he said; 'one day thirty-six of us from the security police were summoned to the office of the Minister of State Security where we were given our orders by the Minister himself flanked by a Soviet adviser. Every one of us was assigned a person to arrest and interrogate. One of us refused—the next morning he was dead. There were no further refusals.'

'When you were under my questioning,' he went on, 'and I minuted things you hadn't said but which I wanted you to say, I had no choice in the matter as I knew that there might be a microphone in the room and everything that passed between us would be listened to. How *could* I do anything but what I did? With *my* past (meaning his career with the gendarmerie and Gestapo) I had to be especially careful!'

Urban I hope you did not show undue concern for his predicament.

Goldstücker I didn't. 'I know,' I said to him, 'that you did not start any of this ghastly business—that you were only a wheel in the machine. But I testified against you quite deliberately because I believe that *anyone* who had his hands dirtied by these monstrous trials deserves to be given the supreme penalty. I very much hope that those who had given you your orders will receive their just deserts.' 'Oh, you are an optimist', Kohoutek answered cynically, and he was right.

Urban What has happened to Kohoutek?

Goldstücker He was pensioned off. I ran into him again a couple of times in the streets of Prague; he was pushing a pram with his grandchild in it—then a few years ago he died a natural death. Doubek's *open* association with the secret police was discontinued, but he was made Director of Personnel at the Czechoslovak Travel Agency, and we know what that means.

Urban When you were being interrogated by these two men, did you feel that they were ideologically convinced of the necessity and righteousness of what they were doing? It is so much easier to beat a man and write out false confessions in his name if you can, temporarily at least, persuade yourself that you are acting under the sanction of superior moral authority—the ultimate good of the working class, your race, or humanity. Nursing a guilty conscience is the privilege of intellectuals—the torturers and executioners like to have a clear one.

Goldstücker Doubek was simple-minded enough to convince himself that he was doing what he was in the name of a good cause. But Kohoutek knew. His attitude was a characteristically Nazi attitude: 'We are soldiers,' he used to tell me, 'but soldiers *twice* over: as uniformed servants of the state and as Communists; and our job is to carry out orders.' And he did.

Urban But given that attitude, was he intelligent enough in his interrogation of you to lay down the Party line, trap you into confessions and make up the plots?

Goldstücker No—but he didn't have to. Every morning he received detailed instructions from his Russian supervisor as to what sort of questions he should put to me and what he should write into the protocol; and every evening he went back and reported what he had achieved. These men had *no* independent brainwork to do. The whole monstrous plan had been laid down by the Russians with the precision of a military exercise.

After the trial

Urban Let me jump ahead of your story again for a moment: after your release from prison you immediately resumed working for the Party. Did you think that the Party had changed—that your imprisonment was the result of some colossal misunderstanding?

Goldstücker Yes—I thought the whole thing was a horrible deformation, and that rectifying it and returning the Party to its humanist mission was possible.

Urban Wasn't this a rather generous assumption?

Goldstücker It was—as events were soon to prove. Not only did I pick up where I had left off, but, to my great surprise, I found Communist comrades who had never been in prison much more bitter in their critique of the Party than I was.

Urban How do you explain this?

Goldstücker I was somehow conserved, almost protected, in my views while in prison, whereas they went through the slow, blow-by-blow erosion of confidence in their daily lives.

Urban So, despite the horrors, and despite—or perhaps *because* of—your isolation, you preserved a purer, shall we say, monastic vision of 'socialism'? Faith renewed through retreat from the world?

Goldstücker Yes—I was myself thoroughly surprised. And this despite the fact that I had gone through the most awesome experiences right to the end of my imprisonment.

Urban Was there in all this an element of euphoria at seeing yourself come out alive?

Goldstücker Undoubtedly—I was brought to trial in May

1953, six months after Slansky. The court sat from first thing in the morning until 4 p.m., when the Procurator General demanded the death penalty for me. A demand by him was in those days as good as the sentence itself; only in highly exceptional cases could a lower sentence be passed. My defence attorney had been drawn from a special list of lawyers controlled by the secret police. He came to see me on one single occasion in the presence of a police officer, and the only piece of legal advice he gave me was 'don't curse or use unbecoming language'. I had no further contact with him. His plea for my defence started with the classic sentence: 'The supreme penalty has been demanded for my client, and there is no doubt that he deserves it'!

At 4 p.m. the court retired to consider the verdict, and I was told that sentence would be passed at 9 a.m. next morning. Between 4 p.m. and 9 a.m. I had to come to terms with the possibility of being sentenced to death and hanged within a week. So when at 9 a.m. in the morning I heard that I had been given only a life sentence, my relief at being able to keep my head was very great. As long as there was life there was hope, but if you had asked me how I imagined I would ever get out, I would not have been able to tell you because any such thought was beyond my imagination at that point. So when I eventually did come out under the first post-Stalin revisions of the show-trials, I was euphoric: I had cheated death, I had defeated the hangman's noose, and I have considered life as a bonus ever since. My return to Party work must be seen in the context of all these conditions.

Urban But you must have had a religious type of belief in Communism to be able to overcome the memory—a very recent memory—of your ordeal and return to the fold.

Goldstücker Yes—we flattered ourselves that we were critical intellectuals, but, in reality, we had psychologically manoeuvred ourselves into a position where faith overshadowed critical thinking.

Urban Djilas has recently borne witness to the same process—describing the attitude involved (*expressis verbis*) as 'religious'.

Goldstücker Oh yes, it was. We spoke about this earlier in this conversation, but let me say it again: the type of faith we had, and the older unregenerate Stalinists still have, expresses a new form of *religiosity*, if not religion. As long as you are in the grip of it you cannot be reached by rational argument.

Urban Is your *current* assessment of all this completely rational?

Goldstücker It is—but, of course, it is easy to be rational in *retrospect*—

Urban —but *is* it?

Goldstücker Oh, it is; it is.

Urban Wouldn't your attitude, even in retrospect, be a little like the memory of one's first love, or one's first creative effort—which one can never think of with complete impartiality? Also, there is a great reluctance in all of us to admit that something we have devoted our lives to for thirty years has been wasted—that we have been fooled by a cause, or a woman or, worse, ourselves?

Goldstücker No, I don't suffer from any of those things—not any more. They have become matters for cool and detached analysis. At the same time I don't think that everything I have done has been wasted. I am still convinced that the next stage of historical development is socialism—but in the sense I have indicated, in the sense in which we set out to change the existing system in Prague in 1968.

Urban What happened after Leopoldov?

Goldstücker I was put in chains again and transported to Prague in a prison van divided into minute and unlit cubicles. In Prague I was put in an absolutely icy cell, deep underground, and completely cut off. I was sitting or lying down there, for seventeen days, on a wooden bench, freezing and suffering from a spinal trouble I had contracted at Ruzyne where, as I've told you, I had been kept half-naked for two winters.

Urban Half-naked?

Goldstücker Yes—our clothing consisted of a pair of long underpants with nothing except our hands to hold them up with—the tapes had been removed in case we decided to hang ourselves—and a pair of felt mules (heelless slippers) to prevent us from running with any efficiency. We had a collarless shirt and a prison smock made of crude sacking. By the time I arrived in Prague again I was barely able to stand up. After this seventeen-day interlude I was once again bundled off in a bus, fully chained, this time to the uranium mines in Joachimsthal. These mines were worked by convict labour drawn from the concentration camps in the area and, of course, the prisoners were exposed to constant radiation. The mines were under the direct management of Soviet engineers, and every piece of uranium was transported to the Soviet Union in special trains under heavy Soviet guard.

Such was my physical condition that I could not be sent down the mines, so I was put to work sorting uranium. I had to pack the ore into small boxes, but because the specific weight of uranium is extremely high, some of these boxes weighed 100 kg. Later I was made to cart uranium rock to a sorting centre and carry the bits that were rejected to a huge waste heap. Under the strain of all this I finally collapsed: I could no longer walk; I was, like a dog, crawling on all fours, and I was unable to take food. I ended up in the sick bay, from where I was eventually sent to the district prison hospital.

Urban How did your faith in 'socialism' stand up to these experiences? Some years ago I read with particular surprise one section in Alexander Weissberg's reminiscences of his imprisonment in the Soviet Union at the time of the great terror. We find Weissberg sitting in a prison cell, together with other Communists, in unspeakable conditions, waiting for the Stalinist machine to chew them up. But far from hatching some plan to escape from this hell, he and his fellow inmates indulge in endless ideological discussions on the nature of the Soviet system, the dialectics of their arrest, Stalin's (as they thought) ignorance of what was being done in his name, and so on. Well, I reflected, these Communists are not only children of faith, but also inveterate scholastics with a Jesuitical temper.

Goldstücker There were three of us Communists in the Joachimsthal concentration camp, and we often discussed the character of the system which had reduced us to the condition we were in. None of us had any illusions left about Stalin, the Soviet system or our own leadership. It was absolutely clear to us that the entire system as it existed at the time was evil; that we were being made scapegoats;

that Stalin and Gottwald, far from not knowing what was being done in their names, were deeply and personally involved. At the same time, however, we were convinced that none of the things that had happened to us proved the bankruptcy of socialism. What we saw was the bankruptcy of Stalinism and the need to rescue socialism from its multiple degenerations. But we all thought that the socialism *we* envisaged was worthwhile—something we had lived for and wanted to go on living for.

And when the sentences passed on us under Stalin began to be revised (my first re-hearing was conducted in the presence of two members of the Party Secretariat, which I interpreted as a token of the seriousness of the change) and it appeared that such injustices as could still be made good *were* going to be made good, I for one believed that the end of despotism was in sight.

Urban The last time I had the pleasure of meeting you before the 1968 upheavals was at a seminar on European unification at Grenoble University early in 1967. I was already under the impression that the speed of events in Prague was pulling at your entire system and releasing Soviet fears, and I asked you whether you didn't think you were heading for trouble rather on the Hungarian pattern.

No, you said, the Soviet comrades were aware that everyone in Prague was completely loyal to socialism, and that the improvements which were being sought would modernise socialism and make it more attractive to the Western world. This, you thought, was well understood in Moscow, the more so as there were people in the Soviet leadership itself whose ideas were similar to those of the Prague reformers.

I marvelled at your optimism. What makes a man, I asked myself, who has spent many bitter years in prison and is nobody's fool go *on* thinking that the Soviet leadership would tolerate any challenge to its authority, whether ideological or geopolitical? And I am still intrigued by—although I also respect—your profound trust in the soundness and inevitability of 'socialism'.

Goldstücker We committed an error in 1968 by not subjecting our impressions of the political situation in the Soviet Union to a more rigorous analysis. We assumed that the process of de-Stalinisation was continuing—whereas, in fact, it was not. The curve of de-Stalinisation in Russia started to rise in 1953, reached its apogee in 1956, and continued by fits and starts until about 1964. Khrushchev's fall meant *re*-Stalinisation, and the evidence was there for everyone to read, for example in the trial of Sinyavsky and Daniel. Why were we being misled? Because in Czechoslovakia the process of de-Stalinisation had been delayed until 1963, so that in 1968 we were out of phase with what was happening in Moscow. We were caught in the trough of the wave while imagining not only that we were acting in the interests of socialism, but that the men in the Kremlin would *recognise* our merit for doing so.

But should we have held our horses if we *had* known where Moscow stood? Would *I* have acted differently—*should* I have acted differently if I had been more sceptical than I was? No. *If you are given a chance in history your duty is to take it*. In 1967 and 1968 I was frequently asked: but can you *guarantee* that if we take step A it will result in step B—that this or that reform *will* come off and not get us into worse trouble than we're in already? I could, of course, guarantee no such thing. Life offers no certainties—no one can *guarantee* that crossing the street I will not be struck down by a falling brick; yet nothing will stop me from crossing it.

Urban You quoted, at the beginning of this conversation, the first sentence from Kafka's *The Trial*. Let me end it with an episode taken from the last pages of the book.

On the evening of Joseph K.'s thirty-first birthday two plump, frock-coated gentlemen arrive at his lodging. K. is invited to follow them, and is frog-marched to a deserted stone quarry. Even now, his escorts are impeccably observant of the courtesies expected of the representatives of authority—the Court, which K. has never seen, and the Judge, who has never heard his case.

One of the two gentlemen carries a butcher's knife under his frock coat. The two of them have laid K. down on the cliff-side near a loose boulder, but they do not immediately set to work. 'Once more the odious ceremonial of courtesy began, the first handed the knife across K. to the second, who handed it across K. back again to the first. K. now perceived clearly that he was supposed to seize the knife himself. . .and plunge it into his own breast. But he did not do so. . . .' He was, Kafka tells us, slaughtered all the same, 'Like a dog!'

Hasn't this concluding scene of Joseph K.'s trials a symbolic relevance to what happened in Czechoslovakia in the spring of 1968?

Goldstücker Well, the butcher's knife was (politely and less politely) brandished before our eyes time and again—at Dresden, in the five-party letter, at Cierna and Bratislava—and it was the Soviet leaders' fervent hope that some group would be found within our Party to perform the role of Quisling, so that the men in the Kremlin would not have to wield the knife themselves. But when, despite the Stalinist sympathies of several of our Politburo members, no such group came forward, the job was nevertheless ordered to be done—with rather less ceremony than in Kafka.

But nations and societies, unlike human beings, cannot be 'killed' unless they are physically exterminated. They may suffer privation, humiliation, suppression, even self-inflicted wounds or wounds of the kind faint-hearted or traitorous governments inflict on them—but they survive to fight another day.

Antonin J. Liehm

Eurocommunism and the Prague Spring

Invaders

Urban My theme is the impact of the Czechoslovak Reform Movement on what has come to be known as Eurocommunism. Throughout the Prague Spring, and already during the last two years of Novotny's leadership, the West European Communist Parties took a keen interest in Czechoslovakia's cautious attempt to reform its institutions, and some of them, especially the Italian and Spanish, followed it with undisguised sympathy.

I am curious to know what accounted for this interest and sympathy seeing that there was, on the face of it, little in common between the conditions in which the Czechoslovak Party found itself in 1968 (Soviet control, Stalinist leadership, command economy, constraints of the Warsaw Pact) and those in which the West European Communist Parties were able to operate.

Liehm The West European Parties had their sympathies well prepared for the Prague events by one all-important element which they shared, and had shared for many years before 1968, with all the world's Communist Parties: Russian control and Russification. To grasp the full measure of this control, and the anger with which, openly or covertly, the West European Communist Parties reacted to it, one has to look at some of the details. The Stalinisation of the world's Communist Parties in the 1930s was not merely a matter of foisting on them the despotic device of 'democratic centralism' and of forcing them to follow Soviet directives on every imaginable issue, but also a matter of imposing on them typically Russian policies and experiences. For example, every West European Communist Party had a Soviet type of internal police force built into its organisation (and there was no attempt to hide its existence) which kept an eye on members' activities and enforced discipline. All this created enormous resentment.

Some of the West European Communist Parties were, mind you, willing enough to install their *own* brand of Stalinism (the post of dictator has never gone begging), but what they found very hard to stomach was the mindless imposition of an alien and wholly unsuitable model. Soviet control and Russification were, then, one fertile source of restiveness.

Another was the democratic, and essentially Social Democratic, milieu in which the West European working class had been nurtured, and which took for granted certain elementary liberties: freedom of opinion, freedom of speech, democratic elections, and the like. All this ran diametrically counter to everything the Leninist/Stalinist parties stood for. The Communists, therefore, found themselves in an environment which treated them with great mistrust and which made it difficult for them to make any decisive headway, no matter how well some of them might have done at individual elections.

Ironically, they fared best when democracy was suspended and they had to fear no competition or contamination from the non-Communist sections of West European society. For example, the French Communist Party had its heyday under Nazi occupation because the rigours of war provided it with an environment in which the Party's own dictatorial and conspiratorial methods fell into place rather naturally—gone was the need to apologise for 'democratic centralism' which was now merely matching like with like; gone was the danger of infection as democratic political life had ceased to exist; and there could be, under occupation, no dissensions within the Party. Nazism provided the natural setting for the monstrous logic of the Stalinist type of Communism to come into its own.

For the *leaders* of the West European Parties fidelity to Stalinism was a matter of self-preservation; Khrushchev's report to the 20th Party Congress, therefore, came as a profound shock to them. Thorez, for example (as we now know) bitterly complained that 'first, the Soviet Party forced a line on us which no Party dared to transgress, and gave us a version of Party history which no Party dared to disbelieve. Now, without any warning, Khrushchev has given the lie to everything we have been enjoined to consider as true and infallible and have demanded of others to consider as true and infallible'—or words to that effect.

The Party rank-and-file thought otherwise. They were hoping that Khrushchev's revelations were the first steps towards a democratic renewal of Soviet society. This, as we know, did not happen. On the contrary, the 1956 Hungarian revolution was brutally put down on the pretext that it was a counter-revolutionary uprising organised and financed by Western interests. Such was the speed of events in the autumn of 1956 (what with Suez coinciding with Hungary) and so cleverly was the character of the Hungarian events manipulated by Soviet propaganda, that the Soviet story was (despite ructions among intellectuals) eventually accepted by the French Communist Party and, with some doubts and hesitations, by the Italian Party too.

Urban It has never been clear to me why the Italians fell in with the brazen untruths put about by Moscow. I should have thought that even a cursory examination of Imre Nagy's programme would have revealed a marked affinity with what was stirring, and was indeed very soon to take shape, in Togliatti's mind.

Liehm This is a legitimate observation—*ex post facto*. At the time, however, Stalinist discipline and the myth of Soviet infallibility were still too strong in the Italian Party to permit an open defiance of Moscow. By 1968, however, the Italian Communists had gone far enough on the road to polycentrism and independence to be able to repudiate the Soviet contention that the Prague events, too, were potentially at least a counter-revolution. The years between 1956 and 1968 were momentous for the history of the Communist movement, because they saw the collapse of the central authority of Moscow and a proliferation of Parties with grudging, or weak, or no loyalty at all to the Soviet Union. The Italians, for their part, decided to play the parliamentary game; their rejection of the Soviet account of what had taken place in Prague was a matter of both intellectual integrity and electoral prudence.

Urban At the risk of making a slight (though I believe relevant) detour, it might be profitable to widen our search for the roots of Eurocommunism by looking into the relationship between the Prague Spring and the Hungarian revolution.

I recall an extremely courageous commemoration of the trial and execution of Imre Nagy and his associates in the 13 June 1968 issue of *Literarni Listy* of which you were the political editor. Written by O. Machatka, this was an overt condemnation of both the Stalinist system to which Nagy had reacted, and the reasons offered by Khrushchev and the other 1956 Soviet leaders for the suppression of the Hungarians. It was crystal clear from Machatka's whole argument that in praising Imre Nagy's reforms at the time of his first (1953–5) premiership and his intended reforms at the time of the second, Machatka was making a case for the legitimacy of the Prague Spring:

> Nagy . . . wanted to return parliament to its true role, and to turn the government into a full-blooded instrument for the management of the affairs of the state. The intelligentsia and the peasants were to be rehabilitated socially, while there was to be legal rehabilitation for the victims of tyranny. . . . Through his criticism of totalitarian dictatorship and through his humanistic concept of socialism, Nagy became a prominent exponent of the democratic and national principle of socialism. He based his thinking on recognition of the fact that a totalitarian regime, the mechanical copying of foreign examples and servility were inadvisable. He wrote that the people's democracies had lost their popular and democratic character due to their copying of Soviet experiences. He therefore related the return of democracy to respect for national peculiarities and to the idea of specific paths to socialism. He considered a country's sovereignty and independence to be an indispensable condition for the preservation of these national peculiarities. . .

—and so on.

Liehm It will strike you as strange—and in retrospect it strikes *me* as *inexplicable*—that we Czech reform Communists had not properly studied the 1956 Hungarian revolution. We tended to shove its lessons out of our minds as though the revolution had never happened; and those who *were* familiar with it did not think it could have any bearing on what *we* were trying to do. It was only in the summer of 1968 that the relevance of the Hungarian story became increasingly clear to us—

Urban This does not quite accord with what Ota Sik tells us in another dialogue (pp. 165–7). Sik's contention was that he and his colleagues in his Institute of Economic Research had realised clearly enough that the Hungarian precedent was relevant—ominously relevant—but whereas they thought that the Hungarians had failed because they had tried to reform the system by frontal attack, they, the Czech reform Communists, would smuggle it in step by step through economic reform. In the event, however, the Russians found the *sotto voce* Czech approach (which turned out to be not so *sotto voce* after all) just as unacceptable as they had found the Hungarian uprising.

Liehm Sik and his staff may have been aware of the dangers of an open confrontation, but I very much doubt that they had analysed Nagy's programme any more than we had—more of which later.

One day Machatka came to my office with a suggestion that we ought to devote a short article to the tenth anniversary of the execution of Imre Nagy and acknowledge some of our debt to the Hungarian precedent. Now Machatka was a very minor figure—a scholarly reviewer of books with a job in one of our institutes—and no great fighter. It seemed to me at the time that the article he was suggesting would be at most an interesting footnote to the Reform Movement, so I encouraged him to write it.

I did not realise, nor did anyone else—and this shows the extent of our naivety—that a review of the kind Machatka had in mind would prove to be not at all a footnote but very much part of the main text! Well, Machatka's article turned out to be no different from a great many other articles we published in those days. We did not want to make a great splash of it so we published it in a subordinate position in the international section of the paper and not as a political article.

Urban You didn't think the Russians would prick up their ears and say: 'Aha, the Prague reformers are justifying the Hungarian counter-revolution and are therefore well on the way to counter-revolution themselves'?

Liehm Not only did we *not* feel that, but we didn't feel another thing either—a blunder of great proportions for which I feel responsible to this day (I don't think it would have changed history if we had not made it, but one should nevertheless avoid making mistakes of this kind): Machatka's article was published on the day of Dubcek's arrival in Budapest on an official visit. We of course did not know that Dubcek was going to Hungary (these things were always kept secret) but, to be frank with you, we *could* have found out if we had really wanted to. The fact is that none of us thought there was anything to worry about.

Well, as Dubcek got off the plane—*there* was Kadar waiting for him with Machatka's piece in his pocket. Dubcek, when he was shown it, was greatly embarrassed because he knew nothing about the article. It was certainly not our intention either to make difficulties for Dubcek or to alienate Kadar—Kadar was, after all, the only leader in the Warsaw Pact who behaved more or less decently *vis-à-vis* the Prague Spring. But *there* it all was: the Western press, and the Russians too, began to engage in wild speculations—the Prague reform Communists, they said, were clearly Imre Nagy's followers and the Machatka article was deliberately published on the morning of Dubcek's visit to Hungary. Conclusion: there was collusion between Dubcek and the Hungarians.

Urban Did the Russians somehow think that Kadar had suddenly reverted to his pro-Nagy policies of October 1956 and embraced (after the Dresden meeting, at that) the programme of the Prague reformers?

Liehm I am not saying they did. It is my speculation that at the back of their minds they might have entertained that kind of suspicion as they were, and are, suspicious of everyone in Eastern Europe. What I do know is that Kadar was very angry and rightly so because he had, of course, nothing to do with any of this, any more than Dubcek.

In the meantime a great myth was being built up around the Machatka article. People who never bothered to read 90 per cent of what had been published in Prague that spring and summer nevertheless know all about the Czechs' alleged Hungarian connection. Poor Machatka was the last to expect that his review would become so memorable an occasion, and I still think it would have had no repercussions had it not come out on the day it did.

Urban Whatever the timing—Machatka and your paper were unambiguously rehabilitating Imre Nagy and, in fact, justifying the Hungarian revolution. When I first read Machatka's article I knew nothing about Dubcek's visit to Kadar, but it was clear enough that Machatka was treading on dangerous ground. Katyn, the Warsaw uprising, Poznan and Hungary in 1956, and now the Prague Spring—these 'unfacts' are deeply buried in the Soviet subconscious.

Liehm *Of course* Machatka's article did amount to Nagy's rehabilitation; *of course* the parallel with 1968 was unmistakable—but remember that in 1968 revelations about the Soviet show-trials and our own were printed daily in our press; we ran Deutscher's *The Unfinished Revolution* in instalments over a long period and carried a great many other items which one might have thought were at least as damaging to Soviet *amour-propre* as was Machatka's article on Nagy. I still believe the article would have melted into the landscape if Dubcek's visit to Hungary had not drawn special attention to it.

Urban Why do you say that for some years after 1956 the Hungarian experience was not thought to be relevant to your programme? Is it possible that even Communists of your own inclinations actually believed that 1956 had been a counter-revolution?

Liehm No, I would not say that was exactly what we believed. We were, right from the beginning, very sympathetic to the Hungarians. At the same time we thought that Hungary was still a predominantly agricultural country with one big city planted in the middle of the vast Hungarian plains—a country which had not shed its nineteenth-century traditions, a country of horses and hunting and all the other paraphernalia of gentry life. And we consequently believed that when, at a certain point in October 1956, the Hungarian authorities lost control, Hungary's old reflexes, its hidden violence and intransigent nationalism, were reasserting themselves. So while we were not thinking of 1956 explicitly as a counter-revolution, we did not believe that we could learn from it. We thought that the democratic traditions and cultural history of the Czech lands demanded a response which would be different from what we had seen in Hungary. In other words, we believed that we could control our liberalisation and render it acceptable to Moscow.

It was only after the Machatka uproar, and eventually after the Soviet occupation, that we began to look at the Hungarian revolution more closely and to discover how fatefully similar the two events really were if one took a large enough view of them. Of course, each country had its peculiarities, its political personality and so on, but the basic similarities were overwhelming. It took us some time to say this openly. I started saying it to my Communist friends in the West soon after my arrival in 1969—and for some time many of them would not accept it. Until 1973–4 even a man like Garaudy would not admit it, and it is a sobering thought that the Italian and French Communist Parties still refuse to concede that Hungary and Czechoslovakia were analogous revolutions, even though many Italian and some French Communist leaders privately recognise the connection.

Urban The question one would want to answer is: Do nations, societies, parties learn from one another's experiences, and, indeed, from their own? There is very little in history to encourage us to think that they do.

Liehm A Czechoslovak film director, Jan Kadur (now in New York), told me the following story.

> I happened to be in Budapest with a delegation during the first stages of the Hungarian uprising, and I told my Hungarian friends—'Boys, you are playing a dangerous game; the Russians will not let it come off.' The Hungarians, all of them Communists whom I had known for years, laughed in disbelief. They were certain that their programme was not only unimpeachable from the Soviet point of view but constructive, and that the Russians would perceive it in the same light. Looking at

Hungary from Prague, one could see where Hungary's train was heading, but the Hungarian Communists would not share that perspective.

At the 1968 Karlovy Vary film festival the roles became reversed: now it was my Hungarian colleagues' turn to warn us that the Prague Spring was going to be squashed and ours to express disbelief. And we did, as I well remember, argue against the Hungarians' dire warnings. We told them that Czechoslovakia was not Hungary; that our reforms were moderate and peaceful which the Russians would understand and indeed welcome, and so on. Well, the Hungarians had a great piece of wisdom on their side. They said: 'perfectly true—Czechs are not Hungarians, but *Russians* are *Russians*!' And they were.

'We are not Hungarians', or French or Italians—this is the mistake all nations make. Americans will tell you they are not Germans, the British that they are not French—words and excuses to cover up a basic flaw in man's collective psyche: his inability to recognise himself in his neighbour.

Urban But how could the sacred cow of national identity, not to say nationalism, be kept alive if an Englishman admitted that he had anything to learn from anyone as outlandish as an Italian? National prejudice is about the only heart-warming feeling left to us in this disenchanted and egalitarian age. Would you want to deprive us of *that*?

Liehm Alas, I have to agree with your conclusion, but not for the reasons you mention—tongue in cheek, I suppose. After the suppression of Czechoslovakia on 21 August 1968, everyone was asking us: How could you have been so blind as not to see that the Russians would clamp down on your form of socialism? My answer has always been that nations are like human beings: they only react to their *own* experiences. A child will not believe that the oven is hot until he has accidentally put his hand on it—but then he will react to the oven with intense caution again and again irrespective of whether the oven is in fact hot or hot no longer. Nations react in the same way. The French, for example, are still highly suspicious of the English because English aggression and occupation have happened to them repeatedly in their history. They have great difficulty in believing that they could not happen again.

Urban But in the case of Czechoslovakia it wasn't that you had no precedent in your *own* and very recent experience. You cannot say that the occupation of 1938 happened to another country.

Liehm Ah, but nations don't think in terms of 'occupations'—they think in terms of their experiences of *other* nations. Occupation by *Nazi* Germany was one thing—but it never occurred to anyone that this should move us to think of *Soviet* occupation as an analogous possibility.

In the 1960s Polish Communists used to visit us and spend long periods of time with us in Prague. They saw the euphoria of the Reform Movement, but their scepticism was intense. Poland was at the time going through the worst of the Gomulka period, and our Polish comrades were highly conscious that the dead hand of Gomulka of the 1960s was the hand of the same man who had raised Polish hopes in 1956 by defying the Russians. 'Look at the state of Gomulka-Poland today,' they warned us: '*we* are your future!'

Well, we didn't of course believe them: 'This is not Poland; things work differently here.' They would shake their heads at us: 'There is one link missing in the Czech historical experience—Russian occupation.'

And these Poles were right. The last 'Russian' occupation of the Czech and Slovak lands happened in the twelfth century, at the time of the Tatar invasion (leaving out of account the Russian presence on our soil during the Napoleonic wars when the Russians were not enemies). We were simply not in the habit of thinking of the Russians as invaders—our historical experience was totally different from that of the Poles and Hungarians whose image of the Russian steamroller was deeply engraved in the national psyche.

Who was responsible?

Urban Shouldn't you have been warned, though, by the political implications of the behaviour of those Soviet troops who occupied Subcarpathian Ruthenia, Slovakia and ultimately much of the Czech lands as allies and 'liberators' in 1944 and 1945? In Ruthenia, for example, one of the first acts of the Soviet authorities was to dissolve the Czechoslovak National Committees and put up Committees of their own which then 'voted' for the incorporation of Ruthenia in the Soviet Union—despite Benes's agreement with Stalin that the pre-Munich borders of Czechoslovakia would be respected. Such were the speed and the extent of Sovietisation that the Czechoslovak Delegate and his staff were put under house arrest and not permitted, under pain of death, to communicate with the London government except through Red Army channels—which meant the Kremlin and Fierlinger. A message secretly sent by a member of the Czechoslovak Delegation to the government in London (28 November 1944) tells its own story:

> The Czechoslovak government's authority cannot be exercised. Where is the Treaty? Czechoslovak property is being stolen in front of our eyes. The Red Army carries even the telephone wires away. Nobody seems to have the courage to oppose them. The NKVD is here and operates. The people see it and cannot feel respect for the Czechoslovak Administrative Delegation. The people are puzzled. The officers of the political service of the Ukrainian Front Command direct the propaganda of the Communist Party. The destiny of the Delegation is in your hands. If you do not intervene in Moscow, we cannot master the situation. It is forbidden to communicate with you. I am calling in secret. Your answer must be worded cautiously. Signed: Krucky

And a day later:

> The risk of calling directly is mounting. I am perhaps calling you for the last time. We are under pressure. Only your démarche in Moscow can save us. Whoever refuses to volunteer for the Red Army is in danger and has to take refuge in the mountains. Many do. The same happens to those who refuse to vote Communist when local or district Committees are being formed. The terror

is directed by the political service of the Red Army. Try to send a courier plane and bring me to London. You should know everything. Signed: Krucky.

Liehm I don't dispute your evidence. The Soviet forces behaved just as badly in Ruthenia and Slovakia as they did in Hungary and Germany, trying to muscle in on the political scene, looting, raping and so on. But by the summer of 1945 they had left Czechoslovakia and the impact of the excesses you have cited remained limited to those who had been personally affected. The kind of occupation *we* had was vastly different from the Russian occupation of Poland, for example, which lasted for centuries and involved Russification as a long-range imperial policy.

In other words—I am not disputing the facts of Soviet behaviour in Czechoslovakia in 1944 and 1945; what I am disputing is the impact it had on the mentality of the people of our country. Who in Prague thought that whatever the Russians may have done in Ruthenia in 1944 ought to be a factor in our assessment of how the Russians might behave in 1968? None of this was being given serious consideration.

The *Hungarians* knew that if once they raised the banner of national resistance, as they had done in 1848, it was the Russian army that would be sent in to crush it. But in Czech history nothing of the kind had happened, and it was very hard to believe that it would happen in 1968. *Now* the gap has been closed, and you can be sure that the Czechs in their relationship with Russia will never be caught on the wrong foot again.

Urban Are you saying that between 1945 and 1948 Czechoslovakia was fully sovereign because it had, after the summer of 1945, no Russian troops on its territory?

Liehm I am talking of popular perceptions: as there were no occupation forces in our country, it was easy to believe that we were not 'occupied'—that we were masters of our destiny, which in fact we were not.

Urban You have said that the Czechoslovak experience of 1938 was not relevant—or that it was, at any rate, not incorporated in your calculations in 1968 because Russians were not Germans. But surely that extremely bright and knowledgeable section of the Czechoslovak intelligentsia which led the 1968 Reform Movement—your own group and others—must have realised that the geopolitical position of Czechoslovakia was in Moscow's assessment very similar to what it had been in the eyes of Hitler in 1938?

Liehm That is the way one would see the Prague Spring from the outside and after the event, and I grant you that from the strategic and geopolitical points of view your analogy is obvious, *sub specie aeternitatis*. But for those of us who were deeply involved in the day-to-day conduct of the Reform Movement, the parallel was less easy to recognise. Let me give you chapter and verse of my *own* shortsightedness.

When I first arrived in America in 1970 a small party was organised for me by various friends and acquaintances. Among them there was a man who recognised me from a television interview: 'Didn't I see you on American television the day before the occupation of Czechoslovakia? And didn't you say in that programme that there would be *no* Soviet intervention?' 'Yes,' I answered, 'you did, and I was dead wrong.'

What in fact happened was this: in the afternoon of 20 August 1968 a CBS correspondent came to interview me in my office. The brunt of his questioning was: did I think the Soviets would move in on us? My reply was that any such supposition was totally nonsensical, and I gave him my reasons for thinking why it could not happen and would not happen. Well, it did happen within twelve hours of my statement, and I have gone on record with my imbecility and lack of foresight!

My only excuse is that I was not alone in thinking as I did, for it was not only Dubcek and his naive Politburo and a bunch of hopeful intellectuals who thought that the Russians would not crush the Reform Movement; the country as a whole thought likewise. There were *fears*—yes—but our irrational hope that the Russians would leave us alone was rationalised in various ways, until everyone talked himself into believing that they *would* leave us alone for sound practical reasons. And why did this irrational hope gain such wide currency? Because there was in the Czech national experience no historical precedent for a Russian invasion.

Urban To what extent did you rationalise your hopes *as a Communist*?

Liehm Although year after year our illusions about the Soviet Union had been gradually eroded, we still tended to say: 'What would the Russians gain by occupation? We are not threatening their security; we do not want to become their enemies; they would completely tarnish their image if they crushed us and do irreparable damage to the Western Communist parties.' Yes, we rationalised our hopes, and in my CBS interview I, too, rationalised my illusions. The trouble was that my rationalisation didn't work.

Your question implies: all right—you believed what you did because you had, as a Communist, certain residual hopes about the Soviet Union.

I accept that—but why, then, did the *whole of* Czechoslovakia also think as we did? Because *no one* believed in a Russian invasion!

Urban Was the Czechoslovak press free enough in the spring and summer of 1968 to touch on the sensitive issue of a possible occupation? We know that the Czech and Slovak press, radio and television were extremely outspoken, but my recollection is that the threat of a Soviet invasion was perhaps the only topic they avoided talking about.

Liehm Broadly speaking—yes, but since when are nations aware only of things they can read about in the newspapers? I must come back to my earlier conclusion: the Czechs did not believe that the Soviet Union would invade them because there was no emergency warning system built into their national psychology to alert them to this particular danger.

Urban Did some of you in the neo-Communist intellectual vanguard argue that the Russians must by now realise that the Soviet model was inapplicable in advanced Western European countries and that the Soviet leaders would therefore sanction the Czechoslovak experiment? The argument would have been a strong one in its own right, and it might also have served as a cogent rationalisation of your hope that the Russians would let you get away with your reforms in the universal interests of 'socialism'.

Liehm Yes, we did. Wishful thinking is always an important element in political motivation and it was certainly part of ours. We based our hopes on two factors. Firstly, we believed that Khrushchev's move to de-Stalinise the Soviet Union was a considered act of long-term policy, and although Khrushchev was eventually removed from power, we were convinced that the clock could not be turned back. We argued, therefore, that the Czech experiment would be consonant with the general thrust of Soviet thinking, for it would offer proof positive that the system *could* be reformed—quietly, without bloodshed, and without causing tremors in the Soviet–East European community.

Secondly, in 1966, 1967 and 1968 we believed that the whole of Soviet policy was very much in the melting pot, and we thought we had reason to hope that the more enlightened men in the Soviet leadership had a good chance of overcoming the conservative elements. The invasion of Czechoslovakia proved us wrong, but this could not be predicted. Today, most students of Soviet affairs agree that the transition from Khrushchev to Brezhnev ended in August 1968; but between 1964 and 1968 the Kremlin's counsels were flexible—by Soviet standards, anyway.

On the basis of these two assumptions we were persuaded that the Prague Spring would be tolerated. Dubcek expressed this belief in almost religious terms—the intellectuals in more rational and often cynical language—but everybody shared the view that sooner or later the Russians would put up with our experiment because they would come to understand that we were also acting in their own long-term interests, or, to put it at its lowest, not *against* their interests.

Urban Were you, in fact, saying: the Russians will sanction our ideas because we are offering the *only* type of Communism which can have an impact in Italy, France and the rest of Western Europe?

Liehm Communism . . . Communism . . . we were not thinking in terms of *Communism*! Ironically, I had to come to the West to hear the word used at the drop of a hat, and to be made to use it myself—

Urban —let's call it 'socialism' then. We need not go into the semantics of the two words for we know what we mean—except perhaps to say that neither the Czechs nor the Russians claim that they have as yet entered the promised land of Communism or that they know what it will be like when they do.

Liehm This type of vocabulary is scholastic prattle. It has not been used in Eastern Europe since the death of Stalin, and it would be misleading and nonsensical if I tried to interpret the Czechoslovak Reform Movement in terms of 'Communism'. Splendid theories about the 'stages of socialism' and the arrival of the classless society! Why, they have been laughed out of court in Soviet Eastern Europe since the mid-1950s!

What we *were* vaguely hoping to do was to combine democracy with a broadly conceived socialism, and by so doing offer one possible example, not so much to the Communist parties in Western Europe as to Western society as a whole.

Urban You were trying to answer the problems of advanced, urbanised, mass industrial societies, or so I have heard some of your comrades say—after the event, to be sure.

Liehm Yes, that was the general thrust of the Prague Spring, without anyone realising it at the time. When Dubcek took over in January 1968 we had no model in mind. To be frank with you, we didn't have the vaguest notion where we were going. The whole Prague Spring was one long improvisation, but that is what one has to expect at a time of revolutionary change.

Our principal objective was simple and practical—to improve the country's situation, and more particularly to do something about our disastrous economy. But as more and more people from abroad came to visit us wondering whether we knew what we were doing, we were forced to rationalise our muddle and appoint a 'model'. That is how 'socialism with a human face' came into being—rather late in the Prague Spring—more in response to inquisitive foreign journalists and academics who were anxious to detect a 'trend' and pin a label on it, than to any spontaneous domestic need. The phrase was not much in use in Prague until well after the occupation.

Urban I still marvel at your optimism. Take the case of Cestmir Cisar with his remarkable speech on 6 May 1968 to commemorate the 150th anniversary of the birth of Marx.

What he was saying was simple enough: the 'monopolistic interpretation' of Marx by Lenin was unacceptable to the Czechoslovak Party. It had created a rift in the world Communist movement which could only be healed if the monopolistic interpreters changed their ways. Either the Soviet Communists joined Prague's side of the argument or Prague would go its own way.

Although Cisar's speech was decked out with the usual disclaimers ('anti-Sovietism is and remains a weapon of imperialism . . . and the Czech and Slovak peoples have nothing in common with it') his message was a clear challenge to Soviet authority in Eastern Europe. So clear indeed was the challenge that on 14 June 1968 Academician Konstantinov answered Cisar in *Pravda*. Leninism, he wrote, was not just a Russian but an international Marxist theory. Its validity was world-wide. Only the enemies of 'socialism'—right-wing revisionists, splitters, Maoists—could argue otherwise.

This was, to my mind, an unmistakable indication that the Soviet leaders would brook no attempt to weaken their control over Eastern Europe. And we must admit that you *were* challenging Leninism—the *raison d'être* of the Soviet Communist Party and perhaps of *any* Communist Party.

Liehm None of this was self-evident at the time. For one thing, the Soviet Communists had themselves demolished one of the supports of the system—Stalinism—and it was not unreasonable to assume that we could widen and enrich Soviet political thinking: Khrushchev's policies had run their course, Khrushchev himself had been removed, and the Soviet leadership was trying to plot out a new course—we thought we could help them.

For another, we could see that the Russians were not completely inflexible in their East European dependencies. They were tolerating a powerful Catholic Church in Poland; they had accepted Polish private farming, and made other concessions of a kind that would have been unimaginable in the Soviet Union itself. Why would they not accept reforms by a thoroughly trusted, friendly Party, especially as these reforms represented, as we thought, the creative interpretation of Marxism?

Urban But you do appreciate the criticism, don't you,

that Prague was in too much of a hurry, and that less haste might have given you better results?

Liehm I have heard such words of *ex post facto* wisdom before. My answer is—No. If we had proceeded with greater caution, if the Prague events had been controlled (and I am leaving aside the question whether they *could* have been controlled), we would have arrived at something like Gierek's Poland—not the Prague Spring. That is not what we wanted. The Prague Spring was what it was because it was a free and spontaneous drive for reform—not an exercise in window-dressing. Our critics say that it would have been better if Husak, not Dubcek, had been elected to lead the Party in January 1968, because he would have imposed a slower and controlled liberalisation and avoided offending Soviet sensibilities. That may be so—but if that is your choice of the means, then you cannot say that your objective is a thoroughly reformed socialist system. Husak, as I say, would have led to a Gierek type of Czechoslovakia, and my estimate is that sooner or later the Russians would have imposed their 'Treaty' on a more or less willing Husak too.

Urban —I would say more rather than less. An important document has recently come to light which shows Husak, in 1944, to have been a vociferous advocate of the incorporation of Slovakia in the Soviet Union.

Liehm Yes, in 1944 Husak was an unambiguous Moscow loyalist. The point I would emphasise is that the Czechoslovak people decided to act as if they were in a position to act freely. They found themselves in the clutches of an antiquated and totally inadequate political and economic system which they knew had to be thoroughly changed. This could not be done unless they resolved to look neither left nor right but to go ahead and do what they thought was right and necessary. I grant you that we may have been naive from the geopolitical and strategic points of view, but my point is that no Prague Spring would have come into being if the people of Czechoslovakia had kept a worried eye on how the Russians might react. Revolutionary change is not brought about by careful circumspection.

Urban But surely after the Dresden meeting there was

no excuse for *not* knowing that the Russians considered Prague to be their *internal* affair and would act accordingly?

Liehm The wagon was rolling down the slope and no one had the power to stop it. You could only derail it—and that is what the Russians eventually decided to do. But I am firmly convinced that at the end of the slope, which was near, the Reform Movement would have levelled out to the great benefit of the Soviet Union as well as Czechoslovakia.

Urban Would it not have been politically wise, certainly after the Dresden warning, to seek Western support—not in any military sense (which was not on the cards) but in that of trying to make it politically and economically expensive for the Soviet Union to march on Czechoslovakia? Would it not have been reasonable for you to argue: if the penalties of invasion are made sufficiently clear to the Soviet leadership, the more liberal elements in it will find it easier to press home their case against the killing of our experiment?

Liehm No, we were careful to do no such thing—partly because we had learned from the Hungarian precedent that even a declaration of neutrality would be read as a direct challenge to Soviet hegemony, and partly because we knew that without active Soviet concurrence our chances of success were nil.

I remember having lunch in Prague with a highly placed American, and later with a German politician. Both asked me the same question: 'Is there anything we can do to help you?' My answer was 'No', which was, come to think of it, perhaps another poorly thought-out response. Mind you, it was obvious from both conversations that neither the American nor the German was thinking of offering us any *active* help. 'If you can work your reforms with the Russians, fine—we'll be with you, but don't get yourselves into a Hungarian-like situation'—this was the drift of their reasoning.

I suppose we *could* have said: 'it would be very helpful if President Johnson quietly warned the Russians not to interfere with us'; but the fact is that we didn't even say that. We believed that our only chance of success was that the Russians would, for one reason or another, accept what we were doing. This was certainly my personal conviction.

'What would you do if the Russians *refused* to understand your position?' I was asked by my CBS interviewer. 'If the Russians don't understand, we will have reached the end of the road and lost, and I personally would no longer want to live in this country.'

That is why I left Czechoslovakia.

Urban Should Czechoslovakia have offered armed resistance?

Liehm This question has often been asked with undertones of a certain disapproval: 'the Yugoslavs fought, so did the Israelis—why didn't you?' Well, Czechoslovakia's situation was very different from Yugoslavia's both during the war and in 1948. For one thing, the most important, Dubcek, unlike Tito, was not in command of the Czechoslovak armed forces. These were in Russian hands and had been, under the Warsaw Pact, for twenty years. We could have organised large-scale resistance by the police and by civilian organisations—a fine gesture but also an act of suicide. As to the parallel with Israel—since its foundation as a state, Israel has had one of the world's superpowers, the US, to back it with the full weight of American diplomacy, and to supply it with arms. Without them Israel would have vanished from the map many years ago.

No one was ready to help *Czechoslovakia*. I get a little annoyed when I hear people say, first, that we had acted far too precipitately and committed *psychological* suicide, and then accuse us in the same breath of lacking the courage to commit *physical* suicide as well!

Urban But isn't it one of the conditions of keeping a sense of nationhood alive that national independence, if mortally challenged, should be defended with all means at a nation's disposal, including the lives of its sons and daughters? 1938, 1948, 1968—aren't these grave-stones on the road to national self-liquidation?

Liehm We have all been searching our hearts on this question for a whole decade. What you say sounds like stirring stuff, but it does not, precisely because it is so beguilingly simple, do justice to the problem we were facing.

First, there is nothing peculiarly Czech about non-resistance. The German attack on Norway, for example, hardly met any resistance, and one could quote other examples. More important, it is my considered opinion that the responsibility for everything that happened in Czechoslovakia in 1968 and 1948 goes back to 1938. The non-resistance and defeat of Czechoslovakia did not arise from an enfeebled Czechoslovak national consciousness; much rather were they the end-results of a crime for which responsibility must be laid at the door of Britain and France who delivered Czechoslovakia to Hitler in 1938 and destroyed the Czechoslovak people's and the Czechoslovak Army's will to resist. Our occupation by the Soviet Union in 1968 was not due to détente or Yalta, but to the 1938 Munich Agreement which demonstrated the Western powers' unwillingness to do anything for a state which they had themselves created.

By abandoning it to Nazi Germany they were abandoning it, in fact, to Soviet imperialism as well, though the Western statesmen, such as they were in 1938, were much too short-sighted and uninformed to foresee that that was what they were doing. No matter how critical one may be of Benes on this or that issue, he was absolutely right not to permit Czechoslovakia to be launched on a course of self-destruction. He found himself abandoned by his allies, and he very reasonably concluded that he would not have Czechoslovak blood shed for British and French duplicity and cowardice.

The Czechs and Slovaks had, of course, their own guilt to answer for, and they have had a terrible price to pay for it—but they were *accomplices* to the crime, not its originators. Suicide would not have helped them any more than it did the Poles who were repeatedly massacred for their courage in the nineteenth century. The Czechs did not fight and did not get massacred; but they were in the same boat with the Poles when Hitler was ruling Europe, and they are in the same boat with them now.

Urban Yet the myth (or is it the reality?) of national character survives, and perhaps this is not always a bad thing. In 1956 the Poles and Hungarians had the traditions of 1848 to draw on. Without it the 1956 uprising might have taken a very different course or not occurred at all.

Liehm *Of course* national myths are important—and their destruction, I might add, is often as important as their survival. A few years ago Max Ophuls made an important documentary film about France under German occupation—*Le chagrin et la pitie*—which I periodically show to my American students here in Philadelphia as part of their education in contemporary history. Their reaction is invariably: 'God, we didn't realise that the French were such a cowardly nation under the occupation—we thought every Frenchman worth his salt was in the Resistance and fought the Nazis to the bitter end!' The film, as you know, shows wartime France in unflattering but entirely truthful colours.

Urban Yes, I saw it, surrounded by a hushed audience, in a small Parisian film theatre.

Liehm Well, after every one of these filmshows I spend hours trying to explain to my students that France was *not* a cowardly country; that there is no such thing as a cowardly *nation;* that the human condition has a way of landing individual men and women in predicaments from which there is no honourable escape or no escape at all. Young people find this hard to understand.

National self-image and stereotypes of other nations are almost indestructible. Ophuls's film could not be shown on French television because it offended—at any rate in the eyes of the official keepers of French national self-respect—the self-image of France as a nation of stalwart resisters. It had to be shown in private cinemas almost to the exclusion of the public, but the fact that it could be shown at all deserves one cheer (and no more than one cheer) for French democracy.

No one likes to see his national myths shattered. In Poland, Vajda's films—*Ashes and Diamonds* and the rest—cause an uproar almost every time they are shown because they run against certain ingrained notions the Poles hold of themselves as a people carrying a set of untouchable virtues. Anyone who tries to put down *Czech* national myths also runs into trouble. The Germans suffered from an especially virulent variant of the same disease, but the Second World War and its aftermath put them through a thorough cure. It is, I think, important that from time to time every nation should take a fresh look at itself and burn its totems and shibboleths.

But, to return to the point that trapped us into the

discussion of national myths and prejudices, it would be quite unjustified to say that the Czechs did not fight because there is a piece of machinery missing from their national psychological equipment—

Urban —yet, ironically, this is what Marx and Engels thought of the Czechs: 'They kissed the rod that had chastised them until the blood came', Engels wrote (on 16 February 1849) of the defunct Prague uprising—

Liehm —Marx and Engels wrote some very bad history, especially about the non-Polish Slavs. But, to repeat, it would be a complete misjudgement to claim that the Czechs did not fight because they were congenitally weak or so conditioned to subjection that subjection had become second nature. They did not fight because in 1938 they had been delivered on a platter to Hitler's Germany, and as a result of that betrayal they found themselves after the Second World War locked in the embrace of the Soviet Union. When Britons and Frenchmen tell us nowadays that on 20/21 August 1968 we ought to have stood up to the Russians, my answer is very simple: 'Have *you* searched your hearts about the cowardice and shortsightedness of Chamberlain, Daladier, *The Times* and your political class at the time of the 1938 Munich Agreement?' Any questioning of the responsibility for 20/21 August 1968 must start with Appeasement and the Munich surrender.

The expropriation of the Communist state

Urban We have digressed—what was the heart of the appeal of the Prague reforms for the West European Communist Parties?

Liehm The Prague Spring had one great attraction for them: unlike the Hungarian events in 1956, it was entirely the work of a Communist Party, even though by June–July 1968 our Party was not fully 'Communist' in the traditional sense. The Italian and Spanish Communists could, therefore, identify with it with a perfectly clear conscience, recognising in it everything they themselves were most anxious to achieve: the democratisation and de-Russification of socialism, headed by a Communist Party which was of good report in Moscow. This was the *Italian* and *Spanish* attitude—but not the French. The French Communists, as could be expected, faithfully followed the Soviet line and were extremely hostile to us. Nevertheless, the Prague events caused a stir among French Communist intellectuals, and Waldeck Rochet's attempt in the summer of 1968 to call a European Communist conference at which the French would have mediated between Czechs and Russians may well have been a response to that. The conference never materialised: the Czechs feared that the conference would put them under Soviet pressure via the French Stalinists and, for reasons of their own, the Russians too were reluctant to participate. We still don't know whether Waldeck Rochet *was* acting for the Soviet Party or whether he launched the idea on his own but ran, for one reason or another, into Russian objections—objections he apparently regarded as a grave set-back, so much so that the eventual collapse of his health and the end of his political career have been variously ascribed to it.

The point to remember is (and I am deliberately repeating myself) that in the eyes of the West European Parties Prague offered the first opportunity to de-Russify socialism without getting into conflict with Moscow. Eurocommunism and the crisis of the West European Communist Parties started with that expectation, and the *shattering* of that expectation. The Western Communist Parties clearly could not—and did not—accept the Soviet explanation that the Prague Spring was paving the way for an imperialist take-over of Czechoslovakia. For the reasons I have already given, a similar fabrication about the 1956 Hungarian Revolution could, just, be made to stick, but in the case of Czechoslovakia it could not. From then on it was clear that the de-Russification of West European Communism could be achieved only in the teeth of Soviet opposition, and this meant that Eurocommunism was to be first and foremost a matter of emancipating the Western Communist Parties from Soviet control and Russification.

Urban But has Eurocommunism not by now gone way beyond that—to de-Leninisation, as for example in the case of the Spanish Party?

Liehm I am not sure that it has. The Russification of the

Communist Parties was a wide-ranging process. Its influence will prove very difficult to eradicate. In the 1920s the all-important Soviet *avant-garde*—the Russian painters, writers and poets—were very close to those in Western Europe. They influenced their Western counterparts as much as they were influenced by them. The intellectual leadership in the two camps was virtually interchangeable: Alexander Blok was as important in Paris as Gide was in Russia. Stalinism put an end to all this. It foisted not merely a particularly odious Russian type of despotism on the organisation of all the world's Communist Parties, but it also perverted and degraded their life-styles, their manners and culture by demanding that they be modelled on Russian life-styles, Russian manners and Russian cultural stereotypes. This, more than anything else, made Soviet leadership of the world Communist movement entirely intolerable, and especially so for the West European Parties.

I keep coming back to this point because it explains both the Prague Spring and the attraction it had for the West European Communists. De-Leninisation, if it comes, will be a bonus. The Spanish do appear to have de-Leninised to some extent; the Italians uncertainly so; the French not at all. We could see before the 1978 French elections that the French Communist Party willingly risked throwing away the Left's chances of electoral victory because it feared that cooperation in government with a strong Socialist Party would subvert its Stalinist organisational structure and undermine its ideological orthodoxy. Its innate Stalinism and its loathing of the Socialists proved stronger than its will to defeat Giscard.

Urban What particular lessons have the West European Communist Parties drawn from the Prague Spring? I have especially in mind the promise, clearly implied in what was being said and done in Prague in 1968, of a multi-party system. You did yourself imply it in various articles you wrote at the time. In *Literarni Listy* (13 June 1968) you called for a new Constitution to be endorsed by a referendum. 'After its final adoption,' you argued, 'political life would develop within a new framework which I would not venture to predict at this juncture.' But you added that the enactment of the new Constitution 'would also mark the end of the mandate entrusted to the enlarged National Front'.

Liehm I don't think it took much reading between the lines to get my meaning. I stood for a multi-party democracy without equivocation.

Urban Yes; but are we to assume that today's Eurocommunists, if they came to power, would permit a genuinely multi-party parliamentary democracy to exist? The Prague events were not allowed to advance far enough to give any indication whether your reforms would have resulted in a multi-party democracy as the phrase is understood in Western Europe, or in a National Front of some kind, in which case the Communist Party would have retained its supremacy and the other parties would have functioned more or less on sufferance within the limits of 'socialism'.

Liehm You have put your finger on the principal problem: would the Eurocommunists *permit* a genuine democracy to function? You are clearly assuming—and I dare say you are, if we think of the French Communist Party, assuming quite correctly—that if and when the Eurocommunists came to office they would want to be in a position to *permit* or *not to permit* a multi-party system. This is the whole question: as long as there is any talk of a West European Communist Party arrogating to itself the right to permit or not to permit this or that thing to happen, there is *no* Eurocommunism—there is only a prolongation of the life of the old and unregenerate type of Communism which may, once it has secured complete control over the state, permit a little leeway here, and some concession there, but will basically allow nothing to interfere with one-party rule.

The hallmark of a genuine Eurocommunism will be precisely its willingness to take the basic decision not to stick to the Russian rules of the game but to give up the whole principle of one-party control and join the adult section of the human race. Many Eurocommunists are fervent supporters of this civilised variety of socialism, but the politburos of the various West European Communist Parties are still deeply torn by the question whether a Party that has given up the idea of single-party rule can go on calling itself a Communist Party.

Urban Once these Parties have genuinely de-Leninised

and decided to stick to the words of Marx alone, I cannot see why they should balk at the prospect of a multi-party system. Marx insisted that there could be no such thing as a Communist Party, much less a one-party state ('The Communists do not form a separate party. . . . They do not set up sectarian principles of their own . . .'). At the same time he qualified his objection to a Communist Party by observing that Communists do not form a separate party '*opposed* to the other working-class parties'; that they have no interests '*separate* and *apart from* the proletariat as a whole'. These qualifications of Marx are strong enough to justify the limitation of even a genuinely multi-party Eurocommunist system to those parties which are prepared to work within 'socialism', and this is in fact what Eurocommunists like Lombardo Radice broadly envisage.

Liehm True, Marx did not support the idea of a Communist Party, but he spoke, unfortunately for us, from the historical experience of the eighteenth and nineteenth centuries—from the experience of a strong centralised state which dominates the political scene: whoever controls the state, controls its economy and its social structure. Therefore the creation of a socialist society, too, depends on the control by the proletariat of the whole apparatus of the state. Now Marx does not say that this take-over requires a centralised force called the Party—he talks of the dictatorship of the proletariat instead. But you cannot have a dictatorship by *five* parties—hence the logic of Marx's whole strategy carries in it the demand for the rule of a single, dictatorial party.

Urban But surely this dictatorship was meant to be transitional—one station on the way to the classless society—

Liehm —'classless society'—this is airy-fairy stuff. The truth is that Marx does not say what the dictatorship of the proletariat is transitional *to*. Lenin too is very hazy on this point. What we *can* see is that the withering away of the state and the promised land of 'Communism' have been postponed *ad Graecas kalendas*, but the Soviet state is strong and getting stronger.

What is most striking about Czechoslovakia today is not only that the Party is in sole control of the whole of the country's life, but that the Party *owns* the country.

Urban —a return to the patrimonial state well known to us from Tsarist times—

Liehm —it means that, too. The crucial point is that the nationalisation of the economy leads inevitably to the one-party state, and that to dictatorship. As long as your ideology demands the conquest of the state and through it the conquest of the national economy, you cannot talk of a pluralistic polity, much less a multi-party system. Locke pointed out a long time ago—and nothing has happened since his time to refute him—that the basis of political pluralism is the pluralistic ownership of property. This is not a plus or minus point for capitalism or communism. It is a fact of life that pluralism within a socialist order can only exist if the principle of the plurality of ownership is upheld.

The Prague Reform Movement challenged the ownership-role of the Communist Party. It did not challenge it immediately. In the early stages of the Movement the idea was to change the Party, and through the Party the system. 'Democratisation of the Communist Party' was the slogan when the wagon started rolling, and this was followed by calls for the democratisation of the press, culture, the judiciary, and so on. Only much later was it realised that none of these things could be achieved without the democratisation of the economy. Eventually the call came for what I regard as the key element in the whole Reform Movement—the call for the *expropriation of the State*.

Urban In Ota Sik's version of the history of the Prague Spring the economic reforms came first and political liberalisation followed, in a rather Marxist sequence, as their necessary concomitant. Having learned from the 1956 Hungarian example that the Russians would not tolerate a frontal attack on the system in the shape of *political* reforms, the Czechs, he hinted, decided to ease *their* reforms in through the economy.

Liehm Sik and his collaborators had to weigh the probable consequences of following the Yugoslav model of economic *decentralisation*, and that gave them justified cause for anxiety. Why? Because in 1966, 1967 and 1968 the Czechoslovak economy was in very deep trouble. It needed decisive leadership—and that meant *centralised* leadership—to pull it out of the mud. If you install workers' control, self-management and the like at a time of great economic weakness, your chances of rescuing your economy from collapse and of putting it on its feet again are negligible. For all these reasons Sik's reforms were meant to be *centralised* reforms which did not, in their original form, threaten the patrimonial role of the system. But that was not the end of the story.

We had realised for quite some time that our first step to ensure that the Russians would not interfere with us was to isolate those elements inside the country who saw their personal interests threatened and were preparing to undermine the Reform Movement even to the extent of calling for 'fraternal assistance' from the Soviet Union. (We imagined in our naivety that without a call of that kind the Soviets would not find it possible to invade us!) We therefore went about isolating these people without using any violence, and I think you will agree that in this respect at least our success was complete. When the crunch came on 21 August 1968, there were no Quislings among us.

But how was the isolation of these potentially pro-Soviet elements to be achieved? By June and July we realised, and Sik was among the first to realise, that a pro-Soviet *putsch* could only be warded off if more power was immediately transferred to the workers. In July and August Sik and his colleagues admitted that they had been wrong: power, including, of course, economic decision-making, had to be decentralised and vested in the Works Committees. It had to be done, not for *economic* reasons (the state of the economy militated, as I've said, *against* any such move) but for extremely urgent *political* reasons. With the devolution of power and 'ownership' to the Works Committees, the first steps were being taken to *expropriate the 'Communist' State*. It is an instructive reminder of the great popularity of this measure that when the Soviet forces invaded Czechoslovakia, these newly formed Works Committees were the last to knuckle under to Soviet control.

Urban 'Expropriating the expropriators of the expropriators' (to reverse Marx's famous formula for the dictatorship of the proletariat)?

Liehm Yes, if you like—expropriating the state—

Urban —which the Russians would inevitably describe as restoring capitalism—

Liehm —to which I would retort, with Trotsky, that the Soviet system is state socialism—

Urban —a point the Italian Communists are now also making.

Liehm Yes—the Italian Communists have learned one important lesson from church history: terminology matters. By describing the Soviet system as 'state socialism' they are implying that other forms of socialism are possible and desirable. Also, by talking of Marxism *and* Leninism—not Marxism-Leninism—they let it be known that *Marxist* socialism need not be a *Leninist* type of socialism as well.

What did we have in mind when we began to see the expropriation of the 'Communist' Czech state as our target? Our starting point was to say that socialism is about the democracy of the workers: the people who produce should decide what happens to the things they produce. We, therefore, perceived our task to be a thorough reform of the existing relationship between production and ownership, realising (though we were slow in coming to this realisation) that every economic reform implies a political reform, and every political reform an economic reform. Hence we decided that—with the exception of certain public services and industries such as railways, electricity, mining and so on—property should be taken out of the hands of the state and turned over to the Works Committees as the producers' rightful representatives. We were confident that the pluralisation of property-ownership would lead to the pluralisation of political interests, and that to the pluralisation of the system.

The question we have to ask the West European Communist Parties, and especially the Eurocommunists, is this: are they prepared to accept the existing West European mixed economies and work for a *progressive* transformation of property relationships? Will they agree that a truly socialist society presupposes a plurality of ownership, and that this in turn rules out any idea of a dominating social bloc, 'hegemony' and the like—to say nothing of a one-party state?

Or do they still believe (in good nineteenth-century

fashion) that socialism means the nationalisation of the economy—the expropriation of capital for the benefit of the state—in which case Eurocommunism will amount to little more than a de-Russified form of dictatorship by the Communist Party?

This is the basic issue posed by the Prague Spring, and I don't think it has yet been properly understood by the West European Parties—not even by some of the Eurocommunists.

Urban But this was not clearly stated at the time—perhaps it *could* not be clearly stated?

Liehm It was not stated in exactly these words but it was implied. Our problem was that the idea of the expropriation of the state and the resulting pluralisation of the system did not come up until very late in the Prague Spring. We had, as I have said, first to defeat the economic reformers' argument that the only way in which the country could be put on its feet again was through maintaining a strong, centralised economy.

There is one observation in Marx which has great relevance to the point I am making. Marx says that the transition from one socio-economic order to another occurs at a time when the new order is already fully grown in the womb of the old one[1]—

Urban —you are stressing the non-violent strand in Marx's conception of social change, whereas the dominant emphasis in both Marx and Engels is on revolution accomplished by violence. Engels was still fighting for the dictatorship of the proletariat shortly before his death in 1891, and even a Eurocommunist like Carrillo, writing in 1977, said that 'the revolutionary violence of the exploited classes is a sacred right, in certain conditions, so that those classes can liberate themselves and put an end to oppressive violence'—a catch-all formula vague enough to leave all of us free to interpret it in any way we like.

Liehm Yes, you are quite right to say that I am stressing

[1] The passage referred to occurs in Marx's Introduction to *A Contribution to the Critique of Political Economy*: 'No social structure ever perishes before all the productive forces for which it has room have developed; and new, higher relationships of production never appear before the material conditions for their existence have formed in the womb of the old society itself.'

the peaceful strand in Marx's conception of social change—and that is precisely what the Prague Spring was about. But even the 'violent' strand in Marx is merely preparatory, as a woman's labour is preparatory, to the birth of a new life. This is the meaning of Marx's metaphor.

But to return to the question of pluralism—the Eurocommunists will have to tell us whether they still believe that socialism means the nationalisation of the means of production, which must, as we well know, end in the death of pluralism and ultimately in the despotism of a single party; or whether they believe the Marxist principle I have emphasised to be right and will therefore opt for the piecemeal change of the existing system by promoting workers' participation and workers' control so that a new socialist society may eventually emerge from the existing one.

As things are at the moment, I do not trust the Eurocommunists. Their vocabulary is still one of 'taking over' the state and changing society from top to bottom. This sounds to me like the old ventriloquist! Western Europe provides daily illustrations of the fact that in the 1970s no government can govern without the cooperation of the trade unions. In Britain, for example, to take the most extreme case, union power and the abuse of union power have greatly contributed to the country's miserable economic performance. Why? Because the British unions have clout but little responsibility. They can cripple the British economy in the name of fighting for the working man's interest and at the same time disclaim responsibility for the economy. In a participatory democracy leading to socialism the unions would be vested with a good deal of responsibility. They would, therefore, have to make their economic decisions with a great deal of circumspection.

Czechs and Italians

Urban Aren't you a little hard on the Eurocommunists? Certainly the Italo-Communists, with their honourable record of resistance to Stalinism, at any rate since 1956, and Gramsci as their home-grown mentor, would agree with part of your conception of socialism even though their notion of 'hegemony' is suspect.

Liehm The nature of Italo-Communism is not easy to read. On the one hand, the Italian Communists were shaped in illegality, in constant contact with other forces of the opposition, which made it possible for them to avoid the grosser forms of Stalinism. (The fully Stalinist Parties, such as the French and Czech, all come from countries in which Communist parties lawfully existed between the two world wars.) On the other hand, the Italian Communists were heirs to the spirit of Catholicism—they needed, and built, a Church. (I incline to believe that Catholic political culture is more conducive to a strong Communist movement than Protestant political culture. If Protestantism means the abolition of intermediaries between God and the individual and is thus hostile to ecclesiastical structures, then it seems to me clear that there can arise no mass Communist movement in any Protestant country—as, in fact, none has arisen.)

Thus the Italian Communists escaped Stalinism while at the same time they are enjoying mass support by virtue of an element of 'catholicism' (with a small 'c') in the Italian national tradition. And then—they had *Gramsci*: a national Leninist, or, if you like, a national Marxist and Leninist thinker of undoubtedly great intelligence.

But how does any of this help them? The question which the Prague Spring has posed and tried to answer—more particularly, the problem of pluralisation through the expropriation of the state—are problems for the *1980s* and *1990s* and beyond, while some Italian Communists are still trying to find Gramscian answers to Italian society as it was in the *1920s* and *1930s*! The problems we are concerned with cannot be solved with Gramscian means because in Gramsci's day they did not exist. There are many things in Gramsci that are worthy of respect, but there are few Gramscian solutions to the problems of West European society at the turn of the twenty-first century.

The Italian Communists are, therefore, in a dilemma. With one half of their selves they can see that such socialism as is open to man to realise must be a slow and pluralistic affair. But the other half of their split personality confronts them with the question: if we abandon the idea of taking power in the name of the working class, if we no longer pursue socialism via the state, but, on the contrary, content ourselves with the democratisation of ownership—aren't we abandoning the revolution? Are we still a Communist Party?

There they have a problem, and I'm not going to answer it for them.

Urban Surely Italo-Communism *does* mean abandoning the revolution?

Liehm It does and it doesn't. The Italian Communists have de-Russified themselves, if we can believe their public utterances, but now they just don't know which way to go. They are torn in different directions and there is a great deal of hot air being generated about all of them.

Urban Shouldn't ideological parties stick to their guns while they are in opposition or, at any rate, not in office?

Liehm It is certainly true that once an ideologically inspired opposition party has attained power it tends to become institutionalised and drift to the centre, and it then risks being overtaken both on its left and on its right. One may reasonably argue that the Italian Communists drifted to the centre even though they were 'in opposition,' and that this is why they find themselves in an ideological and political vacuum. Whatever the cause, their Eurocommunism as it is at the moment does not carry enough conviction, and this will not change until we can see it clearly laid down what precisely Eurocommunism stands *for* —whether it stands for a political party which would act like any other, accepting without reservation the rules of parliamentary democracy, or whether Eurocommunist rhetoric is a disguise for the Party's unchanging ambitions. Promises will not do. The least we can ask the Eurocommunists is to give us their doctrine. But this is precisely what they have not done.

Urban It has been argued that in the 1945–48 period Gottwald himself was, potentially at least, a kind of proto-Eurocommunist, and there are in fact dozens of statements he made in that period which appear to prove the point—statements in support of the multi-party system, of Czechoslovak national traditions, of respect for the Constitution and so on. Yet after the take-over in February 1948 all this went by the board.

I should like to put it to you that Gottwald was a prisoner of Stalin, a victim of the enormous might of the Soviet Union sitting on Czechoslovakia's frontiers, and of the unwillingness and inability of the Western allies to thwart Stalin's ambitions. In other words, Gottwald's failure to live up to his potential Eurocommunism was due to the whole post-war situation in Central Europe—*therefore*, I would argue, we cannot deduce from Gottwald's disappointing performance as a 'Eurocommunist' that Berlinguer, if he reached office, would behave in a like fashion, because the Italian Communists' geopolitical situation in the 1970s is totally different from the Czech Communists' in 1948.

Liehm We don't know whether Gottwald *was* a prisoner of Stalin or whether he was a highly willing accomplice. He and most of the other post-war Czech Communist leaders had been members of the Comintern; Stalinism for them was second nature. The contrast, at this level, with the Italian Communists is certainly striking because none of the current Italian leaders has spent time in Moscow. They are children of entirely Italian conditions—of the Italian resistance and, let us face it, of Italian Fascism, because some of them hail from the Fascist movement.

The psychology of extremism, I might add in parenthesis, is all of a piece; the rules of mass-psychology are stronger than the programmes of political parties. Take the example of one of Italy's traditional areas of radicalism—Bologna, which is a Communist stronghold in the 1970s, having been a Fascist stronghold in the 1920s and 1930s.

Much as I should like to believe that Berlinguer's intentions are different from Gottwald's, I should not want to swear that on the day of reckoning he would live up to his promises. I would want to see a Eurocommunist programme laid down point by point before I could answer the question whether the Italian Communist Party *has* changed. As long as Leninism is tacitly sustained—as long as the Italian Communists have not clearly declared that they don't want to grab the state and run a centralised, monolithic economy—there should always be a suspicion that they may be heading for totalitarianism even if some of them do not realise it. They have as yet not learned the real lessons of the Prague Spring.

Urban One of the red threads running through the articulations of the Prague Spring is the idea that change must take place within the 'socialist' framework. Even those reformers who saw pluralism and a multi-party system as clearly desirable still insisted on this context. Let me take your own example. In the summer of 1968 you strongly (and I might add brilliantly) argued for the renewal and extension of the National Front, 'not as an end in itself, but merely as a means through which the democratisation process works'. At the same time, however, you suggested that the proposed Constituent Assembly should be elected on a single slate because 'elections of this kind . . . are the only ones which . . . can be held within the foreseeable future'. And all this, you wrote, would have to take place within the 'Czechoslovak socialist community'.

Now the Italian Communists, working in an entirely different context, make a point of emphasising their conditional acceptance of parliamentary democracy. But if you confront them with the question: would they peacefully leave the corridors of power if they were voted out of office, they tend to question your sanity. This kind of supposition, they will tell you, is unrealistic—could any electorate want to exchange a higher form of society—socialism—for a lower? (Lucio Lombardo Radice expressed this very view in another discussion.[1])

Putting these two examples together, I cannot help feeling that, at a subconscious level, even the most reform-minded Communists are prisoners of certain unquestioned articles in their ideology. Surely, they assume, no man of goodwill or reason can doubt that socialism is *the* desirable condition to which everything in human nature aspires?

Now a free society, to which the Eurocommunists tell us they subscribe, includes by definition the freedom to reject the entire socialist context, or else the word freedom is meaningless. How, then, is one to read the arrogant assumption that 'socialism' is the *summum bonum* of human life which only fools or knaves would dare to question?

Liehm To stick to the Czech case: a great deal could be said in our press in the spring and summer of 1968, but

[1] *Eurocommunism*, pp. 32–57.

there were certain parameters which people more or less respected according to their temperament and sense of political responsibility. In the six months preceding the Soviet invasion we had an absolutely free press, radio and television, but, as you rightly say, nothing during that time appeared in our media that questioned the socialist basis of society. Was this the result of a genuine consensus? Of national discipline? I don't really know. People were arguing pretty dangerous things in our newspapers—why, then, were they not insisting on the freedom to reject socialism?

Perhaps we were all suffering from a subliminal fear of the context in which we were working—more probably one had to accept socialism in order to be able to transcend socialism. When Wycliffe and John Huss started the Reformation their staple boast was their loyalty to Rome. Not only that, but they really *meant* to remain faithful sons of the Church; only the popes understood much better what Wycliffe and Huss and Luther were about than the Reformers themselves: the popes knew that the Church would never be the same again if the Reformers were given their head.

If you look at the life of Solzhenitsyn, or Maximov, there again you can see men who believed in their youth in Communist society, until their own experiences, followed by incipient doubts about certain aspects of the regime, eventually led them into frontal and decisive critiques of the entire system. The *language* of these critiques, as we well know from Church history, has initially to be kept within the vocabulary of the prevailing orthodoxy. But that does not mean that the critiques themselves stay within the limits of orthodoxy.

Add to this another factor, equally important. In a single-party state pluralism and opposition do not disappear: they take shape *within* the single party, for they have nowhere else to go; and the drive to reform and perhaps to overthrow the regime also comes from critics of the system *within* the single party. For this to be successful, the opposition has to respect the prevailing jargon. I invite you to remember that the present Prime Minister of Spain was a leading member of Franco's Falange and that the Left-radical leaders of the Portuguese upheavals came from Salazar's army elite.

Urban On this showing Stalin was right to have Bukharin and Zinoviev shot, and Brezhnev was equally justified in the pre-emptive suppression of Czechoslovakia.

Liehm Given the grotesque rationale of an inequitable system, they were undoubtedly right—but we do not accept the premises of that system. We do not accept that Soviet socialism *is* socialism; that the denial of freedom *is* freedom; that the suppression of democracy *is* democracy.

Urban Nevertheless, it is clear from what you have told me in this conversation that you were ultimately aiming at a multi-party system not at all necessarily within 'socialism'; that you were working for the expropriation of the 'socialist' state—accompanied by the freedom of the press, assembly and the rest. If you look at all this from the point of view of Soviet national (not to say imperial) interest, can you blame Brezhnev for having acted as the popes had acted against the Protestants, recognising better than you did yourselves that you were, in effect, preparing to undermine the Soviet system?

Liehm The Soviet leaders were not only acting absolutely rationally, but were, from their point of view, absolutely right—and we were absolutely wrong not to perceive this. From the very beginning our quarrel with them centred on one point: is the system you have in the Soviet Union 'socialism'? Is it the only form 'socialism' can take? And when the Soviets answered 'Yes', we ought either to have left it at that, or to have prepared ourselves for armed conflict. But, for the reasons we have already gone over, we did not want to face up to that choice.

Urban The Reformation, of course, did not end with the suppression of the Protestants. Jumping ahead a few centuries, it is also true to say that the 1956 Hungarian revolution did not end with *its* suppression—as the case of Kadarite Hungary well demonstrates.

Liehm Yes. Whatever the fate of individual Protestants might have been, the Reformation came to be established and accepted. The parallel with Hungary is rather different. Kadar's system is pushing the Leninist-Stalinist type of police state and state-socialism as far as they will stretch without openly disrupting them. The Prague Spring was overstepping these boundaries, and that is why, in the

Soviet Union as well as in Western Europe, the boundaries of the Soviet system are now fundamentally questioned. The end of the Prague Spring is not yet.

Urban If you were to name one single aspect of the Prague Spring that induced the Soviet leaders to invade and to suppress Czechoslovakia, what would it be? My personal impression has always been that it was the freedom of the press and of the other media that struck the Kremlin as particularly fraught with danger. The habit of censorship is easy to fall into but very difficult to relinquish—as the whole history of Russia, and not only Russia, shows.

Liehm The freedom of our media was certainly a very powerful irritant. Our press in those six months under discussion was, I think, freer than the press in any other part of the world for the simple reason that we had burst the husk of one system without having fitted into any other. While the interregnum lasted, there were no guidelines, no established habits and conventions—everything could be said, and was said. The Russians, if they had been wise, would have understood that with the stabilisation of the Prague Spring the press too would eventually have shaken down and observed the kinds of restraint which the Finnish media observe out of a sense of national responsibility and prudence. Other restraints would have imposed themselves by virtue of the fact that the press would eventually have become *somebody's* responsibility—a trade union, some guild, a council or association—and as soon as you have, no matter how liberally, institutionalised your media, *some* of your freedom is lost. This was to be expected. What we were determined *not* to have was political censorship. The Soviets were right in thinking that here our position was not open to negotiation.

Urban But, taking in the whole landscape of our discussion, would you not say that, making allowances for their perverse terminology, the Soviet leaders were right in claiming that Antonin Liehm and his associates were preparing to hand Czechoslovakia over to the bourgeoisie and capitalism?

Now—remembering the state of Czechoslovakia in 1968, I personally believe that you could have done a lot worse than hand Czechoslovakia over to capitalism; but were you as a Communist not sensitive to the charge? Are you as a socialist not sensitive to it today?

Liehm I don't suppose I need tell you again why this charge was and is complete nonsense. Not only did we not want to restore 'capitalism' but there is, in fact, no constituency for capitalism in Czechoslovakia. No one wants it. The peasants on their collectivised farms are better off than they have ever been. The industrial workers, though they have massive grievances and may want to change their situation in a thousand ways, would have little time for anyone who suggested restoring the Bata works to Mr Bata. What there *is* a great constituency for in Czechoslovakia is: individual liberty; the abolition of all nannying and censorship; justice and dignity. And the demand for these things grows with the slow but nevertheless real increase in Czechoslovak prosperity.

Was I sensitive to the Soviet charge?

When you are young and inexperienced and dependent on what your headmaster or supervisor thinks or says of you, you get into the habit of putting a damper on your conscience and watching your words. For a long time we acted in that manner in Czechoslovakia. We were always extremely conscious of how the Party and Moscow would respond to whatever we chose to say or not to say on any particular issue.

But in the 1960s we began to grow up, and by 1968 we came to feel that our sense of integrity demanded that we pay no more attention to what anyone in Moscow might think of us—and speak the truth. This was also my personal position. I felt that life had become too short for the charade to continue. We were—as we can now see—set on a collision course, but we were right not to allow ourselves to be diverted.

Zdenek Mlynar

August 1968

Illusion and disillusion

Urban You described the Soviet Union in a recent article as a despotism; *'Eine Despotie braucht Untertanen und nicht Bürger'*, 'A Despotism needs Subjects and not Citizens', was the title of your study in *Frankfurter Rundschau* (28 January 1978). Coming from a former Stalinist who rose, in 1968, to be Secretary of the Central Committee of the Czechoslovak Communist Party, one, moreover, who participated in negotiating the Moscow 'Protocols' and did not leave Czechoslovakia until 1977, your statement seems to call for some explanation. When did you arrive at the view that the Soviet system was a despotism?

Mlynar It did not arrive with a sudden impact; it grew on me gradually, beginning with Khrushchev's criticism of Stalin at the 20th Party Congress; but I lost my last ideological illusions only very *late* in the day, after the invasion of Czechoslovakia and, to be precise, only after we had experienced the 'normalisation' process, that is to say in the early 1970s.

We were misled (and perhaps we willingly misled ourselves) by several factors. Our first mistake was to believe, right up to Khrushchev's fall, that the Soviet Communist Party was not only well disposed towards reform but was the spearhead of liberalisation itself. After Khrushchev's dismissal we failed to notice that the policies followed by his successors were veering back towards a form of Stalinism, so that the reform ideas expressed between 1956 and 1961 in a large number of Soviet statements and documents were being effectively abandoned. The result was that the acceleration of our reforms went side by side with the deceleration, and then the complete reversal, of what we understood to have been Khrushchev's policies.

Urban I am glad you are putting it so cautiously, because we now know from Veljko Micunovic's diaries that Khrushchev's own critique of Stalin was much less radical than most of us thought at the time—indeed he repeatedly reproached the Yugoslav leaders for adding criticisms of their *own* to what had been said by himself at the 20th Party Congress: 'We in the Soviet Union know all about Stalin's errors much better than you do, but there is also another side to the picture', and so on.

Mlynar Another factor which was responsible for our misanalysis has historical roots. Czechoslovakia escaped Soviet occupation (if, that is, we discount the brief stay of Soviet forces on our territory in 1944–45 in pursuit of Hitler's troops). Hence our Communist Party never felt that Czechoslovakia was a Soviet dependency similar to Hungary, Poland and the GDR. We thought of ourselves as the Communist Party of a sovereign nation which would not be denied the opportunity of independent policies. Throughout the 1960s our reform-thinking was bound up with these assumptions.

1968, therefore, came as a complete shock for us, because it suddenly made us realise that Soviet policies were solely governed by the USSR's interests as a world power, that Moscow was prepared to enforce these interests with military means even against a friendly Party within the Warsaw Pact, and that the pursuit of Soviet power had nothing to do with the pursuit of world socialism.

Urban Shouldn't you have been warned by Soviet attitudes to Yugoslavia in 1948, Berlin in 1953, Poland and Hungary in 1956?

Mlynar Of course, of course—but certain lessons of history do not sink in unless we have been made to experience them ourselves. Narrative accounts are not enough; explanations are not enough. We were the prisoners of illusions—the illusion, for example, that in 1956 the Hungarians had committed certain grave errors which *we* would not commit; the illusion that the Hungarian Revolution was not justified and hence its suppression was; the illusion that our own step-by-step approach would be understood and tolerated, and so on.

Urban But didn't your consciousness of the lessons of history as a Marxist alert you to the need to look at your situation in the light of Soviet behaviour in the whole of Eastern Europe since the war? The slogan which the Soviet leaders employed against you in August 1968—'We will not permit the results of the Second World War to be altered'—was the *same* slogan they had employed in 1956 against the Poles and Hungarians and, again and again, in their various disagreements with Yugoslavia even under Khrushchev's 'liberal' stewardship.

Mlynar I would not agree that our reading of post-war events in Eastern Europe was lacking historical perspective. What I would say is that our perceptions were too simple. There is a tendency in all of us to see only what we want to see—what supports our pet theory or gut-reactions. This was the error we made in 1968, but it was unavoidable.

Urban I suppose the annals of revolution would be an empty page if revolutionaries acted on some fine calculation of all the chances of failure and success—

Mlynar —even everyday political action cannot be taken in that manner. You need, if you are an active Communist, a certain unreasoning enthusiasm, a revolutionary ideology, which may, in the end, prove illusory, but without which you are completely immobilised. But the possession of such an ideology also means shutting certain things out of your field of vision. The unfortunate thing is that by the time you realise that you have subjected yourself to a delusion—it is too late. It *was* in our case in 1968.

I discuss some of these problems in my new book (*Nachtfrost*, 1978), and one of the points I stress is that ideology imposes on one extraordinarily lasting inhibitions. I realise that my role in 1968 as Secretary of the Central Committee of the Communist Party cannot be considered in isolation from my life as a young Stalinist in the 1946–48 period or in the 1950s. One has to take it all as a single package and try to explain how and why our ideological illusions were eventually overcome by a more rational political analysis. But when I look back on the illusions I did entertain—I'm horrified! Did I really believe all that Stalinist stuff?

Urban You were in, say, 1948, a completely convinced and dedicated Communist—

Mlynar Oh, indeed I was.

Urban And you believed that you had a foolproof blueprint for a just and superior social order?

Mlynar Certainly, and we swallowed the blueprint whole. Every time we were confronted with the failures, shortcomings and injustices of socialist society we argued, as was expected of good Communists, that these were untypical of socialism—that they did not flow from the *system*, but were, rather, the negation of it. Looking back on this perversion of reason from where I stand today, I simply cannot explain how we could have stuck to it for so long. For it is now absolutely clear to me that these failures and abuses didn't run *counter* to the system but were its logical and necessary consequences.

Urban But, as you say, the power of ideology must have been quite formidable to induce so many highly intelligent people to suspend their critical judgement.

Mlynar It *was* formidable. It is a sad fact about human nature that we are not sensitised to the full evil of lies and deception until we have experienced them on our own skins. We used to believe in grand ideological justifications: 'Objective historical necessity' demands that everything and everyone be judged according to the interests of the world proletariat, the state and the Party. The 'subjective' sufferings of individual people, even the mistakes committed by socialist governments, are unimportant in the light of higher historical necessity. History will justify the sacrifices, and so on. But, once you have seen the results of these 'mistakes' and 'sacrifices' in your own environment you change your mind very quickly and acquire a sceptical, not to say contemptuous, view of the alleged designs of history. But this discrepancy between Utopian commitment and the crimes committed in the name of Utopia is, of course, not a specifically Communist problem—it is as old as religion itself.

Urban You are provoking me to raise a well-flogged but still surprisingly challenging question: how could an allegedly scientific world-outlook assume, especially in the minds of allegedly sceptical 'intellectuals', the characteristics of faith bordering, as it would seem to me, on superstition?

Mlynar A puzzle indeed. Well—Communist ideology is supposed to be scientific (itself a most dubious supposition), but the fact that it *is* an ideology, that it claims to be a body of unalterable truths, is proof enough that it is a *credal* affair first and foremost and 'scientific' only in the nineteenth-century sense.

But once the credal side of it is accepted, one has an *interest* in believing certain things to be true and possible, and others not so. When I was a devoted Stalinist I *had* to believe (as I did) that certain mistakes that had been made in the Soviet Union would not be repeated in Czechoslovakia. If I had clearly foreseen that, the system being what it was, the failures and abuses we had witnessed in the Soviet Union would unavoidably strike home in Czechoslovakia too, I could not have taken a single step along the road to socialism.

Urban My father often told me about the enormous amounts of drink he and his men in the Austro-Hungarian Army were offered the night before particularly dangerous infantry attacks on the Russian front in the First World War. If these men had been sober enough to foresee that half of them or more would bite the dust within twelve hours, perhaps they could not have been driven over the top.

Mlynar This is putting a somewhat exaggerated gloss on my point, but I take your meaning.

Now let me at once add that our illusions and disillusion have not been completely wasted. As a result of 1968 and the Soviet 'normalisation' process things have come to such a pass in the West European Socialist and Communist Parties that it has become very difficult to find any group of any significance that would still consider the Soviet model as even vaguely acceptable. In 1975 and even in 1976 this was not so—the faithful on the European Left still saw a connection between socialism and the Soviet Union. This has now been killed stone dead.

Urban But don't you think that Leninism and even Stalinism have retained considerable strength in the West European Communist Parties? This is patently true in France, but in Italy and Spain too orthodoxy seems to have a powerful grip on large numbers of Communists, especially at grass-roots level. These people do not see the Soviet model as irrelevant to their concerns.

Mlynar There is in every Communist Party some discrepancy between the political/ideological base of the Party and the policies actually pursued by the Party leadership within the constraints of political realities. This is abundantly so in France, but, as you say, to some extent in Italy too. This *need* not mean that the orthodox/Stalinist element has a privileged escalator to the corridors of power within the Party, but in most cases it *does,* especially where the Communist Party has become the ruling party.

Our own experiences between 1945 and 1948 offer a relevant example. In those three years our Party was using the same 'Eurocommunist' tactics for attaining power as the French Communist Party is using today; our Party leaders made firm commitments that the multi-party system would not be tampered with, that agriculture would not be collectivised, that nationalisation would be restricted to companies employing a work-force of more than fifty people, that the Constitution would be scrupulously respected, and so forth. And, indeed, for some time after February 1948, a 'coalition' of sorts ruled the country. But as soon as the first economic difficulties began to affect us, the Stalinist pseudo-radicals (for they were radicals only by their own perverted definition) came forward with the argument that the source of all our troubles was the survival of capitalism in our society; hence—stop cooperating with compromise-happy socialists and opportunists and show some radical mettle. And this popular demagogy was being listened to because it offered easy solutions. People who entertained a rational conception of democracy were sacrificed to it, and the Party was set on its way to despotism.

What I am saying is that a Communist Party in power is always highly vulnerable to the demands and demagogy of its Stalinist component. I hope the West European electorates are aware of this.

Urban Isn't it true, though, that the secret of the success of any Communist Party is its professed extremism? Radicalism, like violence, appears to have its own immanent 'magic' which attracts people of a certain chromosome structure to Fascism or Communism or both. The history of Italian Fascism and Italian Communism offers evidence that some of the rank-and-file members as well as some of the elite of both movements were (and perhaps still are) interchangeable.

I am, in fact, inclined to read your own fanaticism as a young Stalinist (described by yourself in *Nachtfrost* with daunting frankness) as a clue to fanaticism in general—whether of the far Left or the far Right. 'Faith in the Communist ideology,' you wrote, 'which I and tens of thousands of comrades of my generation adopted in 1945, included from the very beginning a tacit authorisation to wage a crusade against the infidel. . . . It presented us with an enemy (in the shape of a "class"), and our job was to fight him with the clear objective of liquidating him radically and without any compromise. . . .'

For 'class' read 'Jew' or 'Communist', and my meaning is clear.

Mlynar This personality-type exists—the born radical, whether of the Left or Right, is an important element in any society. I think it was Göbbels who made the famous remark: 'We can never hope to turn a Social Democrat into a National Socialist, but a Communist is the right material for us.'

But the typological explanation, though true, is insufficient. Social contradictions—extremes of wealth and poverty, privilege and under-privilege—are also important agents in radicalising society. Where there is a strong Social Democratic Party, the Communist appeal is more or less limited to the radical sections of society. Moscow used to be able to exploit this as long as these natural radicals could be persuaded (or persuaded themselves) that the Soviet Union stood for radical policies. Before the Second World War all European Communist Parties based themselves on this assumption, and some of them still do.

But all this is now in the process of rapid change. More and more of the Left-radical groups see the Soviet Union as the embodiment of a deadening bureaucracy, conservatism and immobilism. More and more often they switch their allegiance to Maoism, anarchism and other radical poles of attraction—all of them *away* from the Communist Party of the Soviet type.

Of course, where Social Democracy is weak, as in Italy, the Communist Party can broaden its appeal and attract large numbers of Left-orientated votes. This is how Eurocommunism has arisen, but the context and the rules of the game for a Eurocommunist Party are totally different from those under which the pre-war Communist Parties operated, and some Moscow-centric Parties still operate.

Urban If Eurocommunism is not a misnomer, its appeal should cover the whole of Europe. Does it?

Mlynar I'm not at all certain that it does or that it is likely to. Eurocommunism stands no chance of universal success unless we understand it to mean a deliberate attempt to heal the split which occurred in the international working-class movement as a direct consequence of the October Revolution. Eurocommunism, therefore, either means the reunification of the socialist movement, or it means nothing at all.

If it *does* succeed in creating a single stream of socialism, then it may, under certain conditions, have a measure of success. But I would, under whatever circumstances, find it hard to imagine that a Eurocommunist type of socialism could make headway in the Federal Republic of Germany, Austria, Switzerland and the Scandinavian countries. The Eurocommunist phenomenon in Italy and Spain is a function of very specific social and historical circumstances which do not exist and are most unlikely to arise elsewhere.

Urban Wouldn't the type of Eurocommunism you have in mind be more easily recognised as Social Democracy?

Mlynar That is slightly oversimplifying my meaning, but one may put it like that for an easy answer. Naturally, even in a reunited socialist movement unity of purpose and organisation will probably never be fully achieved. There are, and will always remain, historically and culturally determined differences such as those existing today between Latin socialists and Germanic socialists. But I can well imagine, and I fervently hope, that despite these divergences, a politically and ideologically homogeneous socialist movement might arise which would once and for all discard the misleading perspective of revolution, the dictatorship of the proletariat, and all the other paraphernalia of the Soviet model. Whether a socialist movement of this kind would formally assume the name and organisation of a single party, I do not know, though it would be clearly of advantage if it did. It is also possible that a united socialist movement would be short-lived, that it might again split into two, with one stream joining the Social Democrats and the other re-joining the Soviet side.

Urban What bits of political and ideological furniture would the Eurocommunists have to jettison in order to qualify for membership in your unified socialist movement?

Mlynar I have not given this matter any detailed thought but, obviously, they would have to take a firm stand on behalf of political pluralism. In other words, a Eurocommunist or Socialist party would have to accept, in good faith and without reservations, the rules of parliamentary democracy: the majority party forms the government, and if and when the majority is lost, the party retires into opposition. This is of crucial importance, for it rules out single-party rule. All this has, of course, been well accepted by several Eurocommunists in their public utterances, but whether they, and, more important, their parties would, in fact, act on these principles remains to be tested by their behaviour in office.

Then there is another piece of ideological and political furniture which they would have to get rid of.

The Eurocommunists never tire of telling us that they would scrupulously respect the rules of parliamentary democracy. At the same time, however, they never stop mouthing slogans about solidarity with the Soviet Union in fighting American 'imperialism', freeing the third world from colonialism and neo-colonialism, and supporting struggles of national 'liberation'. In other words, the Eurocommunists are still slaves to the idea that in matters of 'imperialism' and 'colonialism' the growth of Soviet power and influence is a blow struck for progress.

But this is absolutely not so. Eurocommunism will have to repudiate, not merely in theory but in practical action too, the whole idea that Soviet Communism has anything whatever to do with socialism, the liberation of unfree or semi-free peoples, and so on. Not only is the growth of

Soviet influence in the third world *not* identical with the advance of socialism, but it means the *reversal* of the chances of socialism. It is a directly *reactionary* force which has led to the division of the world into two power blocs and has acted as a brake on the independence and sovereignty of every nation it has as yet reached.

Urban You said at the beginning of this conversation that the Soviet Union is a despotism. Are you now saying that it is an imperialist power too?

Mlynar That is what I'm saying, though not in the Leninist definition of imperialism. A country and a system which have set themselves unlimited power as the overriding objective of national existence, and which are prepared to use military force and dictatorship in order to attain and sustain it, cannot be called anything but a form of imperialism.

Urban Your unified socialist movement would, then, have no reason to quarrel with NATO—as Carrillo and Berlinguer have clearly stated?

Mlynar It wouldn't. I don't think one would look upon NATO with any great enthusiasm, but one would accept it as a necessity so long as Europe and the world are divided.

'Consumer-socialism'

Urban While still on the political furniture that would have to go overboard: what would your unified socialist party do about Marxism and Leninism, not to say Marxism/Leninism?

Mlynar Well, we have to be quite clear about it that Lenin's policies—'Leninism'—were responsible for the destruction of the unified socialist movement. Not only that, but Leninism was a response to very specific *Russian* conditions and, as the Spanish Communists have rightly stressed, to very specific *world* conditions. It is therefore grotesque to make a party's or an individual's loyalty to Leninism the test of his 'revolutionary' socialism at a time when neither the conditions of Russia in 1917 nor those of the world in 1917 obtain.

Urban You would, then, quietly bury Leninism; but

might you repudiate Marxism as well, as the German Social Democrats have done in their Bad Godesberg programme?

Mlynar Repudiate Marxism . . . well, Marxism *has* been repudiated—by the *Russians*! The basic revision of Marxism and Leninism was the work of Stalin. What, after all, is left of the 'Soviet' state from which the *soviets* have been effectively eliminated?

But I don't want to go into a theoretical discussion of the corruption of Marx and Lenin in Soviet hands, for I see the crux of the problem elsewhere.

I have now arrived at the conclusion that no Communist society can be built on what Marx has written. Think of Marx's dated theories: that the division of labour will cease under socialism; that the state will wither away; that the poverty of the working class will rapidly increase under capitalism, and so on. These are ideas drawn from the state of society and the state of science in the mid-nineteenth century. They did then, perhaps, have some relevance. But they have none today. Consider the absurdity of trying to base the programme of a political party in the late twentieth century on Utopian ideas which Marx culled from his socialist predecessors or produced himself in the 1850s! Think of the absurdity of building, in the name of such Utopias, a society which can only achieve the 'liberation' of man—by enslaving him!

Marxism as a political programme for the 1980s and 1990s is an absurdity. When, therefore, Soviet propagandists tell us that the touchstone of our 'socialism' is our willingness to subscribe to Marxist theory, we ought to treat them with the contempt their demagogy deserves.

Urban Much has been said and written about the ideological cynicism of the Soviet leadership. Yet I find it a little difficult to believe that men utterly lacking personal charisma should be able to sustain their power to rule over two continents without *some* sense of feeling that their power is legitimate and that it is so regarded by a large part of the Soviet population. You have said that if you had not, in the 1940s and 1950s, believed in the ideals of 'socialism' you would not have been able to take a single step as a Communist. Should one not assume that somewhere at the back of their minds the Soviet leaders are similarly motivated—and for practical purposes I don't think it greatly matters whether they are willing or unwilling prisoners of their ideology?

Mlynar No, no—I don't believe the Soviet leaders have retained any faith in Marxism, or that they even bother to think about it.

Novotny, who is—wrongly, as I think—always described as a Stalinist, did maintain his faith in Marxism, and that, paradoxically, is the key to understanding why, under Novotny, a certain tentative liberalisation of the regime could nevertheless be put in train: at the time of Khrushchev's leadership Novotny came to the conclusion that Khrushchev's policies did after all represent an authentic form of Marxism and he subordinated himself to some extent to them.

But the men now sitting in the Kremlin are without any such conviction. Their sole criteria for action are the criteria of power—personal power at that. The question is: should one approve or disapprove of this?

Urban I should have thought the answer was, from your point of view, obvious—

Mlynar —not so very obvious if you broaden the question and ask: does the collapse of ideological motivation represent progress or regression in human affairs?

I am of the opinion that the loss of any value-system is a retreat and a defeat. Even though the Soviet interpretation of Marxism was honeycombed with distortions and had, in the final analysis, very little to do with what Marx had written, it nevertheless gave the citizen certain moral guidelines for his private and public life. Many of these laws and regulations were grotesque, but they did represent a recognisable order. One could be for it or against it, but it was difficult to remain indifferent to it.

Now we are faced with the paradox that the impact of pragmatism, modern technology, and rational planning have led to the collapse of ideology in the Soviet Union and, to the extent that it ever existed, in Eastern Europe too. In one sense, this must be rated as a highly positive development, but it is also a regression in the sense in which the erosion of the Christian value-system, too, was a regression in human affairs: the signposts have been removed, and we are threatened with chaos.

One could observe this very clearly in Czechoslovakia. The nine years I spent there under the post-invasion regime demonstrated two things. First, that trust in the legitimacy of socialism, even of the reformed type, has completely evaporated—evaporated, I might add, as a result of the ordinary citizen's daily experience. Second, that nothing has taken the place of the Marxist/totalitarian value system. There is a vacuum: an empty, self-serving, unprincipled pragmatism has taken over. That, too, is a very bad thing.

Urban Aren't we, then, in the happy position of seeing the Communist and non-Communist worlds converge in one shared state of disorientation, for modern Western society, too, has again and again been accused of being unable to put an overall value-system in the place of the Christian ethic—or so at least has run the standard charge against us since Victorian times?

Mlynar The Western system may be flawed in many social respects, but it is, after all, a fully operational democratic system, not a dictatorship. I would certainly agree that the Western democracies, too, are now without a universally accepted value-system, but whereas the loss of such a system in a live democracy is balanced by the interaction of a broad variety of democratic institutions, the loss of ideology in a totalitarian society means the complete collapse of the morale of that society, because the sole justification of totalitarian rule *is* the ideology on which it rests.

Urban What, then, apart from naked force, sustains the Soviet bloc in the 1970s?

Mlynar We are witnessing a curious dilution of totalitarianism. What we see in Czechoslovakia and some of the other Central and East European countries is not a return to Stalinism in the ideological, fideistic sense, but a dictatorship slowly deflated by the demands of the consumer society.

Urban I can well believe that the people of Czechoslovakia, Hungary and even Poland may be content to live without any overriding faith or ideology so long as the privatisation of life is tolerated and consumer expectations are satisfied. We can already see some of this in action in

Hungary. But I am a little doubtful whether a withdrawal of paternalism would work in Russia. Privatisation, personal liberty, individualism, democracy have no obvious appeal to the Russian character (if you will permit me to make so grand a generalisation); firm rule, regimentation, even despotism have. I am sure you wouldn't as a Marxist want to ignore 90 per cent of Russian history.

Mlynar I wouldn't; yet I am opposed to your formulation: 'The Russian people *is*, or *needs* to be treated like this, that or the other'. All we can legitimately infer from Russian history is that *so far* the specific conditions of Tsarist imperialism and Soviet rule have involved the use of tyrannical methods. But I would never agree that any people is predestined to live in a police state, much less that it has some inborn desire to do so. I am convinced that in the long run—and perhaps only in the very long run—the Soviet Union, too, will move closer to Western models of a more liberal polity, retaining, of course, much of Russia's specific character.

That said, I would agree that in the *short* term the evolution of Soviet society will be very different from that of Czech, Hungarian, Polish or East German society. I don't believe that reform Communism has a constituency in the Soviet Union. I am, therefore, not at all hopeful that the Central and East European countries have much to expect from Moscow, and if they have to mark time until Russia, too, is ready for change—well, that would be a national disaster. Mind you, nations are known to have been overtaken by national disasters—I am not excluding the possibility. But if a cataclysmic *dénouement* is to be bracketed out of our calculations and we assume a *rational dénouement*, we have to be clear that change in the fortunes of the Central and East European countries can only come about if the Soviet Union is put under pressure as a world power and *made* to loosen its hold on its satellites.

Urban Don't you think that some of this loosening has already taken place—partly perhaps as a result of détente, partly because the Soviet leaders are willing to put up with a modest amount of unadvertised dissent from their models as an exercise in experimental prophylaxis?

Mlynar Some loosening *has* been in progress since

1956—studded, however, with gross reversals such as the suppression of Hungary in 1956 and the occupation of Czechoslovakia in 1968.

In preparing our reforms in the 1965–68 period we did carefully consider the amount of change the Soviet leaders might be able to assimilate, and we came to the conclusion that, in the light of Yugoslavia, Hungary and the break with China, the Kremlin, too, might have learned certain lessons, and that it was not to be expected that reasonable attempts to reform the system would *always* be brutally put down. 21 August 1968, however, proved us wrong in this expectation.

Urban The limits of what the Soviet leaders would overtly accept are narrow on any showing. A free press is excluded; freedom of public discussion and assembly is excluded; a multi-party system is excluded; tampering with democratic centralism in the Communist Party is excluded—in other words, most of the reforms you were anxious to put into effect in 1968 were non-starters.

It would, however, appear to me that a great deal can be achieved by not challenging the system frontally—by not *saying* in so many words what you are trying to do, but simply doing it by stealth, by bending or ignoring the rules, or by simple corruption. One preserves the existing institutions but renders them meaningless. The Hungarians, with their traditional expertise in pulling the wool over the eyes of Turks and Austrians, have gone a long way towards making life tolerable under the Soviet system by the commendable device of corrupting it.

Mlynar This is all very well in the case of countries which do not possess a profoundly Western liberal-democratic tradition. If you are socially and culturally somewhat backward (and I am now, of course, thinking of Russia rather than Hungary), any device to outwit or sabotage the system is an improvement on your existing condition. But if you are a West European country with a long democratic history behind you, you like to think that there are more straightforward and more rational ways of promoting legitimate change than by subterfuge and trickery.

Urban But wherever this is not possible corruption is surely a blow struck for liberty—

Mlynar I suppose it is, but the limits of what you can

achieve by navigating between the paragraphs are narrow. It is perfectly true that there is much more liberty in Hungary today than there is in Czechoslovakia—that it is much better and easier to live in Budapest than in Prague. I am nevertheless convinced that the Hungarians have run themselves into a cul-de-sac.

Why do I say that? Hungary under Kadar seems to me to be in a situation not unlike that of Czechoslovakia during the last years of Novotny's regime—for it is (as I've already said) a great mistake to think of Novotny's rule after, say, 1962, as the rule of Stalinism. Czechoslovakia under Novotny in that period was an increasingly liberalising society, and all of us now living abroad because of our opposition to the present regime began to think and speak openly and publicly about the need to reform the system *under* Novotny in conditions of considerable freedom. But when it came to the point of pushing these reforms over the hump, the whole movement came unstuck—and we had Soviet occupation. The Hungarian people are aware of all this; they have the examples of 1956 and 1968 before them to remember, and that is why Hungary is quiescent. They have learned how to play the system, and they are playing it successfully. But they, and their government, know well enough that there is a strict limit to the distance they can travel. They are liberalising on the sufferance of the Soviet leaders, and this sufferance may come to an end whenever Moscow feels that it should. Liberalising by stealth, evasion and corruption has no institutional impact, and it is, in the last analysis, institutional change alone that matters.

American connivance

Urban You were, as Secretary of the Central Committee of the Czechoslovak Communist Party, a member of the Czech team which 'negotiated' (if that is the word) your settlement with the Soviet Union at the end of August 1968. Did the Soviet leaders' lack of faith in their principles show up in the arguments they used, or failed to use, in their talks with you?

Mlynar Oh, yes—their lack of ideological conviction wore several faces. The first expressed itself in the massive fact that we were in Moscow under duress, negotiating virtually as prisoners on behalf of a country which had just been occupied by the very men we were facing at the conference table. There could, under such conditions, be no question of conducting 'negotiations'. I remember Ponomarev bluntly telling us: 'If you won't sign these documents today, you'll sign them tomorrow, and if not tomorrow, then the day after—*we* have plenty of time!'

This tone was the tone of a leadership which would brook no contradiction and was clearly in the habit of using muscle to enforce obedience.

We had an even more significant demonstration of all this on the last day of our so-called negotiations. The entire Soviet and the entire Czechoslovak Politburo were meeting in joint session when Dubcek got himself involved on some point or other in a heated argument with Brezhnev. Obviously irritated, Brezhnev got up and said: 'What are you waiting for? Do you expect anything is going to happen to help you? No, there is going to be no war—you might as well take note of that. I had an enquiry sent to President Johnson asking him whether the United States would respect the Yalta and Potsdam agreements, and on 18 August I received his reply saying that as far as Czechoslovakia and Rumania were concerned the US would unquestionably honour these agreements—the case of Yugoslavia, he said, would have to be the subject of negotiations. So what on earth are you marking time for? I will tell you what *is* going to happen: Tito is going to make a speech and Berlinguer is going to sound off—but so what? Do you think speeches made by West European Communists have any significance? For fifty years now they have not mattered one way or the other!'

Brezhnev then went on to compare our situation with that of Poland in 1956: 'All right, I can understand that you have emotional difficulties in accepting the facts. But remember Poland: in 1956 Gomulka was dead set against our suggestion that we assist him with Soviet troops. But if I now so much as dropped a hint that Soviet troops might be withdrawn from Poland, Gomulka would take the first plane to Moscow to implore us to do no such thing.'

It is clear from all this that nothing could be more distant from the thinking of the Soviet leaders than concern with principles and ideology. Brezhnev's was the voice of power-politics in its crudest form. He didn't even waste time on confronting us with the standard charges which the Soviet press had been under instructions to make against us—that we were preparing a counter-revolution, that we wanted to restore capitalism, and so on. He simply said: 'You lost control of the situation in Prague, and we saw our interests threatened. You put the results of the Second World War at risk. That our Western border is on the Elbe today has been paid for by the blood of our soldiers. We cannot allow this to be jeopardised, least of all because you have irresponsibly decided to *experiment* with socialism without so much as bothering to consult us.'

Urban I have recently had occasion to talk to a number of leading Americans who were deeply involved in directing US foreign policy under President Johnson: Dean Rusk, who was US Secretary of State at the time of the Soviet invasion;[1] George Ball, who was the President's ambassador at the UN;[2] and Eugene Rostow, who was Under Secretary of State for political affairs.

I did not know, at the time, of Brezhnev's claim that he obtained, as you have said, *carte blanche* from President Johnson to do as he pleased with Czechoslovakia. Nevertheless, this kind of thing had been darkly rumoured for some time, and I incorporated it in my questioning. The denial of these rumours was uniform and categorical, and when I asked Mr Rusk for a written clarification, this is what he said: 'The idea that the United States gave the Soviet Union some sort of "assurance" or green light to go into Czechoslovakia in August 1968 is simply ridiculous. For their own purposes the Soviets have tried to pass this word around and, indeed, some Czech circles have also done the same. Soviet intelligence and their political leadership probably made the accurate judgment that the West would not go to war against the Soviet Union over Czechoslovakia, but

[1] *Détente*, pp. 243–61.
[2] Ibid, pp. 229–42.

that was a very different thing from supposing that we had in any way encouraged the Soviet Union to take that action.'

Did you think Brezhnev was speaking the truth?

Mlynar I could not judge that; I can only tell you what he said to us at the joint session of the two Politburos shortly before the 'Protocols' were signed. The form of words he used implied that he had addressed himself personally to Johnson—but what mechanism he had used for doing so, and whether he had really received an answer on 18 August 1968—I don't know.

You see, Brezhnev opened with the question: 'What are you waiting for? . . . there is going to be no war', and he went on to use the message which he said he had received from President Johnson to underpin his point that we'd better sign on the dotted line quickly, for resistance and procrastination were hopeless. But he added in the same breath that Johnson's assurance was not all *that* important because 'we would have sent our troops in even under the threat of a conflict with the United States, because we were and are determined not to allow the results of the Second World War to be altered in any way'.

Urban Did you yourself believe that the Russians were prepared to go to war over Czechoslovakia?

Mlynar Well, this is the sort of thing they had been vaguely hinting at months before the invasion. Bilak said that he had been given a warning of this kind when he was in Moscow in May 1968. But these were words, allusions, propaganda—we have nothing to prove that the Soviet leaders would or would not have gone to war if the West had taken a different line.

Urban But you would agree, wouldn't you, that the Prague Reform Movement was dynamite for Soviet rule in Eastern Europe, and very possibly for the Soviet Union itself?

Mlynar That is true of Poland and the GDR. Gomulka and Ulbricht saw their positions gravely threatened—and the best proof of how right they were to feel threatened was that within two years of the Soviet invasion both were removed from their posts. In Poland there were students openly expressing their hope of seeing a 'Polish Dubcek' lead their country, and there was, both in Poland and East

Germany, a great eagerness to benefit from whatever successes we managed to achieve.

But it is quite absurd to argue that our reforms represented any threat to the internal *status quo* of the Soviet Union. What happened was that certain Soviet bureaucratic interest groups, which had already been gravely alarmed by Khrushchev's reforms, saw the writing on the wall and decided to take no chances.

Urban But wasn't the integrity of the empire at risk?

Mlynar Soviet imperial interests *were* threatened, but then the Soviet Union as a socialist state is not supposed to have imperial interests!

It is perfectly true that if the Czechoslovak example had spread, the entire web of relationships between the Soviet Union on the one hand, and Czechoslovakia, the GDR, Hungary and Poland on the other (Rumania and Bulgaria are different cases), would have undergone profound change—and this was something the Soviet leaders were, and are, quite unwilling to countenance. In other words, I don't believe for a moment that we would have had any impact on the domestic politics of the Soviet Union, and I don't believe the Soviet leaders seriously feared that we would. But they feared for their world-power position and acted exclusively on that consideration.

Urban You have said that the presentation of the Soviet case in Moscow was crude and unprincipled. Did the Czech side use a more sophisticated approach?

Mlynar Let me, first, say that nothing of any importance was said at these so-called negotiations that had not been said in the five-party letter and our reply to it in July 1968. To the extent that principles and socialism were at all 'discussed', they were raised by Dubcek and Cernik at the joint session of the two Politburos. But Brezhnev had very little time for any of this. His attitude was that of a schoolmaster lecturing a bunch of imbeciles: this and that are the true facts; take them or leave them; but if you do leave them, remember that you have asked for what is coming to you. This was the context in which the so-called Moscow Protocols—a Soviet ultimatum, in reality—were eventually signed. In trying to change various formulations in the text we did, here and there, argue from ideological principle, as we were anxious to keep the road open for a measure of Kadarisation, but basically nothing was added to what we had said in our reply to the five-party letter in July.

Urban Was it your impression that Brezhnev was speaking as his own man? There were reports at the time that the decisive factor making for intervention was the college of Soviet generals, and Brezhnev was their spokesman rather than their leader.

Mlynar The Soviet generals were, without question, enthusiastic supporters of the occupation of Czechoslovakia. My own impression was that initially Brezhnev had been against intervention, but by the time we came face to face with him in Moscow ranks had been closed and he spoke with complete conviction. I don't think it makes a great deal of sense to draw a strict distinction between Soviet generals and Party leaders. The problem of Czechoslovakia was seen by all of them as a challenge to the strategic and political authority of the Soviet Union. Brezhnev came to share that perception—but then he had no choice.

Urban What is your reason for saying that?

Mlynar Because, while his leadership seemed uncontested, his hands were tied in some respects. Let me specify.

Bohumil Simon, a member of our Politburo, was in Moscow on 7 November 1968 as head of our Party delegation at the anniversary celebrations of the October Revolution. He was one of those six men who had been arrested by Soviet troops on 21 August and transported to Moscow. But he was on friendly personal terms with Brezhnev, so that in November he could have a frank conversation with him. This is what (according to Simon's account) Brezhnev told him: 'Do you want to know where the Dubcek leadership committed its greatest error? In thinking that power makes it possible for you to do whatever you like. But, in politics, this is just not so. I can myself only carry out perhaps 30 per cent of the policies I'd like to. For example, if I had not voted for Soviet armed assistance to Czechoslovakia you would not be sitting here today, but quite possibly *I* wouldn't either.'

I incline to think that when the Soviet leaders put the matter of intervention to the vote, the post of Party General

Secretary was also being tacitly put to the test—and Brezhnev knew this. There were successors waiting in the wings.

Two worlds

Urban We know from various sources that the Warsaw Pact did not present a completely uniform front either before the invasion or after it. The Hungarians and Rumanians were, for reasons of their own, most unwilling to see your reforms and your independence squashed.

How important were the differences?

Mlynar It became crystal clear at the Bratislava meeting that Kadar's attitude to us was different from the rest. One could notice minute *personal* differences in the articulations of Gomulka, Zhivkov and Ulbricht, but nothing that would affect the uniform stand of the Pact as a whole, that is, the stand of the Soviet leadership. Kadar, however, was extremely anxious to prevent military intervention in a neighbouring country. After the Bratislava meeting, Kadar, Dubcek and I had a forty-minute private session together, and Kadar gave us an urgent and very friendly warning. 'Please do *everything* you can to prevent Soviet intervention,' he said. 'I speak from experience. I came to power under extraordinarily difficult circumstances. . . . You have no idea what it means to be in the sort of situation we were in in Budapest in 1956. . . . You must take a different road. . . . Try and prevent the kind of disaster that hit us.'

Quite obviously, Kadar reckoned with Soviet military intervention as a very real possibility. Not only was he anxious that there should be no such intervention, but he told us in so many words that he considered it to be of great importance for the future development of *Hungarian* socialism that our reforms should be allowed to succeed. He had, quite apart from a certain general sympathy for us, a clear interest in seeing us through. But, then, *he* was not making Soviet policy. When the Warsaw Pact troops finally invaded, Kadar had no choice but to send along some Hungarian units, but this was a symbolic gesture which we understood.

Urban Did Kadar draw your attention to specific features of the Reform Movement to which the Russians were particularly sensitive?

Mlynar We didn't really have a chance to go into details, but it was clear enough that it was the freedom of the press that was causing most offence in Moscow.

I was, at the time, of the opinion that a cautious limitation of the freedom of the press and an early Party Congress (I had in mind a May or June Congress) would put us in a stronger position *vis-à-vis* the Soviet leadership and give our reforms a better chance of success. Today, however, I am convinced that, although greater caution might have made intervention more difficult or delayed it, basically it was impossible not to come into a head-on conflict with Moscow. By August we were facing an either/or kind of choice: we had to decide whether to maintain the momentum of democratisation or opt for the kind of policies followed by the Husak leadership at the present time. But if we chose the former, as we had to and did, the clash with the Soviet Union was inevitable.

Urban Didn't Kadar also warn you against toying with the idea of a multi-party system? I remember how nervously the Soviet press reacted to 'KAN' and 'Club 21', seeing these, and of course even more so the various gatherings of Social Democrats, as the subversive beginnings of a multi-party system and the collapse of the 'leading role' of the Communist Party. The 1956 Hungarian experience was rich in precedents.

Mlynar The sticking point for the Soviet Union as well as for our Party was the restoration of Social Democracy. We were against it.

Urban The monopoly of Communist rule was to remain untouched?

Mlynar The principal and, really, the only objective of the Prague Spring was the renewal of the existing system—not change in the control of power. Our ambition was to liberalise the Communist Party by subjecting it, through a number of new institutions, to social control and making it accountable for its actions. This meant pluralisation within the existing order. For example, we intended to, and did, separate the trade unions from Party control, and we began to vest the civil service, the judiciary, economic planning and so on with a certain institutional autonomy.

These were, for us, far-reaching measures, and we decided that we would first have to see how these reforms worked out in practice before asking ourselves the next question—namely whether the system thus reformed was ripe for extension, and whether unlimited freedom of the press and political pluralism, including possibly a multi-party system, could be accommodated. My position was, and is, that a multi-party system of some kind was probably desirable—but not in the first phase of reform. The reasons for this were twofold. First, no party which had enjoyed dictatorial control for twenty years could be expected to commit political suicide (quite apart from the fact that our abrupt abdication would have landed the country in chaos). Second, and more important, it would have been utterly hopeless to try to convince the Soviet leadership that suggestions for a multi-party system and the simultaneous surrender of the leading role of the Communist Party could have meant anything but counter-revolution.

A multi-party system was, therefore, not on the agenda of the Reform Movement. We never discussed it seriously, and I do not think that any of our reformers was looking far enough ahead to articulate opinions about it.

Urban Did your discussions with the Soviet leaders touch on the desirability of giving the 'parties' within the National Front some real independence?

Mlynar Well—*any* mention of a multi-party system struck the Soviet leaders not only as rank heresy but as a direct call to counter-revolution. So poor was their understanding of how a free press operates that they could not begin to understand how individual journalists could express a wish for this or that kind of a political development without direct orders from the Politburo. And if journalists *did* utter opinions that did not agree with the Soviet line—well, that, of course, was interpreted as a sign that the Czech Politburo had lost control. One could not, and cannot, really talk to the Soviet leadership about these matters. Their minds operate on a different wavelength.

To give you a small example: one of the Soviet negotiators (I cannot now recall who it was) said to us that he had clear proof that the Prague Reform Movement was a well-prepared counter-revolutionary plot—how else, he asked, could the Czech road-signs and street-names have been painted over within twenty-four hours of the arrival of Soviet troops? You see, the Russians take it so much for granted that everything in Soviet life is done by higher order that they simply could not imagine that when ordinary Czechs and Slovaks saw the Soviet troops invade our country, they went out on their own initiative to take down or reverse the road-signs and paint over the street-names as a gesture of defiance!

For another example: as you know, members of our Presidium—Dubcek, Smrkovsky, Spacek, Simon, Kriegel, Slavik, Sadovsky, Jakes, Kapek and myself—were arrested in the building of the Central Committee while we were in session on the night of 20/21 August by a special detachment of Soviet paratroops. A paratrooper was stood behind every one of us pointing a loaded machine pistol at the back of our heads. Well, at about 9 in the morning a group of Soviet officers and Czech security agents arrived and bundled off Dubcek, Kriegel, Smrkovsky and Spacek to face a 'Revolutionary Tribunal' headed, as we were told, by Alois Indra. Those of us not taken off were left in the room, with the paratroops still pointing their guns at us. At midday, suddenly, the air-raid sirens went off, and the Soviet soldiers got nervous. 'What's all this?' the young lieutenant guarding me asked. I had, of course, no idea what was happening in the streets of Prague but assumed (rightly, as it turned out) that the workers had sounded the sirens as a token of protest against the invasion. So I told him just that. The lieutenant was perplexed and indignant: 'Are you trying to tell me that the workers have sounded the sirens without someone in the leadership ordering them to do so?'

Well—how *can* you communicate with people who think like that?

Urban I suppose your leadership's enforced visit to Moscow was not the ideal opportunity to persuade anyone in the Kremlin that the Prague Spring had been an attempt to reform the system on behalf of the Soviet Union as well—but no doubt you did try to present your case in that framework at earlier stages of your negotiations?

Mlynar Yes, at Cierna Dubcek and others did argue, forcefully and at length, along those lines. But Brezhnev and his colleagues dismissed it all as naive, idealistic and dangerous prattle. And I will concede that to *them* it must have seemed dangerous. Given the terrible oppressive system which they run in their country, their elbow-room for experiment was very small. They rightly suspected that the slightest change in Prague might set off tremors in their whole empire. The staggering fact is that they wanted, and want, to keep the system exactly as it is.

Urban Santiago Carrillo, speaking on French television on 13 July 1977, said that if Soviet tanks ever reached Spain to suppress a Spanish Eurocommunist government, the Spanish people would fight. And Manuel Azcárate, the Spanish Party's 'foreign minister', talking to me in Oxford recently, voiced a similar opinion. Asked whether he thought Czechoslovakia ought to have offered armed resistance in 1968, he said—Yes, '*we* would have fought', and he stressed that we should be conscious of the lessons of Yugoslavia: Stalin knew that Tito would fight, which, he said, removed the danger of Soviet intervention. This is no doubt treating a complex problem in simplified form—but would you agree in retrospect that Czechoslovakia ought to have fought, even if the odds were hopelessly against her?

Mlynar I am not concerned with what the Spanish Communists might do in a highly hypothetical situation, but on the question of our own resistance let me say this: by August 1968 it was far too late to organise military resistance. A country of the physical shape of Czechoslovakia could not be effectively defended even if timely preparations *had* been made; but add to our geographic indefensibility the facts that our battle order under the Warsaw Pact was facing west, that our armed forces were under Soviet command, that our command structure, communications system and military technology were entirely in Soviet hands.

We *could* have organised local resistance, a type of guerilla warfare on the Hungarian pattern, and this is one of the things we did consider in the Presidium on the night of 20/21 August. But we rejected the idea because we were persuaded that the purpose of Soviet intervention was precisely *that*: once the shooting had started it would have been very difficult to establish who had fired the first shots or to contradict the Soviet argument that Czechoslovakia was in the grip of a counter-revolution. We wanted to show the world with absolute clarity that it was the Soviet Union that had committed unprovoked aggression; and the only way in which that could be done was to refuse to be provoked into armed resistance of any sort. In this limited but important objective we have, I think, fully succeeded.

Political resistance was a different matter. That, too, was discussed by us on the night of the invasion, but no satisfactory decision was reached. A motion calling for political resistance was rejected by four of the voting conservatives (Bilak, Kolder, Svestka and Rigo) helped by Indra, Kapek and Jakes who did not have the vote but were influential enough to exert pressure.

Let me impress on you one important factor which, ten years after the Prague Spring, tends to be more and more forgotten. The Dubcek leadership was *never* united. It always contained a strong group of conservatives who would simply not hear it mentioned that our reforms might lead to a conflict with Moscow. Dubcek himself was absolutely convinced that none of the proposed changes could be brought to fruition unless we carried the Russians with us. The entire political perspective of the Prague Spring was anchored in the assumption that the Soviet Union had no cause to be apprehensive about our programme, and the last thing we wanted to do was to challenge the Soviet leadership. In *retrospect* we may well say that this was an ill-considered perspective—but this *was* the perspective we had at the time, and given that perspective any idea of preparing for a military conflict with the Soviet Union just did not come within the realm of possibility.

I was, on the fateful night, personally very conscious of the enormous responsibility we carried in having it in our power to send or not to send thousands of our young men to their deaths. I had in my political career never consciously taken a single decision that would have harmed human life, and by the early hours of 21 August 1968 I was convinced that no political result that looked remotely attainable if we ordered our forces into action was worth the life of a single Czechoslovak soldier. It was far too late.

One could wish it had been otherwise—but it was not.

Ota Sik

Egalitarianism in Socialist Society

Urban Re-reading the 1968 Czechoslovak press and recalling what was being said on radio and television, one is left with the impression that the Prague reformers attributed their country's troubles in rather summary fashion to the survivals of Stalinism personified in Novotny and his close collaborators. Yet their complaints bear an extraordinary resemblance to criticisms made of the *Western* system by Western observers—about the evils of centralisation, the over-weening presence of bureaucracy, the dehumanisation of work, the depersonalisation of the individual and the dangers of a mindless egalitarianism. The Czechs pinned the bulk of the blame for the unhappy state of their country on a convenient whipping boy—Stalinism. But one wonders whether they would not have been in for a great disappointment if, after the successful reformation of the Czechoslovak economy and body politic, they had found that a good deal of their troubles was due, not to the abuse of power by a few men and perhaps not even to the Communist system, but to the exigencies of mass industrial society.

I, for one, found it difficult to escape the impression that, for all the abuses they had been made to suffer, the Czechs in 1968 were an optimistic people, for they were led to believe that the 'good life' could be attained by the removal of bad leaders, the reform of the economy, the elimination of certain rules from the Party statutes, the return to a purer form of Marxism, and so on. There is no question that Novotny's rule must bear the brunt of the blame for what went wrong in Czechoslovakia. The question is, how much blame should be apportioned to Stalinism, over-centralisation, faulty planning, etc., and how much to the nature of modern industrial society?

Sik You have profoundly misunderstood the Czechoslovak Reform Movement. I don't think that either our economists or our political scientists and philosophers imagined for a moment that the Western world, the so-called capitalist world, had a positive alternative to offer to Stalinist bureaucratic socialism. I must say a word here about the semantics of the problem, for it is too easy to assume that Stalinism is somehow coextensive with the cult of J. V. Stalin. It isn't. Social phenomena have to be given a name, and when we talk of Stalinism as a bureaucratic system, we are simply saying that this system is neither progressive nor socialist. But in criticising it we never implied that Western capitalism was the answer; we never imagined that the West would be without its own grave contradictions—social conflicts, bureaucratisation, alienation and the rest. Stalinists, to our mind, are communists who ignore the basic objectives of socialism and protect their vested interests in the form of a particularly damaging dogmatism. I will, therefore, go on using the word Stalinism even though I do not, as I say, want to restrict the term to the cult of Stalin or the policies of the actual followers of Stalin.

Now, in Stalinist eyes, the Stalinist system is something diametrically opposed to Western society; we, on the other hand, believe that the bureaucratic order of Stalinism is not only *not* opposed to Western bureaucracy but is bureaucracy carried to its exponential extreme. When we talk of the problems of Western Europe and the United States we refer to the bureaucratisation of society, the socially mismotivated pursuit of growth, the alienation of man and so on. Stalinism, however, far from remedying any of these phenomena, has taken them to absurd lengths. It has, in fact, fashioned state-monopolism into its *raison d'état*. This means that the monopolistic system, which in the West is surrounded by a number of checks and balances, has become the sole legitimate order in Communist society. It means that under Stalinism there is a cast-iron hierarchy of disciplinarian relationships, that the economy is completely subordinated to the demands of heavy industry and arms production, and that the resulting alienation of man is incomparably greater than it is in any Western country. Our critique of the state-monopolistic system of Stalinism was therefore not accompanied by any naive expectation that the monopolistic system of private capitalism would offer us a valid alternative—we were opposed to both.

Urban I noticed with great interest that a remarkable specimen of self-criticism of the kind you have just made was in fact published in Czechoslovakia after the Russian occupation. I am referring to a volume edited by Pavel Machonin, *Ceskoslovenska Spolecnost*, in which egalitarianism, bureaucratism and technocracy are shown to be the dangers threatening industrial society. I would hate to belittle the sins of Stalinism or exaggerate the virtues of Western industrial society but, as the contributors to this book argue, technocracy resembles socialism in its respect for technical competence, but it also resembles bureaucratism in its lack of democracy, and thus stands half-way between the two: the evils of egalitarianism and bureaucracy aid and complement each other. I am stressing these points merely to show that technocracy, bureaucracy and egalitarianism overlap, and it is quite possible to think of a highly inequitable social order in which bureaucracy is the child of technocracy and not of the single-party system, although I would agree with you that the evils of a technocracy-led bureaucratisation, which we are beginning to experience in the West, do not compare with the evils of a *totalitarian* and *politically* motivated bureaucracy.

Sik It is certainly true that the rapid industrialisation of the Western countries has created its own technostructure, and it is also true that the social ethos of this technostructure reflects the methods of production every bit as faithfully as the small capitalist enterprises used to reflect theirs at an earlier stage. The difference is that today's technostructure is extraordinarily powerful, so that it can heavily influence consumer choice. Mind you, I believe it has always been the case that consumption was a function of production, but today the size and concentration of industry have spawned a bureaucracy which can no longer cope with the vast variety of activities it is supposed to oversee and administer. For the ordinary citizen, who is at the suffering end of this process, this means fragmentation, depersonalisation, poor motivation, and the rest.

And yet the picture is not wholly black. I have been in the West for some years now and I speak from personal experience when I say that, despite the growing power of Western monopolies, despite the technostructure and the bureaucratisation of the economy, the market forces are still of decisive importance. Here is where I tilt lances with J. K. Galbraith. Of course, there has never been a time when supply and demand have been perfectly balanced by market forces alone, but it is, in my opinion, vastly preferable to have an imperfect market economy than to have none at all. The growth of monopolies and cartels has certainly distorted competition in the market economies; nevertheless, neither bureaucratisation nor the power of the vast national and international companies has been sufficient to annul consumer choice. The large Western enterprises still have to gear their production to the needs and tastes of the consumer, they still have to produce economically, and they still have to improve quality if they want to stay in business. These are three important factors which have ceased to matter in the Communist economies because the free play of market forces has been suppressed there. When that happens, bureaucratisation becomes an article of faith, consumer interests are violated as a matter of economic philosophy, and the consumer is simply told: '*This* is what we are going to produce because we have laid it down in the Plan, and *that* is what you are going to consume.' The consumer is helpless.

Urban What exactly was the point at issue between yourself and Galbraith?

Sik We met at a conference in Zürich on the subject of the manipulation of man in modern society—a well-trodden path by now. I gave a paper on the manipulation of the consumer in the East European states, in which I tried to show how the East European consumer has become prostrate in the face of the all-powerful and ever-hungry Moloch of bureaucracy. Galbraith countered my analysis with the argument that there is no difference between manipulation in the East and manipulation in the West, that bureaucracy in the West is just as powerful as it is in the East, and that there is really nothing to choose between the two. Well, I could not agree with him: one cannot put an equation mark between the ordinary man's manipulation in the West and his manipulation in the East European societies where bureaucracy has become a monster. If you do that you are making covert excuses for the East European variety, because the implication of what you're saying is that if the Western citizen can live with *his* bureaucracy—which is, as we know, unpleasant but not unbearable—so can the East European. But this is simply not true. Galbraith is clearly not familiar with Eastern Europe; if he were, he would not be making such facile comparisons. We all know that there *is* manipulation in the West, but there is also a self-corrective mechanism which limits the scope of manipulation: there is competition between the various companies even though competition is often rigged so that the consumer's choice may be illusory. But rather than taking up the cudgels against manipulation, Galbraith seems to be content with throwing up his hands in horror and declaring—with great wit, mind you, and great eloquence—that this is a wicked world which we cannot hope to change. An elegant gesture, but is it helpful?

Urban Galbraith is also one of the main spokesmen of the idea that industrial societies converge because they share a common rationale. Would you say that this common rationale exists, and that industrial societies are, as it were, ineluctably driven into sharing a common social and cultural structure?

Sik I have my own theory on this point. There are two ways in which societies may converge, and it is my earnest hope that the first of these will not materialise, but of course the possibility that it will cannot be totally excluded. The first is the bureaucratisation of the whole of society, and this is Galbraith's point: if convergence consists of the fact that on both sides of the divide the market is disappearing, that planning is universally adopted, and all industry is becoming so interconnected that it is, for all practical purposes, centrally directed, then we can talk of convergence of a kind. However, this convergence would, in my opinion, be an entirely negative affair, for it would mean the absolute bureaucratisation of society, and the price for it would be paid by the man in the street. Let me hasten to add that this sort of development is viewed with sympathy by power elites both in the East and in the West, because elites look upon ordinary people with a good deal of contempt.

The second possibility of convergence—and this is the one I would support—is of a more positive kind and consists of two elements. First, it would eliminate certain important causes of alienation by giving people direct access to decision-making. This means self-management, for it is through the representation of the citizen in all organs of economic planning, social planning, local government, etc. that the conflict between power elites and the powerless masses may eventually be overcome. All this sounds very sketchy and idealistic if one tries to summarise it in a few sentences, but we had a detailed blueprint for all this in Czechoslovakia with which I will not burden you.

The second element of my solution has to do with finding a balance between planning and the free play of market forces. I would definitely not want to have the market replaced by planning because the cost would have to be borne by the consumer. I would keep the market as a countervailing force to balance the monopoly-interests of the state. Planning would, by and large, be restricted to those parts of the economy in which market forces are unable to serve the long-term interests of society—clearly, market forces are short-term forces, which cannot be expected to serve social interests. Here again I cannot agree with Galbraith when he claims that planning is bound to remain the preserve of the producers. I should like to see producers and consumers represented, on a basis of parity, wherever planning is done, from the state down to the small enterprise.

Urban Are you hinting at participation (codetermination) on the Austrian/German pattern, or would the more radical Yugoslav example be closer to your thinking? What is interesting to observe is that although the Yugoslavs make great play with the Marxist provenance of workers' self-management, Marx and Engels never refer to workers' councils in their writings in so many words. I suppose they would not have been against them, but it is intriguing that they should not have given us at least a broad outline of how they would like to see workers' councils operate in modern conditions.

Sik I don't agree. In *The Civil War in France*, where Marx tried to generalise from the lessons of the Paris Commune, there is a clear reference to associations of workmen taking possession of the factories—

Urban —of abandoned workshops and factories 'under reserve of compensation' to the owners. A war-time measure, and I should have thought a flimsy precedent to build on.

Sik Nevertheless Marx was showing that workers *can* manage their factories, and he was implying that self-management can be coordinated with social planning. This is the sort of thing we had in mind in Czechoslovakia. Nor can one say that Lenin has not written about workers' self-management. When the Soviet Party was preparing for its 7th Congress in 1918, Lenin suggested that all factories should be run by workers' councils, using this very term. It is, therefore, well established that the Marxist classics were not silent on the idea. In 1919, however, Lenin began to veer away from the councils. He said: 'We recognise neither freedom, nor equality, nor labour democracy if they are opposed to the interests of the emancipation of labour from the oppression of capital', and after the Kronstadt uprising Lenin changed his attitude very drastically; he began to feel that workers' self-management was a danger to the supremacy of the Party. At the 10th Congress there was a memorable discussion of the role of the trade unions, and Lenin coined the phrase 'anarchosyndicalism' to brand the Workers' Opposition (led by the former Commissar of Labour, Shlyapnikov, and by Alexandra Kollontai) and, with it, any independent trade union activity. All of a sudden Lenin seems to have forgotten that he has himself been the proponent of the workers' councils. All of a sudden he emphasises the leading role and personal responsibility of the enterprise director, throwing, in fact, the baby out with the bathwater. Instead of saying that while the workers' councils could not *replace* management, they should nevertheless complement the work of management in a supervisory capacity, Lenin simply rejected the whole idea, and from this rejection it was only one step to installing an almighty Party bureaucracy which made the enterprise director a beneficiary of the favours of the Party *apparat*. There was no question of the director being elected by the workers. There was no question of his independence.

In Czechoslovakia we were hoping to do exactly what Lenin decided he would *not* do—install a system of self-management.

Urban But is it, do you think, possible to have democracy at the grass roots without having it in the whole polity? In Yugoslavia self-management is a safety valve: the polity is not democratic, there are no political parties and there are no free elections. Nevertheless the workers enjoy a certain autonomy. Can such a system last? Can democracy be part-time any more than marriage? Can one restrict freedom of choice to the shop floor?

Sik Our plans were rather different from the Yugoslav model precisely because we would have followed through from self-management in the economy to pluralism in the political sphere. A single-party state makes it impossible for conflicting interests and ideas to be adequately represented. In the Western countries the power of bureaucrats is restrained by the play of market forces and by the checks of political democracy. These may be imperfect, but they are there.

In Eastern Europe the Communists took a very critical and high-minded view of what they thought was a mere *show* of democracy in the West and decided to pour new wine into this old bottle. But instead of doing just that, they broke the bottle in the process. So now we have no open conflict of interests, opinions or pressure groups. The only interest that can and does assert itself is that of the bureaucrats both in the state and in the Party. These men make all the decisions, wield all the influence and rule the masses without the masses' consent.

Urban Trotsky's attack on Stalin centres precisely on the charge you make against Stalinism, namely, that Stalin's rule was the rule of bureaucracy, and we know how this rule emerged gradually from the Workers' and Peasants' Inspectorate of which Stalin was the Commissar before he became General Secretary of the Party. Lenin saw the dangers of the very great power which Stalin wielded through his functions as Commissar of the Inspectorate, and one important reason for his break with Stalin was Stalin's inability—or unwillingness—to check the bureaucracy. So in this sense your critique is entirely in line with Trotsky's accusations and Lenin's fears.

In another sense, however, I think the Party programme which you worked out in Czechoslovakia ran counter to a good deal of sound Marxism and Leninism. What do I mean by that? The Czech Party's discussion of its future at the Vysocany Congress, and especially of the new party statutes, came back time and again to the problem of egalitarianism in socialist society, and to my surprise your demands were not for *more* equality, as one would have expected of a socialist conference, but for *less*. Some of the comment waxes quite indignant on this point: 'Egalitarianism has little in common with true socialist equality and justice, especially if it amounts—as it did in our country—to egalitarian distribution of inadequate resources.'

This is a curious assertion: I should have thought a shortage of resources was the best possible argument for their even-handed, egalitarian distribution, especially in a 'socialist' polity. Now all this strikes me as not being entirely in line with Marx's and Lenin's thinking. I would not care to defend your proposition in a debate with Vladimir Ilich, for of Lenin's three fundamental points about 'socialism' the most important was precisely the principle of equality which you deny in your statutes. Lenin insisted on the election of officials and, most importantly, on the principle that the salaries of officials should be 'reduced to the level of the wages of the average worker'. He was echoing the lessons which Marx drew from the experiences of the Paris Commune: universal suffrage in the election of municipal councillors, revocability of councillors at any time, and public service at 'workmen's wages'. Now, it may well be that the Czechoslovak experience demanded a drastic change in the Marxist and Leninist view of what constitutes socialism, but if so, perhaps the Vysocany Congress ought to have said so, and given us a fuller explanation of where Marx and Lenin had gone wrong.

Sik Again, I can't agree that either the discussion at the

Vysocany Congress or our new statutes were rejecting Marx or Lenin, but we did refuse to look upon their ideas as dogma. Both Marx and Lenin suffered from a certain fixation when it came to discussing the material rewards of labour. Marx makes the point repeatedly that officials should be paid no more than workers. I believe he arrived at this conclusion after insufficient reflection. In practice, an egalitarian wages policy is entirely untenable. Lenin abandoned it fairly early in the game because he discovered that, without due financial incentive, people will either not work at all or not give their best. As I say, Lenin was at first obstinate on this point but soon learnt from reality. Today in the Soviet Union the need for material incentives is fully realised, and the pay differentials between a workman and a senior civil servant are very large—much larger than in most capitalist countries.

Our rejection of egalitarianism attempted to answer a specific problem. Egalitarianism in Czechoslovakia was a very thorough-going affair; it carried the equality of men—appropriate perhaps in a primitive workers' democracy—to such extremes that the most highly qualified professional and the least qualified labourer earned about the same money. No one had any incentive to work harder or to improve his qualifications, because neither hard work nor a diploma could help him to better his personal condition. It was a common thing for a highly qualified engineer with many years of hard study behind him to earn less than a skilled worker; foremen were more poorly rewarded than the men who worked under them, and so forth. This was an invitation to apathy, conformity, mediocrity, idleness and a general reluctance to tackle anything but the easiest and least responsible jobs. People accepted the fact that they earned little, and their answer to poor pay was to give very little in return. This is why we had to emphasise the dangers of egalitarianism; we had to solve a specifically Czechoslovak problem—a hangover, perhaps, from the egalitarianism of the Bohemian Taborites and other millennial sects in our history (in no other socialist country did this problem arise in such acute form). We realised that if we wanted to provide the economy with qualified engineers, competent managers and administrators, we would have to pay them accordingly. We discovered after two decades of bitter experience that at this particular phase of the development of our society the majority of people will not work harder or better unless they can get more money for their work, and unless the goods they want to buy with their money are available. Ignore this rule and your economy is heading for ruin.

But we also drew another conclusion. We could see that it was not enough to pay people according to their work, but that it was also important to reward them according to the social usefulness of what they were doing. One of our big headaches under the Stalinist system was lack of control over the actual fulfilment of the Plan. Once a Plan was *officially* fulfilled, no one was in a position to say whether the items foreseen in the Plan had really been produced, and no one cared very much whether the articles produced were geared to consumer demand. The Plan was calculated on the basis of very primitive indicators. Wage scales were predetermined, hence the social economies and diseconomies of production could not be measured. Now *we* were saying in our reforms that the market provides the only practical indicators of the social profitability of work, i.e. whether a shoe or a pan is of the size and quality that the consumer really needs. Therefore we demanded material incentives, and we suggested that the economy should be forced, through the free play of market forces, to serve the real interests of society. All this sounds plain common sense, but in the Stalinist system common sense too was in short supply.

Urban I am struck by a word much used at the Vysocany Congress—'self-fulfilment', or 'self-realisation'. Talking of the future structure of Czechoslovak society the new Party programme said:

> A socialist society must reckon with the factual inequality between those on the one hand whose jobs give them only a very limited opportunity for free self-fulfilment as human beings, whose working hours and wages make it almost impossible for them to achieve this outside their work, and who therefore depend on the mass-consumption system, and those on the other hand who do work

> that possesses, in however limited a fashion, features of genuine human self-fulfilment. . . .

Let me reflect on this for a moment: the people whose jobs give them 'only a very limited opportunity for free self-fulfilment as human beings' are the vast majority of the population both in the East and in the West. They may no longer be the hewers of wood and drawers of water, but they still have the moronic, the soulless, the repetitive fatigues to perform. Psychologists tell us—and I am sure common sense tells us as much—that creative leisure as a compensation for soul-killing work is a figment of the social reformer's imagination. I am myself sceptical whether one can be free and a slave, ill and well, passive and creative in the same person; for work is not part of life—it tends to be life itself. Marx's idea of the rounded man (one who would 'hunt in the morning, fish in the afternoon, raise cattle in the evening, criticise after dinner . . . without ever becoming hunter, fisherman, shepherd or critic') is a captivating vision, but it is utopian. The division of labour is a function of modern society and not, as Marx imagined, of the ownership of the means of production. Specialisation since Marx's day has developed beyond what the most prophetic minds could foresee even fifty or thirty years ago.

Nor is it proven that the automation of the more tedious tasks in modern industry is an answer to work-alienation. We know perfectly well that even if automation were applied continuously from craft to machine-tending and to conveyor belt technology, it would not answer the problem of alienation. It has been estimated that in the optimal American case automation would affect not more than 8 per cent of the labour force, that the cost would be astronomical, and the results would be felt only after several decades, because only 8 per cent of American jobs are conceivably ripe for automation. James Bright's study of American automated plants shows that automated machinery requires not more but less skill, thought and initiative, in the same way as an automatic car takes less skill to drive than a manually operated one. I would therefore suggest that there is nothing that we know about capitalist or socialist industrial society as it really is that would support the Vysocany

Congress's claim that our alienation will decrease and our chances of self-fulfilment increase. If in your economic reforms you decided to recognise the weaknesses of man, offering him material incentives to make him work harder, why not recognise his ordinariness and fallibility throughout? I find it interesting that a congress which blazes a trail, in some respects, towards a hard-headed conception of 'socialism' should still feel the need to pay homage to some very old-fashioned—and untenable—assumptions about the goodness, selflessness and creativity of man.

Sik You were reproaching us a minute ago for not having adhered closely *enough* to the socialist classics—now you are saying that we have adhered to them *too* closely! You support my conviction that we struck the right balance!

We must distinguish between short-term and long-term objectives, the short-term plans being more realistic and the long-term ones more theoretical. No one said in our discussions that alienation would end tomorrow or the day after. The long-range plans set us tasks for the future; they tried to contribute to a better understanding of certain problems which have been on the agenda of the socialist movement ever since socialism was first thought of. Yet I would not say that our long-range goals are unattainable simply because so far we have not been able to attain them. All of us need creative outlets of one kind or another. This is a psychological fact about man, and the hobbies we pursue in our leisure time are just one expression of this creativity—

Urban —some of it very destructive creativity—

Sik —that comes into it also. All we wanted to say was that man is an active rather than a purely passive animal, and self-fulfilment requires creative activities on a great many levels. I can well imagine that in the somewhat more distant future—which will certainly be a very complex future—the working week will be reduced to four days and later perhaps to three days, and the working day will be shorter than it is today. This will bring with it an enormously increased amount of time for creative leisure, and I think this time will be used for self-education. People will demand to know much more, and on the basis of their new knowledge their interests will branch out in many new directions. Some of this is already beginning to happen.

Urban You will remember that one shrewd observer of our time, John Maynard Keynes, was very sceptical whether this newly won free time would be creatively used. Writing in 1930 Keynes asked:

> When poverty and insecurity have been eliminated from our lives, will we not get up to worse forms of mischief, because we have too much time on our hands, than we did when the daily grind consumed most of our energies? . . . for the first time since his creation, man will be faced with his real, his permanent problem—how to use his freedom from pressing economic cares, how to occupy his leisure. . . .

Sik I cannot recognise this as a legitimate point in our discussion—for or against. Assertions are not arguments. Keynes could not think away from a market economy in which an open-ended spiral of consumption has to keep up with an open-ended spiral of production. He was filled with foreboding at the thought of falling consumption and a rise in savings, because he could not imagine an inverse correlation between human happiness and the health of the market economy.

Urban I should have thought Keynes was referring to something much more general—to our psychological inability, and perhaps unwillingness, to amuse ourselves usefully and creatively. He does not seem to *exclude* the possibility, but he does say that, given the facts of human history, it would be unreasonable to expect that we will make fruitful use of our vastly increased leisure.

Sik These are matters which do not admit of precise argument. We are now touching on questions of faith, on basic human attitudes, on estimates of the nature of man. I must put my cards on the table: I am an optimist and a humanist. I am convinced that our destructiveness, our periodic insanities as individuals and societies, are ultimately anchored in social frustrations.

To put it in a nutshell: I believe man has in him the capacity for good as well as for evil—but this is stating the obvious. I also believe that it is in the power of society to encourage our positive and to discourage our negative proclivities. A society in which the outlets of human ambition are blocked, in which we are estranged from ourselves and our surroundings, in which we feel materially and culturally deprived, in which bureaucracy and fragmentation press upon us from all sides—such a society is the breeeding ground of enormous frustrations, and these, in turn, beget human beastliness in all its forms: hatred, envy, jealousy, *Schadenfreude*, destructiveness, what you will. If, however, the organisation of society prevents such frustrations from arising, or tempers them when they do arise, then our negative characteristics too will find it more difficult to get the better of the positive ones. This is a perennial problem and we can't begin to do justice to it in a few sentences.

But coming back to our long-range objectives in Czechoslovakia, I must stress again that these were *very* long-range and somewhat idealistic targets. What we were trying to say by setting our sights so high was that production and consumption are not goods in themselves, and that they must not be allowed to become the ends of human endeavour. Our purpose was to show that work must prove its social usefulness, and as part of that general proposition we were suggesting that modern technology has given us the means to serve socially desirable ends with less pain, less work, less *dirigisme* and fewer broken heads than we could have done twenty or even ten years ago.

Urban I am still not certain that I understand what you mean by man's 'self-realisation' in your programme. What sort of a man is 'man' whose self-realisation you advocate? This is an important point for I can think of certain types of human being whose self-realisation I would consider highly undesirable. The phrase returns with great frequency in the statutes and the Vysocany discussion. There must have been some ideal type in the minds of the delegates.

Sik We have never imagined that technical progress could eliminate the need to produce and the chores connected with production. But we did think that with the rapid advance of science and technology, and especially automation, man's productive work would become less taxing and much more creative than it has been hitherto.

Urban You don't think that the views I quoted a minute ago are persuasive on this point, viz. that automation does not equal more intelligent work?

Sik No, there are studies that show the opposite. They show that the machine-tending activity of automated equipment is almost as demanding as the designing and manufacture of the equipment itself. The maintenance and repair of such machinery requires sophistication and high intellectual ability. Work of this kind is not only conducive to the development of man's creative faculties but can almost force such creative activity to emerge.

Urban You are, then, in some respects not so far from agreeing with Galbraith that technological work and the habit of rational enquiry that goes with it are agents of intellectual and spiritual liberalisation?

Sik When I say that I don't agree with Galbraith's version of the theory of convergence, I do not, of course, mean to say that I disagree with him on all points. Where I would fault Galbraith in the context of the point you have made is that he does not distinguish precisely between different types of technical or para-technical work. There is a world of difference between the creativeness of the work of a project-engineer or a cybernetics technician on the one hand, and the non-creativeness of an accountant in the tax collector's office, on the other. I can hardly think of a more moronic and soul-destroying activity than the sort of work our own Czechoslovak economists had to put up with in our Planning Bureau.

There is no easy answer to the problem of monotonous and demeaning work. Nevertheless we have made a great step forward from the hard physical fatigues of earlier generations, and I believe we are about to make another great leap by reducing the need for fragmented and alienating labour. It is quite possible to imagine that the more unpleasant kinds of work will eventually be assigned to robots. Another aspect of the same problem is that we can, as I've said, expect the working day and the working week to become very much shorter and our leisure time much longer. When that happens, one of Engels's forecasts may well become reality, viz. that people will voluntarily take turns at doing the remaining monotonous chores of society, exchanging a small part of the working week unpleasantly spent for leisure time in which they can satisfy their interests and fulfil themselves as human beings.

Urban One has to be an optimist to be a socialist, but does one have to be bemused? By the time the average American reaches the age of fifty he has spent 15,000 hours in front of his television set and seen 70,000 acts of gross violence ranging from rape to genocide—which does not seem to me to be convincing proof that, given half a chance, the man in the street is determined to improve his mind. Then, I am also less optimistic than you are that men who spend the money-earning part of their lives in moronic jobs will, when their time for leisure comes, suddenly engage in feats of responsible and creative activity. For a crude example, one knows from army life that the great majority of private soldiers have absolutely no desire to rise even to the rank of sergeant, for they hate nothing so much as having to shoulder responsibility. I am not saying that these are necessary reactions, but if we want to be practical and go by the only evidence we have—the evidence of history—man's proclivity for irresponsibility and idleness is the one thing we can be sure about. Creativity is a bonus.

Sik I think you are a prisoner of our image of ourselves as we are today. But why should we not be able to detach our vision of the future from this image? I hold no brief for the lunatic fringe of the student rebellion, but one good thing the students have helped us to understand is that the army regular's willing subordination to authority and his fear of responsibility are becoming highly untypical of our society. We have to learn to think away from current stereotypes; why should it not be possible to imagine that two hours' work a day will be enough to satisfy our material needs and that the rest of our time will be harnessed to a more worthwhile purpose?

I don't want to treat you to homilies, but it is true that so long as people haven't got enough to eat, the satisfaction of hunger will be their only real interest. When that condition is overcome and the other needs and creature comforts have also been tolerably satisfied, people begin to need music, they demand more education, books, theatre. I am not saying that an increase in leisure will *automatically* hoist us on to a higher level of consciousness. This can only happen if the whole ambiance of our society—our education, the style and quality of our living—challenges us to set ourselves objectives that are different from—and one hopes higher than—the ones we have set ourselves so far.

It is, of course, perfectly true that if you take man as he is today and tell him that his eight-hour day will be reduced to two hours but that he will at the same time enjoy the same wages that he has been earning for a full day's work, he will be at a loss to know what to do with his leisure because he has not been brought up to do anything sensible with it. That is where the inanities of television come in. Television has become a surrogate for the lives people have ceased to live. But this can and will change. Now, back to your question: what does the self-realisation of man mean in the Czechoslovak programme?

It means that man can do justice to the species Man—that is to say, that we should be able to feel ourselves to be, and expect others to look upon us as, human beings. What makes us different from non-human nature is our ability both to adapt to our surroundings and to change our surroundings through the conscious exertion of our intellect, and to find pleasure and satisfaction in so doing. Of course, one can put a mechanistic interpretation on this definition, in which case my conception of man acquires a quality of facile idealism. But if you think of self-realisation not merely as a matter of personal satisfaction, but as something that is socially conditioned and feeds back into the quality of society, then the self-realisation of man is invested with a fresh meaning. When we can do the kind of thing that fills us with joy, when we feel that our faculties are well stretched and our creative energies usefully employed, then, I would say, man has attained a measure of self-fulfilment.

Urban Ignazio Silone once remarked to me that Communism fails to convince as a life-philosophy because it has nothing to say to us on the question of death. I brought up this remark of Silone's in a conversation with Gyorgy Lukacs in 1968. His answer was that Communism seeks to give no explanation to Silone's problem as it regards it as a non-problem. Religion, he said, was a substitute for a poorly lived life, and he quoted Tolstoy's short story 'The Death of Ivan Ilych' as an illustration of his thesis that the secret of the good life is a sensible, goal-orientated and rational existence[1]. This, I should have thought, was *his* definition of 'self-fulfilment'. How would you, as a principal architect of the Czechoslovak Reform Movement and as a former Deputy Prime Minister, react to Silone's question? It is, after all, a question which Bernstein had the foresight to raise much before Silone.

Sik We are now touching upon ultimate issues, and I believe there are no answers to these questions, certainly not in our present state of consciousness. Is there absolute cognition? There isn't, but we can safely say that our knowledge of the world is steadily growing, though it is probably equally true that we shall never be able to exhaust it with finality. Every time we reach the frontiers of knowledge and can probe no further, explanations are sought in the irrational, and religion asserts itself. But as more and more of reality is opened up to scientific understanding, the field for religious types of beliefs narrows. Also, it is clear that people who have acquired the habit of scientific thinking simply need no religion. Now this, in my view, is the long-term trend—the unanswerable questions will still be there, but the demand that the answers should be couched in numinous language will shrink and perhaps disappear.

Having said that I recognise that at the present stage of our social development society still needs spiritual tranquillisers—it simply cannot do without the comfort of the numinous. But, as I say, the demand for these tranquillising agents is falling off.

This still leaves us with the problem of morality. Religion and ethics are usually considered to be two sides of the same coin. True or not, we must concede that the retreat of religion has been accompanied by a moral vacuum which we have, so far at least, not been able to fill. Society does need an ethic, but morality in my view should not be identified with any particular religion or any particular

[1] *Encounter*, October 1971.

ideology. Morality has arisen as the conjoint realisation of certain habits and rules of social coexistence, and at a certain stage of social development it came to be identified with religion. That is all.

In other words, the survival of society depends on the assertion of social interests through a social ethic, and it is this unwritten social ethic that is later translated into written rules and regulations. But as society changes, morality, too—precisely because it is a sophisticated expression of the collective interests of society—changes with it. Now, in our situation today Christian morality has ceased to be effective; the rules of the game of yesterday have no attraction for the young. Their values are in conflict with their fathers' values. Yet a new ethic is very slow in emerging. The old code has lost its charisma but there isn't a new one we could trust—so we are not in a position to answer certain questions which, I am entirely confident, we *will* be able to answer in not too many generations.

Urban The claim is frequently made in Eastern Europe that the fundamental questions of society can only be answered by 'socialist' society, and that these questions are in fact in the process of being answered by the 'socialist' societies of Eastern Europe.

Sik This is absolutely untrue—there is no socialist society that I can see in any of the 'socialist' countries. What we have there is a state-monopolistic system in which man's alienation is more profound than under traditional capitalism. The so-called socialist morality handed down from on high as a substitute for the Christian ethic is not a morality born in the womb of society, not an ethic of the majority, but one which is entirely fashioned by and imposed upon the people by the holders of power. Clearly this ethic evokes no response and has no followers. It will not survive the present form of 'socialism' which is itself unlikely to die of old age.

Urban The reforms contained in the Vysocany programme adjudicate on the large questions we have been discussing in almost the same spirit of 'socialist' idealism in which Kropotkin, Bukharin and Preobrazhensky used to preach at us in 'The ABC of Communism', and you seem to share a good deal of that idealism.

Sik This is not the first time that I have been accused of unwarranted idealism. I hold no brief for an ideal society, and I do not imagine that there *could* be a society from which all contradictions and conflicts have been eliminated. Anyone who assumes that such a society could exist has learned nothing from Marx's dialectic. My own interests are confined to solving certain practical contradictions which put the brakes on the progress of society. We are, in the social sciences, trying to lay bare the nature of these contradictions and to offer solutions without, however, suggesting that once these particular problems have been solved, society would be free from conflicts. My own analysis starts from looking at the contradictions which exist in the so-called Western capitalist countries, and then to proceed to look at those which slow down the development of 'socialist' society, that is to say a society ruled by state monopolies. Having looked at these, I then ask myself how these contradictions may be removed—whether they can be removed by piecemeal social engineering or whether they require a change of system. But whatever the outcome of any remedies I may offer, I would never be so rash as to imagine that a society thus created would be without its own contradictions and that these wouldn't, at a later stage, require their own solutions.

Urban If the Czechoslovak Reform Movement had been allowed to run its course, would it have offered socialist answers to the ills of mass industrial society as well as to the particular problems which Stalinism and the command economy had left you with? My impression was that you were, for understandable reasons, so busy trying to make the economy work that you had little time and energy left to think of dealing with the more fundamental problems. Yet Western Communists were looking to you for solutions precisely in this area. They expected you to give them a model of how Marxism works, not in a backward country such as Russia where it does not work, but in the kind of developed, industrialised society which Marx wrote about.

Sik We tried to set side by side problems which have arisen in state-monopolistic, command economies, and those which have arisen in Western capitalism, and we came to the conclusion that, although here and there the problems arise in different forms and assume different magnitudes, they are variables within the same equation and can be dealt with by the same methods. This analysis then led us to believe that it would make good sense to think of the two systems in terms of a common model, a model which would help us to overcome the contradictions in both the capitalistic and the state-monopolistic types of society. I cannot here go into the details of our work, but we did try to examine all the big questions of modern industrial society, and we did come up with tentative conclusions which the Soviet occupation of our country did not allow us to put into practice. But—and this must be emphasised—we never imagined that our model was a cure-all.

Urban Students of contemporary history and Sovietologists of all descriptions have already spilt a great deal of ink trying to persuade us that the Czechoslovak Reform Movement was—or was not, as the case may be—a matter of economic reforms first and political reforms only as a by-product of the need to reform the country's badly lagging economy. Respectable Czech sources can be quoted to support either view. Some believe that economic renewal and politico-cultural liberalisation played comparable parts in the Prague Spring; others support the idea that political reform was the prime mover, but that it had to masquerade under the guise of economic reform which was less likely to offend the sensibilities of reform-shy Stalinists. Do you as a crown witness of the economic reform programme come down in favour of one side or the other in this debate? If the 1956 Hungarian experience is anything to go by, I should have thought that economic issues were the fuse, but the dynamite had been accumulating over the years in Czechoslovak society, and had only been waiting for an appropriate issue to light the fuse.

Sik I was present at the birth of this movement in 1957; I may perhaps even claim that I was one of its initiators. It all started around a small group of social theorists, but the actual problem we had to tackle as our first priority was that of the national economy. However, it was clear from the beginning that the economic problem itself had a strong national colouring. We realised that Czechoslovakia could have been much further advanced in her social and cultural life if her economy—a basically advanced economy—had not been so disastrously mismanaged, that is to say, if the system as a whole had not driven that economy into absurd self-contradictions. In other words, it was Czechoslovakia's unsatisfactory cultural and economic performance that set us off on our investigations, and our first practical task was to see what could be done to drag the economy out of the trough. But no sooner did we start on that than we found ourselves surrounded by political scientists, sociologists and writers, all anxious to put their bit of reform in motion parallel with ours or, to be more precise, all anxious to show that it was impossible to make changes in one part of the polity without making changes in the others too. And, of course, it *was* impossible. And once it was realised that reform would have to affect the whole structure of society, questions began to be asked about the good life, the ultimate aims of socialism and indeed of human society.

Let me emphasise that when I say that economic reform was the formative influence in the Prague Spring, I do not mean to say that there was any direct economic pressure on the government of the kind we saw on the Baltic coast of Poland in 1970 when poor wages, high prices and other consumer grievances led to direct action of a very bloody kind. No, in our case the reforms were the work of intellectuals. Our ideas had been patiently prepared over a long period of time at a fairly high level of abstraction. There was nothing spontaneous about them. Nor was it an accident that many of the intellectual reformers hailed from the Party Academy. These men were sincere socialists, they had no vested interests to defend, and they were not after power. They were persuaded that the system had to be changed, for they could see that what had been foisted on Czechoslovakia in the name of socialism was not only not offering answers to capitalism, but was *itself* a form of capitalism, driven to absurd extremes, in all but name. That is how things got started.

Urban In what way did the 1956 Hungarian uprising affect your movement? I remember an article by O. Machatka in *Literarni Listy*, written in June 1968, which surprised me at the time because it commemorated the tenth anniversary of the announcement that Imre Nagy and his associates had been sentenced to death and executed. The fact that such an article could be written was significant enough, for it amounted to the rehabilitation of Nagy and the 1956 uprising; but it was even more significant because it ended with the words: 'Even in our country his [Nagy's] ideas, which anticipated so many future events and which probably sound much less far-fetched today, should not remain unknown.'

Sik The writing was on the wall. We could see that a spontaneous assertion of the popular will could only end in suppression by the Soviet Union. We could see that, to avoid provoking Moscow, we had to proceed with great caution, great patience, and great tactical finesse. Looking back on these patient preparations with the wisdom of hindsight, I would still say that we did our best, and I would add that in the circumstances we didn't do too badly. Alas, in the last phase of the Reform Movement things got out of hand. To the moves we had patiently prepared and controlled a new element was now added: a kind of self-combustion which escaped our control. Military occupation followed.

Today the great debate among the former leaders of the Reform Movement is whether occupation by the Warsaw Pact countries could have been prevented if we had managed to keep our reforms more under control. My own opinion is that this would not have helped us, for the real source of our trouble was not so much the spontaneous spread of liberalisation, as the composition of the leadership that came to power after Novotny's fall. For—contrary to popular opinion—this leadership was not a reform leadership but a leadership of compromise and dithering. There were both outright Stalinists and convinced reformers in it, and the occupation of Czechoslovakia was directly due to the fact that some of the Stalinist members of the leadership did not want the reforms to succeed in the first place: they *wanted* Soviet intervention.

When people talk of the 1968 Czechoslovak leadership the names of Dubcek and Smrkovsky are the ones usually mentioned. Yet in the same leadership you had men like

Kolder, Indra, Svestka, Bilak and others whose goals were diametrically opposed to those of Dubcek and Smrkovsky. Well, this split in the leadership made life extremely difficult for the reformers and for the people: under Novotny everyone could see that the enemy was the Novotny regime, but with this new leadership at the head of the country in the spring of 1968, it became very difficult to know whom to fight and whom to support. It was impossible to go against the new team, but it was equally impossible to go along with it. Some of the new leaders were sincerely committed to reform, but others simply sabotaged the Reform Movement. To mention one example, Pavel was appointed as Minister of the Interior to clear out the Russians, but a month later Salgovic, an old NKVD agent, was made Secretary of State to keep the Russians *in* and sabotage Pavel's policies. The Politburo too was split down the middle, with about half its members dead set against the reforms. Our chances of success were not too good.

In any case, various provocations by the Stalinist old guard further embittered the people. Pressure groups were building up on all sides to keep the Reform Movement going and, as I have said, these then began to have a momentum of their own which no one could control. From then on it was only a question of time—of how soon, but not whether, Soviet troops would move in.

Urban Some of us in the West have never been able to understand how old Communists, many of them with years of prison experience under Stalin behind them, could expect to get away with a free Czechoslovak press, free television, and freedom of speech at a time when Moscow regarded such experiments as internal *Soviet* developments which were thought to constitute a mortal threat to Soviet internal stability, and therefore also to the Soviet Union's international power. I had occasion to talk to one of the leaders of the Czechoslovak Reform Movement some eighteen months before the Soviet occupation, and I ventured to express my doubt as to whether Moscow would tolerate the Czech variety of 'socialism'. My interlocutor did not share my apprehension. He argued that the Soviet comrades would not want to prevent an entirely reliable and proven ally from following *its* road to socialism, especially if that road promised to lead to a credible model of Western socialism which might prove attractive to other Western nations. I find such idealism appealing, but I doubt if it has a place in the ugly business of politics.

Sik This is another Western over-simplification. It is so easy to be wise after the event. We were not so naive as not to realise that Soviet intervention was a possibility. But possibility is one thing, necessity another. I do not agree with you that the probability of Soviet intervention was a foregone conclusion; there was an either/or possibility which, of course, we never calculated in percentages. But suppose there was a fifty-fifty chance—I still believe that we were right in not abdicating our responsibility but carrying on with our plans, as in fact we did.

In any case, I believe we did have a very real chance of preventing Soviet intervention, but this chance was thrown away; and *because* it was thrown away the direction of developments slipped out of our hands. The chance I am referring to was a speedy convocation of the 14th Party Congress. Up to April 1968 this was a realistic possibility. The delegates who had been elected were good and experienced and their hearts were in the Reform Movement. I am mentioning April because in April the Russians were, by all the evidence, still undecided whether or not to march on us. They had made their military preparations, but they were sitting on the fence. If we had managed to have our Party Congress, say, in April, I'm personally convinced that we would have elected a new leadership, consolidated our policies, and regained control of the Reform Movement in a way that would have given our Soviet critics every incentive to hold their horses. We could have seen to it that the press, radio, and television did not provoke the Soviet leaders unnecessarily. Of course, I cannot say with certainty whether—if all this had been done—we would in fact have avoided occupation. But there might have been a fair chance. We could have offered the Russians precise guarantees about our reliability as allies, as Western outposts of the socialist camp, etc., while candidly telling them at the same time what we were trying to achieve with our internal reforms. Unfortunately we never reached that point. We could not persuade Dubcek to bring the Party Congress forward to

April. The conflicts between the Stalinist and reformist wings in the Party leadership made Dubcek hesitate, and the Congress was repeatedly postponed. By the time Dubcek realised that we could not carry on without a new leadership and decided to convene the Congress for September, it was too late: the Soviet leaders had made up their minds to occupy us before the Congress. It is therefore not true to say that we were not aware of the dangers—we were. Our fight for an early Congress had in fact become our battle to save the Reform Movement itself.

Urban You were saying that the Russians might have been appeased by certain guarantees. Would they have been amenable to the kind of argument I quoted a minute ago—an appeal to the long-range interests of the world Communist movement, best served by a model 'socialist' state in Czechoslovakia of the kind Marx foresaw but the Soviet Union failed to realise?

Sik You cannot operate with ideological arguments when you talk to the Russians. Dubcek believed one could, and he had to learn the hard way. Stalin's quip about the Pope's divisions is still typical of the mentality of the Soviet leaders. No, we ought to have given them reliable guarantees. Of course it is an open question how far we could have gone in giving such guarantees without jeopardising the Reform Movement. Nevertheless, I am sure that suitable guarantees could have been devised. I don't want to put all the blame on Dubcek, for he was himself a victim of the schism in the leadership; but it is a fact that we gave the Russians no practical guarantees that the Movement would be held within certain limits. All they could see was that the press and television were bringing to light things that seemed insulting to them and hurtful to their interests and that we were not in a position to stop it. This, in their eyes, was a direct provocation, and they acted accordingly. We could see perfectly well that the Russians themselves could do with a new model of socialism, but it was impossible to convince them by ideological means. That is why I attach such great importance to the timing of the Party Congress. For ten years we had inched our way forward step by step without significant reverses. We were patient and cautious because we had learned from Hungary. But when it came to convincing the leadership that the Congress ought to be called in April, we were—for the first time in ten years—defeated, and this proved a fatal reverse. The moment we realised that the Congress would not be called before September, we knew that we had lost. But what was there for us to do? Incite the nation to withdraw its confidence from Dubcek? That would have been an act of desperation and gross irresponsibility.

Urban Would it have been right and realistic to ask the people to fight when the Russian troops arrived in Czechoslovakia?

Sik No, fighting a war is something we can no longer afford. The Soviet tanks got us between two pincers from which there was no escape. Our military predicament was worse than it was when Hitler occupied our country in 1938. Nor was there the slightest hope that anyone would help us. Armed resistance to the Soviet invasion would have spelt the suicide of our nation.

There are Czechoslovak emigrants who now tell us that we ought to have fought. Well, I would not have liked to have taken responsibility for such a decision. Our geographic and military situation was entirely unlike that of Yugoslavia. We were not prepared for military resistance and we would not have stood the slightest chance of making a success of it. And I do not believe that we had the right to ask thousands of our young men to lay down their lives in a token demonstration of our national mettle.

Manuel Azcárate

The Prague–Moscow–Madrid Triangle[1]

Socialism, true and false

Urban Both you, Señor Azcárate, and Santiago Carrillo have repeatedly told us that the groundwork for Eurocommunism was laid by the 1968 Czechoslovak Reform Movement. Would I be right in saying that Eurocommunism owes its existence directly to the Prague Spring? Or did Prague merely act as a midwife to a development that was well under way irrespective of the Reform Movement?

Azcárate When the Czechoslovak Communist Party began to stir in January 1968 twelve years had passed since the 20th Soviet Party Congress and Khrushchev's denunciation of Stalin. We had been given a warning by Soviet party history to be sceptical about 'models' and think out afresh the future of Communism in Western Europe. We had been made conscious that the socialist experience in Russia and Eastern Europe was replete with highly negative examples. [We realised that we had been profoundly deceived by what the Soviet comrades had told us about the state of civil liberty and the purge trials, the role of the police forces and the entire apparatus of repression under Stalin.] We had many friends among the victims of Stalinism—Arthur

[1]The edited transcript of the tape recording on which this chapter is based was submitted to Señor Azcárate for his approval. He requested that various revisions should be made. These have been incorporated, but where the changes seemed to diverge in important respects from what had been said in the tape recording, the original passages have been included in square brackets. The text of this chapter follows the form in which it was published in *Encounter* magazine (March 1979).

London, for example—from whose evidence we could piece together the truth about Stalin's terror in all its beastliness.

We were in this frame of mind when news reached us, towards the end of 1967, of a ferment in the Czechoslovak Party, of Novotny's eventual fall, of Dubcek's election and the Reform Movement's increasingly successful attempt to infuse democracy into the system. This was a breath of fresh air for us, and we shared the Czechoslovak comrades' exhilaration. Prague confirmed what we had been vaguely feeling for some time but did not clearly articulate—namely that the degeneration of Soviet socialism into Stalinism was due to certain specific reasons such as Russia's economic and social backwardness and the absence from Russian history of any democratic tradition.

Czechoslovakia, therefore, was not so much a shock for us as a *recognition*. Here was a promise to renew socialism in the spirit of the same democratic values in which it was born. Czechoslovakia was clearly the only fully *Western* country in the Eastern camp—the only one in which respect for civil liberties, tolerance and compromise had sunk deep roots. We realised that whatever happened in Czechoslovakia was of immense interest to us and to all Communists in Western Europe. [Any success the Czechs managed to achieve in reforming Communism was a challenge to *our* ability to reform it; *their* reaction to Stalinism was a prophylactic warning to *us*.]

We were, therefore, not only interested in the Prague Reform Movement, but enthusiastic supporters of it. I remember articles we wrote in *Mundo Obrero* and *Nuestra Bandera* (of which I am the editor) expressing our conviction that the Czechoslovak reforms were [leading us back to the] showing an authentic pattern of socialism.

Urban Your party was in exile in 1968. Were you in touch with the Czechoslovak Communists—were you reliably informed about the mood of the people?

Azcárate Yes, we were in exile in France, but we had in Czechoslovakia about 150 Spanish Communists who had been expelled from France in the early 1950s, when our Party was outlawed there, too, and had settled in Czechoslovakia. We were, of course, in close touch with these comrades. They had jobs in different parts of the country and we kept getting reports from them—trustworthy people who had fought in the Spanish Civil War—of what was happening in Czechoslovakia. When Moscow began to send word around that Prague was heading for a counter-revolution, we were, therefore, in a good position to nail the lie; we knew from our comrades that the people were supporting Dubcek and there was no sign of any counter-revolution.

Until January 1968 our relationship with the Czechoslovak leadership was intermittent, but after the changes of January we were in close touch. I was myself in Prague on several occasions and established friendly ties with Smrkovsky and Dubcek. We were, therefore, fully in the picture and knew what the Czechs were trying to do.

Urban Let us go back for a moment to the idea that the Prague Spring was only a midwife to Eurocommunism . . . because it seems to me important to establish as precisely as we can that some kind of Eurocommunism was, embryonically at least, in existence well before Prague—not only among the Italian Communists but elsewhere too. Santiago Carrillo says in *Euro-Communism and the State*: 'Czechoslovakia was the straw which broke the camel's back and led our parties to say: *No* . . .'

What camel? What parties?

Azcárate Our criticism of Soviet policies pre-dates the Prague events. But while we could sense that all was not well in the Soviet Union, for a long time we tended to believe that our doubts were themselves open to doubt. We inclined to think that Khrushchev's revelations and the changes he initiated would be much more far-reaching than they in fact proved to be. We had protested against Khrushchev's dismissal; we made it clear that we were gravely disturbed to see that, despite the 20th Party Congress, the leader of the Soviet Party could be removed from his post in [a *putsch*-like fashion] a manner which was nothing short of a conspiracy. But until the 1968 Prague events, our criticisms were tempered by a feeling that perhaps our information was partial and our judgment therefore open to errors.

What made the Czechoslovak events decisively relevant for us was the wholly internal nature of the Prague reforms:

the changes had come about as a result of a vote *in* the Central Committee. We were witnessing a process which was entirely consistent with the socialist system and with the structure of the Communist Party. When, therefore, Soviet tanks rolled into Czechoslovakia to suppress a leadership which had been democratically elected within the framework of the socialist system, our tentative criticism of the Soviet system was at once transformed into frontal repudiation: 'This was intolerable.' It was from then on clear to us that there was a basic contradiction between the policies pursued by the Soviet leadership under Brezhnev, and our own conception of what socialism was about. *This* was the straw that broke the camel's back.

Urban When Carrillo says that the facts circulated by the Russians about Czechoslovakia under 'internationalism' were 'light-years away from reality', what precisely does he mean?

Azcárate Carrillo was referring to Soviet allegations that Czechoslovakia was in danger of returning to capitalism; that the Czechoslovak leaders were traitors; that the Prague reforms were the work of German agents; that American arms had been found near Czechoslovakia's Western border, and so on. I remember reading of a Party meeting (6 May 1968) to commemorate the 150th anniversary of Marx's birth, at which Cestmir Cisar, Secretary of the Czechoslovak Communist Party, said that the Leninist interpretation of Marxism was one-sided and the legitimate interpretation of Marx in our time should lead to a democratic socialism.

Well, Cisar got attacked for his speech in *Pravda* in a quite despicable fashion. [It was alleged that he was trying to disarm the fight against imperialism, that he was a revisionist and a nationalist. This wild misrepresentation of the truth is what Carrillo had in mind when he said that the Soviet case was 'light-years' away from the facts. He was also implying that these untruths were being used to justify certain 'emergency' measures which the Soviets had taken to suppress Czechoslovakia. I was in Paris at the time, and so was Carrillo. We were in frequent touch with representatives of the Soviet Party who tried to win our support for their version of what was happening in Czechoslovakia. We absolutely refused to give it to them, and we told them so unambiguously. But we did more than that.] You will remember that in July and August 1978 Soviet manoeuvres were taking place near the Czechoslovak borders, and rumour was rife that these were a prelude to the invasion of the country. Well, we told the Russians that if they invaded Czechoslovakia we would publicly condemn their action.

I remember talking to Ponomarev in Budapest at the preparatory meeting for the 1969 Conference of European Communist Parties and protesting against *Pravda's* attack on a well-known leader of the Prague Spring. [I had just returned from Czechoslovakia and I remarked to Ponomarev that there were fears in Prague and among West European Communists generally that the Soviet side was preparing to invade the country and suppress the new Czech leadership. Ponomarev was most indignant. 'How dare you impute such an intention to us? What sort of an attitude is this? Of course, we are a little worried, but how dare you say that we want to invade Czechoslovakia?' A few weeks later these rumours turned out to be true. I did, incidentally, find Ponomarev an uninformed and not very intelligent man, and I was wondering how a person with such obvious failings could be in charge of vital matters in one of the world's two most powerful states.]

[**Urban** Was Ponomarev's attitude shared by other leaders of the Warsaw Pact countries?

Azcárate It was—to the extent that Ponomarev really believed what he said. The others believed what Ponomarev said. But that is, of course, begging the question.]

Urban Did you suspect duplicity?

Azcárate I did, but I could not be certain. But to answer your previous question: after the Cierna and Bratislava meetings we thought that the crisis was being defused, so I decided to take a holiday in Poland—Carrillo went to the Soviet Union. Until then we had been in Paris keeping a daily tab on the Prague developments, but we now thought there was a respite. Before going to the Baltic Coast, I spoke to one of the Polish leaders. I told him, too, about the rumours that were circulating, and I said that we as a Party would publicly denounce any military move against Czechoslovakia. He, too, was indignant and strongly denied that any such thing was being contemplated or indeed imaginable.

The invasion of Czechoslovakia took place while I was still in Poland. I decided to return to Paris immediately, and as I was making my seat reservation the Polish Party authorities suggested that they explain matters to me before I left the country. And they put forward the name of the same man I had seen before. My answer was: Yes, I would be very happy to talk to him, but my own and our Party's attitude was unchanged—we were going to make a public denunciation of the invasion of Czechoslovakia. Whereupon I got my seat reservation, but the Party leader in question made no further attempt to see me. I suppose it would have been highly embarrassing for him to argue the *opposite* of the case he had argued to me some ten days earlier.

Urban Did you think the Polish leaders shared the Soviet view of the Prague events?

Azcárate No, my impression was that the Polish Communists were, by and large, witnesses, at worst accomplices, rather than convinced supporters of the invasion of Czechoslovakia.

[**Urban** But wasn't there a certain *Schadenfreude* among the Poles ... 'You thought you could get away with something we couldn't—now we are in the same boat again'?

Azcárate Here and there one could detect signs of that feeling among the rank-and-file. But I don't think the Poles, either in the Party or outside it, actively hoped for the failure of the Prague Spring. The population as a whole was certainly hoping that it would succeed for understandable reasons of its own.

Urban Talking to Ponomarev in Budapest, was it your impression that, his protestations notwithstanding, he knew that preparations were being made to put down Czechoslovakia?

Azcárate I could not be absolutely certain whether the decision to invade had been reached (although, with hindsight, we now know that by July the preparations were well advanced). But the impression I got from our conversation was that, despite his ostensible indignation, he did not consider the suppression of Czechoslovakia as something totally objectionable under certain circumstances.]

Urban How would you, as a senior leader of the Spanish Communist Party and the man responsible for the Party's foreign relations, describe the character of the 1968 invasion?

Azcárate Well, an invasion is an invasion, and aggression is aggression whoever commits it.

It has been argued that the decision to invade was reached under the pressure of worried generals on predominantly military grounds. Others have thought that the Kremlin hawks, with Shelest in the role of the vulture, were mainly responsible. There may be truth in both theories, but the real reasons must be sought elsewhere.

A socialist society of the type which the Czechoslovak Communists were working for—one based on freedom, democracy, the consent and support of the people—was seen to be a threat to the Soviet system. It would have spread, it was feared, to the other East European countries and eventually to the Soviet Union itself. In the Manichean world of Soviet thinking Prague assumed the features of the Devil—and the Devil has to be destroyed. You don't sup with him, you don't argue with him—you kill him.

Already during those brief months of the Prague Spring the Czechoslovak example was exerting a noticeable influence in Eastern Europe—a most positive influence, in our view, because it was showing that it *was* possible to change socialism, Soviet-style, in sensible and non-violent ways.

[Prague, moreover, was not merely a theoretical threat to the Soviet system and to Soviet hegemony—it was a *personal* threat to a small group of men who exercised power in this enormous land by bureaucratic despotism. These men knew that if the ideas generated in Prague were allowed to mature and to spread, they would themselves eventually have to find a different legitimation for holding power, or indeed face the prospect of losing power.]

Their violent reaction to the Prague reforms was, of course, dressed up in ideology. They did not say: 'Our rule is threatened by the Czechs, therefore we will crush them.' No—they said: 'Anyone who is a real Communist and not a traitor to Communism must respect the Soviet interpretation of Marxism-Leninism and accept the Soviet model of socialism; and those who do not must face the consequences.' Whether the Soviet leaders actually believed their own propaganda is difficult to say and historically unimportant. The fact is that they identified [their personal rule] the cause of socialism with the closed Soviet system. Nothing outside the system is tolerated. That was the basis of their attitude to Prague, and that is their attitude to Eurocommunism today.

Urban You are talking as though Stalinism still existed in the Soviet Union fifteen years after the death of Stalin and twelve years after the 20th Party Congress, whereas we know perfectly well that for the man in the street Stalinism in 1968 was a fast receding memory—no more.

Azcárate Certainly the mass repressions had ceased by 1968, certainly there are no longer millions languishing in camps, but the Stalinist conception of the state—the *cult* of the state as the joint embodiment of a powerful bureaucracy, a powerful police force and a powerful army—continued, and continues, to be the basis of the Soviet system. This is a conception in which the 'good' *of* the people is interpreted by [a ruling elite] a small group of leaders, which then imposes this 'good' *on* the people by the apparatus of the state. It is, therefore, preposterous to say that there have survived in the Soviet Union certain 'residues' of Stalinism. No—the dogma of the supremacy of the state apparatus and the continuing repression testify to the survival of a basic form of Stalinism. The invasion of Czechoslovakia was only the most tangible and repulsive demonstration of its staying power.

'The Spanish people would fight'

Urban Santiago Carrillo expressed his puzzlement at the phenomenon you have described in these words: 'If all states are instruments by which one class dominates another, and there are no antagonistic classes in the USSR, there is, objectively speaking, no need for repressing the other classes; who, then, is dominated by this state. . . ?'

Azcárate The answer is clear. Far from having given birth to a free democratic society which might serve as a model to others, the Soviet system has become an instrument of [serving a small group of rulers who have subjected the entire Soviet population to their] bureaucratic despotism.

Urban Carrillo goes one step further when he argues that some of the *formal* features of Stalinism are 'similar to those of fascist dictatorships'. Would you agree that there still exists this *formal* similarity (Carrillo, to be fair to him, stresses that in substance the two have always been different)?

Azcárate Yes, I would—the formal similarities are obvious. But we don't have to go back to Stalin's rule to draw damaging comparisons. Even today, political liberty in [most] some capitalist countries is [much] more extensive than it is in the Soviet Union—to say nothing of Russia under Stalin. Compare, for example, the citizen's ability to obtain information in the capitalist West and in the Soviet Union. Without any question, his freedom to receive and impart information is [infinitely] greater [under capitalism] in several capitalist countries than under the Soviet system—and this freedom to inform and to be informed is, after all, the first condition of democracy.

While our party was in illegality in France we found ourselves in the *absurd* situation that, in our disputes with the Soviet Party, we were able to inform our Party members both of our side of any argument and of the Soviet reaction to it. But the Soviet Communist Party, which has been in power for sixty years and rules the world's largest country, did not feel strong enough to permit *its* public to find out what we were saying!

Urban You were, in fact, freer in clandestinity in an oppressive capitalist society than your Soviet comrades in an ostensibly free and ostensibly socialist society?

Azcárate Not to put too fine a point on it—our discussions with the Soviet Party were not at all, and *are* not at all, discussions between two Communist *parties*. On the Soviet side the argument has always been regarded as the private property of a small nucleus of leaders, whereas on our side the debate has been, and is, wide open.

Urban I notice that when Carrillo was attacked in *Novoye Vremya* in July 1977 you circulated among your members both the text of the Soviet article and your answers to it, among them your own in *Mundo Obrero*. Is this measure of internal freedom part of your established practice? It would not seem to be in line with 'democratic centralism' which you have not repudiated.

Azcárate The freedom of informal discussions has been a well-established practice in our Party for many years; we had it in our underground existence and, of course, we have it now. Let me give you another example. When *Partiinaya Zhizn* used my Report to the plenum of the Central Committee of our Party, in September 1973, to attack the Party leadership and the independent line we had been pursuing in our foreign policy, we published (in illegality) a leaflet giving all our members the entire text of the Soviet attack as well as our own arguments, so that everyone could judge for himself. The problem is, as I've said, that after sixty years in power the Soviet Party does not feel confident enough to tolerate any view other than its own. Its current stance on Eurocommunism, too, cannot be graced with the word 'argument', for it consists of the brandishing of dogma, threats and condemnation. These are methods worthy of the Inquisition—not those of a debate conducted with another Communist Party.

Urban Does all this betray the weakness or the strength of the Soviet leadership? Looking at the decision-making scene in Washington—where decisions are frequently lost among a plague of decision-makers, and where, when decisions are finally made, they are frequently undercut or undone by free-wheeling dissenters of every kind—isn't there a case for appreciating the advantages of the Soviet leadership's brutal but effective methods of government?

Azcárate I don't know enough about Washington to make a comparison, but I consider Soviet dogmatism to be a sign of great political and ideological weakness. The system is closed. It reverberates to nothing outside its own parrot-like recitation of the virtues of itself and the crimes of others. This means shutting out the world as it really is.

To give you one example: Marxist thinking is paralysed in the Soviet Union. The home of creative Marxism today is France, Italy, and even the United States—not the Soviet Union. For many years now no fresh Marxist ideas of any kind have come out of the USSR. What you have in the

Soviet Union is *government* thinking, which betrays great political weakness. [The only type of undertaking in which the Soviets are not weak is the military field—power—but that would take us into another discussion.]

Urban Wouldn't you say, though, that, with all their limitations and dogmatism, the Soviet leaders were, in 1968, acting in the Soviet, and perhaps ultimately in the universal Communist interest, for if they had allowed Czechoslovakia to take off, the whole of Soviet 'socialism' would have been jeopardised?

One is, of course, familiar with the argument that by suppressing Czechoslovakia Soviet interests were protected at a very high price, the price being the accelerated disintegration of what was left of the unity of the World Communist movement and, more particularly, the rise of a new strain of resistance to Soviet leadership: Eurocommunism. But, then, politicians' choices are usually between unpleasant alternatives, and the Soviet leaders can hardly be blamed for having opted for the survival of the Soviet system rather than put their money on the unity of the movement which, by 1968, could not be guaranteed against further erosion in any case.

Azcárate I don't agree. The Czechoslovak experiment was an absolutely decisive move in the history of socialism in that it tried to give socialism an effectively modern and democratic dimension [and put its creative focus back into Western Europe]. It was a move to rescue socialism from the general backwardness which it inherited from the historical accident that the first socialist revolution had taken place in semi-oriental, Tsarist, under-industrialised Russia. [The suppression of Czechoslovakia was a particularly odious demonstration of the fact that the backward and anachronistic force of Soviet socialism has all the power in the world to prevent, if necessary by force of arms, the progressive strain in socialism from making headway. To the extent that the occupation of Czechoslovakia has killed or heavily retarded this development, we can only say that it has dealt a blow to the whole socialist movement, including, of course, its Soviet variant.]

Urban Hugh Seton-Watson, the distinguished British historian, has said that the occupation of Czechoslovakia was an act of 'Russian imperialism', and Milovan Djilas, too, has described (in *The Unperfect Society*) the Kremlin's attitude to Eastern Europe as 'Soviet pan-Russian imperialism'. Would you agree with these judgments?

Azcárate 'Imperialism' for me [for us in the Communist movement] has a very specific meaning. It denotes the monopoly stage of capitalism in which the division of the world among the leading capitalist powers has been completed. The label therefore does not fit.

Urban Would you describe the Prague Spring as a form of national liberation struggle?

Azcárate I would hesitate to do so [because such struggles are directed, in our conception, against colonial imperialism]: the principal aim of the Prague reforms was to inject democracy into socialism.

We have to take a large view. We believe that the October Revolution was an event of world historical importance—the first move in the historical process *away* from capitalism *to* socialism; *away* from a society of exploitation *to* a superior civilisation. But this process was inhibited by Russian backwardness, by Russia's lack of a democratic tradition and all the other impedimenta of Russian history. If the first socialist revolution had taken place in *Germany* rather than Russia, under the guiding influence of people such as Rosa Luxemburg, then the whole evolution of socialism would have taken a different direction, and the whole European scene would be different today. But the fact that socialism was born out of a Russian, rather than a West European, matrix, does not invalidate the significance of its birth.

The general curve of socialism is unbroken, but *within* it there have been serious setbacks, such as Stalinism, which gravely threaten the speedy attainment of real socialism. But let us remember that the French Revolution, too, was followed by many years of Bourbon rule and the passing triumph of reaction; but such instances of a backlash did not invalidate the liberating message of the French Revolution, much less kill it.

Urban You are saying that in due course Stalinism too will appear to have been a regrettable deviation—no more. It did not, in your analysis, rise out of the *nature* of 'socialism'. Here is where non-'socialists' part company with your interpretation.

Azcárate I don't want to excuse Stalinism, much less justify it. On the contrary, I feel very strongly that enormous personal mistakes and crimes on a vast scale were committed in the Soviet Union under Stalin, and that human rights are still being violated and terrible injustices are still being committed there. At the same time we must remember that the October Revolution was, as I've said, a break with the capitalist system which had caused the sufferings of the First World War, and a reaction against Social Democratic policies which had given support to that imperialist war and underwritten colonial oppression. The October Revolution marked the coming of a new world-order although, under Stalinism, its progressive content suffered a profound degeneration. The process which started in October 1917 represents a continuous advance in the history of human affairs, well attested by the various national liberation movements. But the future is open—we don't know how the Soviet Union will behave.

[At the same time I am convinced that if 'existing socialism' can change course and return to its democratic moorings, then the catalytic significance of the 1917 October Revolution will stand out in even stronger relief than it does already. Of course, we don't know what will happen in the Soviet Union. But should there be an evolution in Soviet society analogous to the one we saw in Prague in 1968, then—yes—it would make perfect sense to argue that, despite the degenerations which have rendered socialism suspect in Soviet hands, the process which started in October 1917 represents a continuous advance in the history of human affairs. But the future is open, and we don't know how the Soviet Union will behave.]

Urban Let me return for a moment to the question of whether the rising (as you assume) curve of socialism would have been put at risk if the Czechoslovak reforms had not been killed by Soviet intervention. The burden of your case is that, with all its grave imperfections, Soviet 'socialism' is nevertheless socialism *in posse*. I would therefore argue with the Soviet leaders that, as the Soviet Union is the only power base in the world of any kind of socialism, its defence has to be given absolute priority over any other consideration. Take the Soviet base away, and the world's Communist parties—pro-Soviet, non-Soviet, and probably even anti-Soviet—are left without the political and ideological assurance of which you have just spoken: that in Russia in 1917 the curve of 'socialism' began to rise from point zero and has never stopped rising. And if you believe, as you clearly do, that the curve of a rising 'socialism' is an irresistible and irreversible fact of history, then you have to stand up for its Soviet variant, if it is under attack, because in the Soviet Union alone has 'socialism' been firmly (if not always successfully) established.

This is, of course, an old Comintern argument to which I do not subscribe; but I can quite see that if one accepts the ideological parameters of Communist reasoning (which I do not), the Soviet leaders' case for the 'normalisation' of Czechoslovakia is a powerful one.

Azcárate I firmly believe that the *contrary* of the reasoning you have cited is true. Let us imagine that the Soviets had tolerated the Czechoslovak Reform Movement. What would have been its repercussions? The Western Communist Parties would have been stimulated by the Prague example. The Social Democrats too would have been strongly influenced by it, for the possibility of bridging the gap between Communism and Social Democracy would not have been lost on them any more than it would have been lost on us. A powerful and united Left might have emerged throughout Western Europe. Furthermore, in Eastern Europe, where tensions were (and in some cases are) high, the Czechoslovak model would at once have created a demand for sweeping changes—for freedom, popular participation, pluralism—

Urban —in other words, the East European glacis, and probably the Soviet system itself, would have disintegrated, as the Soviet leaders correctly feared—

Azcárate —you can only use the word 'disintegrated' pejoratively if you think that the existing system is worth preserving. I would say, on the contrary, that the East European countries would have advanced towards an immeasurably better form of socialism. Of course, this would have meant various changes, especially in the Soviet leadership, though not the disappearance of the Warsaw

Pact, because the leaders of the Prague Spring never questioned the military alliance—indeed, they frequently expressed their determination to remain loyal to it. But far from 'disintegrating' in the sense in which you have chosen to use the word, the East European countries would have drawn closer to a healthier, viable, up-to-date and democratic form of socialism.

All this was frustrated by the Soviet intervention [because the leaders of Soviet bureaucratic socialism saw their personal power threatened].

Urban I don't think the Soviet leaders were worried only about a *different* kind of 'socialism' establishing itself in Eastern Europe—although that too must have given them enough cause for worry—but, rather, about the total collapse of *any* form of socialism, first in Eastern Europe and then very probably in the Soviet Union itself. And this would have meant the end of any kind of hegemony—Soviet or Russian. The risks of suppressing Czechoslovakia were, in the short term in any case, *slight*; the risks of *not* suppressing Czechoslovakia were, in the short as well as the long term, *enormous*.

Azcárate If one accepts your hypothesis that the proliferation of the Czech example would have eventually led to the elimination of any kind of socialism, then the *logic* of the Soviet response—that is, the invasion of Czechoslovakia—cannot be questioned from the point of view of crude Soviet power interests.

There are two points to be made here. First, I do not go along with the idea that ends justify means. We must, therefore, absolutely stick to the principle that the invasion of Czechoslovakia was wrong purely and simply because it was an act of aggression. Second, it was by no means a foregone conclusion that the proliferation of the Czech example would cause socialism to collapse in Eastern Europe or in the Soviet Union. There was, on the contrary, a very real possibility that a democratic and modern type of socialism would survive and prosper. Undoubtedly the developments in Prague would have provoked changes elsewhere, but these would have been well within the range of choices socialism offers [and I am fairly certain that if Eurocommunism manages to let down roots in Western

Europe as a significant political force, changes of this kind *will* come about, both in Eastern Europe and in the Soviet Union, under the impact of Eurocommunism].

Urban Your strong words about the invasion of Czechoslovakia seem to imply that the Czechs, in your view, ought to have offered armed resistance. I draw the same inference from what the leader of your Party said about the Spanish Party's attitude to the hypothetical case of a Soviet invasion of *Spain*. Speaking on French television on 13 July 1977, Santiago Carrillo warned that if Soviet tanks ever reached Spain to squash Spanish Eurocommunism in government, the Spanish people would fight. Do you share this view?

Azcárate On your first question—we have often been asked whether we disagreed with Dubcek's record on any point, and our answer has always been: yes—*we* would have fought. We consider that in the situation in which the Czechoslovak Communists found themselves on the night of 20/21 August 1968 they ought to have offered armed resistance.

Of course, militarily this would have been very difficult; it would have entailed a great deal of suffering [and might have set off a major conflagration]. But we are very conscious of the lessons of Yugoslavia. In 1947–48, when the Yugoslavs got themselves into deep trouble with Stalin and were expelled from the Cominform, the Soviets did not invade Yugoslavia because Tito let it be known, and Stalin fully realised, that the Yugoslavs would fight. The Yugoslavs' toughness warded off Soviet intervention, the result being that the Yugoslav experiment—self-management, pluralism of a kind, liberalisation in culture, and so on—has been able to go ahead and has become an important milestone in the development of socialism.

On your second question: Yes—in the unlikely event that Soviet tanks should invade Spain to crush a Eurocommunist regime, the Spanish people would fight. But we are, of course, dealing here with a very remote hypothesis.

Urban In the aftermath of the 1978 French general elections, Jean Elleinstein wrote in *Le Monde* (13 April 1978) that Soviet society is not only not an exemplar which France would want to follow but an 'anti-model' of socialism. Would you agree with that?

Azcárate I would—indeed we have gone further than that. We have stated (and I have said personally) that the Soviet Union is *not* a socialist state. In Elleinstein's view Soviet society represents a form of arrested socialism. We, on the other hand, consider the Soviet state not to be a socialist state at all but rather one which displays many of the worst features of capitalism and oppression.

On liberties, formal and real

Urban One important achievement of the Prague Spring which Soviet intervention did not completely stultify was the federalisation of the Czechoslovak state and of the Communist Party. There is now a separate Communist Party for Slovakia, though, paradoxically, there isn't one for the Czech lands. The reformers' intention was to federalise the Party in the same way as the state. This would have resulted in two national Communist Parties—each with its own Central Committee, Presidium, and Secretariat—which would then share power with the federal Communist Party for Czechoslovakia. The plan could not be fully carried out because it fell foul of the Soviet model—the USSR has no Communist Party for the 'Russian lands', therefore Czechoslovakia was not allowed to have a Party for the Czech lands either.

The Spanish Communist Party's thinking appears to be moving on parallel lines. Although your Party has been (nominally at least) no more willing to repudiate 'democratic centralism' than the Czech Party, it has embraced federalism as one form of democratisation. In your 1974 programme you call for the self-determination of Catalonia, the Basque country and Galicia, and, in fact, ancillary Communist Parties already exist in all these regions.

I remain a little puzzled. Nations and nationalities, in the Marxist view, are transitional phenomena which will, as capitalism is destroyed, give way to a single world community and a single culture. Support for the national ambitions of small nations is to be given only in those cases (and then only temporarily) where a small nation's struggle for independence coincides with the advance of the proletariat as an international force destined for world leadership. There has never been any question of supporting national ambitions as an act of justice and democracy.

Lenin was very frank on this point:

> A struggle against any national oppression—unreservedly yes. A struggle on behalf of any national development, of 'national culture' in general—unreservedly no. . . . Marxists, it stands to reason, are hostile to federation and decentralisation. . . . A centralised large State is an immense historic step forward from medieval disunion to the future Socialist unity of the whole world, and otherwise than through such a State . . . there is not, nor can there be, any path to Socialism.

I gather that you repudiate these views of Marx, Engels, and Lenin—that the Spanish Communist Party's support of the self-determination of the Basques and Catalans is more than a temporary expedient subject to the interests of the class struggle?

Azcárate Our Party supports every minority nation's right to self-government, including of course the use of its language and the maintenance of its culture. However, the political realities in Spain do not make it possible to grant self-determination for the Basques or the Catalans. This could only be achieved in agreement with all Spanish political forces, including the far Right and the Army, and *their* agreement could not be obtained. The new Constitution foresees *autonomy* for these regions, and we support this with the caveat that we have not given up the principle that ideally every nation, no matter how small, has the right to self-determination.

Urban You are supporting the idea of national autonomy within a genuinely democratic state—

Azcárate —Yes, and the Spanish consensus is very encouraging on this question: there will be regional home rule for Catalonia, the Basque country, and so on. The all-important point is the new Constitution—not the fact that we have written wonderful principles on a piece of paper (nothing could be easier), but the provisions we have made to safeguard the Constitution from arbitrary applications, distortions, benign or malicious neglect. Our Constitution enshrines a declaration of human liberties, and we have seen to it that no subsequent legislation can invalidate it or superimpose on it 'interpretations' of any kind. It has often been said by Communists that the freedoms of bourgeois society are merely 'formal' liberties. Well, bitter experience has taught us not to be so disdainful about 'formal' liberties. They tend to be not so formal after all, and they matter enormously.

The new *Soviet* Constitution, too, guarantees individual liberties, national independence, even the right of the national minorities to secede from the Soviet state—but what is the value of such liberties if the operative limitation in the Constitution renders all of them subject to the requirement that they do not run counter to 'socialism'? The 'formal' liberties of bourgeois democracy compare favourably with such liberties as exist in the Soviet Union.

But one has to be fair: we must admit that the October Revolution had, during at least the early period of socialist power, a liberating influence for the more backward Soviet nations and nationalities. If you compare their level of education, the development of their language and culture, not only with what these were like under Tsarism but also with the continuing backwardness of comparable Asian nations and nationalities outside the Soviet Union, then Soviet policies in these [limited] fields must be assessed as positive and progressive.

At the same time, the lack of liberty which characterises the entire Soviet system has had a particularly poignant and malicious impact on the freedom and even the national consciousness of the Soviet nationalities. The initial responsibility for reducing national rights to a formality was Stalin's. Lenin was aware of the problem. In one famous exchange he told Stalin, the Georgian, that there was no worse pest than a non-Russian's Great-Russian nationalism.

Urban 'Scratch a Russian Communist and you will find a Great-Russian chauvinist', Lenin said at the 8th Congress of the Communist Party in 1919.

Azcárate Yes—alas, the Russification process did not stop with the death of Stalin. The feeling that they lack national liberty is widespread to this day among the Soviet nationalities.

Urban The problem, then, is the one we keep coming back to: democracy respected and practised in all its aspects. The problem of minorities of all kinds, including nations and nationalities, tends to fall into place if the system is open to self-correction. In Eastern Europe, the current difficulties of the Hungarian minority in Transylvania are a case in point.

Azcárate Yes, I was virtually brought up on the Hungarian-Rumanian minority question because my father was Director of the Department of Minority Problems in the League of Nations, and he spent a great deal of his time worrying about and travelling to Transylvania. But let me take this on a wider ground. What makes me anxious as a Communist is that the socialist transformation of society is obviously not enough to solve the problems of nationality. This is a serious matter for us because we always believed that once a society's economic and social structures had undergone socialist change, public consciousness would follow suit and the archaic rivalries between various nations would automatically cease. This is not happening. The question is obviously more complicated.

Urban But aren't you rather begging the question? The problem persists because the 'socialist transformation' is, as you have just said, incomplete or non-existent. The Western countries have at least better ways of dealing with minority problems, as the cases of Scotland, Belgium and, oldest of them all, Switzerland, well demonstrate. In all these instances the heat was taken out of potentially explosive situations because there was enough elasticity in these genuinely parliamentary democracies to permit the devolution of power when devolution was seriously demanded.

Azcárate Yes—our emphasis must be on the universal freedom of the polity. But I am convinced that socialist society *can* contribute to solving the question of national antagonisms and has already done so. What impresses me about Yugoslavia is that, parallel with the socialist transformation of society, the various Yugoslav nations have learned to live together in relative peace and harmony. Diverging interests and tensions remain—those are normal—but we can certainly say that the hatreds and hostilities which marred Yugoslav society before the War, and then led to the fearsome massacres of the civil war during the Second World War, have ceased.

Urban The democratisation of Yugoslav society is a tricky problem because it is bound to mean adding fuel to the national self-assertiveness of the constituent nations. I cannot see how Yugoslavia could be further decentralised and 'pluralised' without the emphasis on decentralisation and pluralisation becoming an emphasis on national separateness, if not separatism. It was only a few years ago that many Croatians, including Communists, demanded *under* Tito a separate household management for Croatia and indeed separate representation in the UN. What proportions will such demands assume *after* Tito, even if the Soviet Union were not to encourage the centrifugal ambitions of the constituent Republics? And there is no reason to assume that it will not, seeing that current Soviet policy is both to fuel national separatism and to let it be known in Belgrade that Soviet assistance would be readily available if the unity of the state were threatened. (Soviet 'help' was indeed offered at the time of the 1971 Croatian crisis, as Tito has revealed.)

Azcárate I am not saying that the problem of the integration of the various Yugoslav nations is *solved;* it is *contained*—and that is a great step forward. I am confident that the national interests of Yugoslavia as a whole will prevail, even if Yugoslav socialism is further liberalised and decentralised—as it should be.

What we are trying to do in Spain is a useful pointer to the *limits* of decentralisation. It is not in the rationale of a modern economy to break up the unity of states if diversity within a unitary state can be guaranteed under the rule of law and under conditions of freedom. An unchecked 'cantonisation' would lead to demands for the independence of every region, then every municipality, and eventually every village in the realm. The disintegration of the first Spanish republic in 1873 was due to this sort of process. The new Spanish Constitution guarantees the devolution of power to the Basques, Catalans and other Spanish nationalities and regions—extensive self-government, cultural and language rights—without touching Spain's economic and social integrity as a modern state.

My reading of the Yugoslav situation is that the Yugoslavs have—*with* mistakes and many shortcomings—succeeded in combining decentralisation, which militates for small size, with the requirements of modernity, which militates for large-scale organisation. Compared with the non-solution of the nationality question in the Soviet Union and the Magyar question in Transylvania, the Yugoslav example has much to recommend it.

Moscow and the Spanish elections

Urban One of the encouraging facts about Europe in the 1970s has been the peaceful transition of Spain and Portugal from Fascist types of dictatorship to democracy. It has proved possible for the Spanish Communist Party to emerge from illegality and become a well-accepted member of the political life of Spain. The American 'imperialists' did not object. Indeed they quietly assisted in encouraging and speeding up the process of democratisation.

No parallel transition has yet proved possible in Eastern Europe. What kind of transformation would Eastern Europe have to undergo to match the Spanish example? To stick to Czechoslovakia in 1968: it would have been necessary to demolish, with active Soviet cooperation, the whole of Novotny's dictatorship and to permit it peacefully to transform itself into a liberal parliamentary democracy, with parties of extreme right-wing flavour also admitted as legitimate contestants for power. Nothing of the sort was allowed, much less encouraged, to happen.

What makes a healthy body politic different from a tired or diseased one is that whereas the former can assimilate a great many a-systemic and even hostile agents, a sick body politic hasn't the power and adaptability to do so. If this is accepted—on what grounds (other than *amour propre*) do Communists insist that 'socialism' represents a superior order to bourgeois democracy? Doesn't the comparison between Czechoslovakia and Spain show the opposite to be true?

I can see no curve in history leading mankind from the October Revolution to 'socialism'. What I *can* see is an irregular graph taking us in and out of despotisms of varying severity, with the occasional irruption of free regimes providing the exception and the contrast.

Azcárate To take the concrete example of Spain. Spain's transition from Fascism to democracy was due to two interrelated factors: the growing opposition of the entire population to the Fascist regime, and the Spanish capitalists' increasing awareness that Fascism was breaking down. All this encouraged the more enlightened elements inside the system to initiate certain reforms which eventually whetted popular appetites for more radical ones. In other words, it was not the merit of capitalism that Franco's Fascism or the Salazar regime were democratised. On the contrary: seeing their isolation and impotence in the face of popular opposition, the Spanish and Portuguese capitalists had change *forced* upon them and, of course, they eventually tried to go along with it in the slowest and smoothest possible way.

Urban Whatever the background, the Americans did nothing to prevent the Communist Parties of Spain and Portugal from gaining a very respectable foothold in what used to be Fascist dictatorships wholly committed to the cause of anti-Communism.

Azcárate Yes—the Americans probably felt that broadly based democracies in the Iberian Peninsula would serve them better than having to deal with countries torn by uncontrollable tensions. But your examples are one-sided: what about US aggression against Vietnam and American intervention in Santo Domingo and Chile?

From the examples you have given—the cases of Spain and Portugal versus Eastern Europe, especially Czechoslovakia—one can only make the limited inference that Eastern Europe is dominated by a system that is not open to change, that will have no truck with freedom, and that has, in the case of Czechoslovakia, not hesitated to use military force to keep itself afloat. All this is wholly bad and we do not hesitate to condemn it. But it has nothing to do with the merits or demerits of socialism, for such a [the Soviet] system is *not* socialist.

Urban But this asymmetry between what is possible on the NATO side of the equation and what is possible in Eastern Europe does, you will agree, disturb the power balance? A few years ago Portugal was very close to becoming a Soviet base right in the middle of NATO's Atlantic defences—and there is no question but that the US and the rest of NATO *would* have put up with it. The Soviet government, on the other hand, would not tolerate even a watered-down version of 'socialism' in *its* sphere of influence.

Azcárate I don't accept this balance-of-power argument—it is a *Soviet* argument! I don't agree that we have capitalism on *this* side of the East/West divide, and socialism on the *other*. I see socialism as a world-wide process which manifests itself on *our* side in certain socialist structures such as trade unions and workers' parties, mostly in opposition, and on the *Soviet* side in a distorted type of 'socialism-in-power' which subdivides into certain political institutions which are socialist in name only, and others, especially in the economy, which have a more profound socialist content.

But I emphatically cannot share the idea that the world is and will remain divided into two camps. That two military blocs exist at the moment is an unfortunate fact, and we have clearly stated in our recent *Theses* that the survival of these blocs is due more to the interests of Soviet and American prestige and hegemony than to military necessity. (This point, incidentally, greatly incensed the Soviet Communist Party's representative at our Party Congress.)

You are, of course, right in saying that the repulsive example which the Soviet Union had set in 1968 in Czechoslovakia was not followed by the Americans in Portugal. Nevertheless, when in January 1978 the Italian Communists seemed close to entering the government, the Carter Administration warned against it, which was every bit as scandalous, and effective, as military intervention would have been. After all, the Americans have their fleet in the Bay of Naples—their words cannot be misunderstood.

The interests of those broad strata of people who want socialism require that the military blocs should be reduced, that the siege-mentality between them should cease, and a new international system should be called into being. The progress of the socialist transformation of West European—and East European—society assumes, and will further add to, the exhaustion and irrelevance of bipolarity.

Urban But disregarding for a moment the narrow interests of the Spanish Communist Party and of Eurocommunism generally, would you not agree that the West is at a permanent political disadvantage in its dealings with the Soviet Union because the internal structure of democracy will not permit certain crude power-political measures, such as the military occupation of a defecting ally?

Azcárate I don't think this is a weakness. It could, indeed, be a sign of strength: it might mean that the countries in NATO have sufficient political flexibility to deal with their problems in ways very different from those obtaining in Eastern Europe.

[They have enough economic self-confidence, enough political and social cohesion to keep their system in fair working order without having to resort to military interventions. *Per contra*, there is no such flexibility in the Soviet bloc because the hegemony of the Soviet Union is based neither on the agreement of the peoples who live under Soviet rule nor on any economic or social strength that could keep the Soviet-ruled territories in a state of good repair. The Soviet substitute for an acceptable social order is crude military power. Soviet dogmatism is *empty* of content. The Soviet Communist Party is a public-relations office churning out ideological pap. The Western world has no need or room for any such thing. With all its faults, it has preserved sufficient flexibility to survive the strains of its internal contradictions.]

Urban Is it in the Soviet interest to have the Italian, or French, or Spanish Communist Party in power?

Azcárate I cannot judge what is and what is not in the Soviet interest, but it seems to me that at the present time the Soviet leadership has no desire to see any of these Parties in office.

Urban Would they upset the delicate equilibrium of what is left of détente?

Azcárate Possibly, because in the Soviet view détente equals the *status quo*. The Soviet leaders want one thing above all: complete and permanent immobilism. They probably feel that a socialist Western Europe, in which the Eurocommunist parties would undoubtedly play a part, would exert a kind of influence on Eastern Europe which a capitalist Western Europe cannot exert. So what would they stand to gain? They can obtain vast credits from the West under the *present* arrangements. They can get technological transfers, grain shipments—everything without letting themselves in for the dangerous experiment of promoting Communists in office in Western Europe.

Urban Perhaps they can get all these things only because Communists are *not* in office in Western Europe and the capitalist system is strong enough to keep the loans and supplies flowing?

Azcárate [There may be something in that (*laughter*). Some years ago Fidel Castro told us: 'We must hurry up enjoying all the good Spanish ham we can get from you because when socialism comes to Spain it will be very difficult to find any!' (*laughter*)] Well, the economic success of capitalism leaves a lot to be desired these days!

Urban Moscow, then, doesn't want to see you in office?

Azcárate I think not.

Urban You are not just saying this because it is good for your electoral image not to be seen to be supported by Moscow?

Azcárate Not at all. The Spanish Socialist Party, for example, is now very friendly to the Soviet Union, and when Gonzalez was in Moscow he was received much more warmly than Carrillo. Gonzalez must be assuming that his acceptance by the Soviet leaders is a vote-catcher rather than an invitation to electoral defeat in the sense that he can now show his party to be acceptable to both the US and the Soviet Union.

Urban The Soviet attack on Carrillo came shortly after the 1977 Spanish elections, not before. Had the Russians wanted to help you, they would have attacked Carrillo *during* the election campaign. But they didn't—which bears out your reading of Soviet intentions.

Azcárate I am familiar with this theory but I think it is a little far-fetched. True, we did ourselves say that we were annoyed to see that the Russians did not attack us *before* polling day. But I do not credit the Soviet leaders with sufficient intelligence to imagine that they would have thought of *not* attacking us before the elections in order to keep down the Spanish Communist vote. The Soviet leaders [sad to say] do not possess enough sophistication to reason like that. They genuinely believe that when they *attack*, they cause *harm;* when they do *not* attack, they *refrain* from causing harm.

Urban Very revealing.

Azcárate I should imagine they held back during the election campaign because they wanted to prevent any accusation by other prehistoric Communists of their kind: 'How *could* you attack a Communist Party before a difficult election?!' That is as far as their sophistication goes.

The spectre haunting Eurocommunism

Urban Your critique of the Soviet system is clearly far-reaching—would you agree that we might, with a slight perversion of Marx's words in the *Communist Manifesto,* cogently claim in 1978: 'A spectre is haunting Eurocommunism—the spectre of Communism, Soviet-style?'

I am not inverting Marx's words frivolously—I really believe, on the evidence of what you and other Eurocommunists have told me, that the only environment in which Communism can develop and prosper is capitalism. It certainly cannot begin to do so under Communism, Soviet-style.

Azcárate Well—what our liberal critics frequently forget is that the freedom we enjoy under capitalism has been dearly paid for. Their criticism of us concentrates on one point: 'You supported Stalinism—you supported Soviet repression—therefore you are the enemies of freedom!' There is no doubt that we badly misjudged the nature of the Soviet system, and to that extent this criticism is justified. But, at the same time, we were in the forefront of fighting Fascism. The freedoms which now exist are due to the sacrifices we have made. The capitalist system never experienced difficulty in ruling with Fascist methods. Capitalism has never voluntarily surrendered its power to exploit and to oppress. It conferred universal suffrage on the working people only under pressure from Chartists and socialists. It was only under the impact of the struggles of the working class, the October Revolution, the defeat of Hitler and the resistance of enslaved peoples that the colonial era was brought to an end. The human rights record of capitalism was very poor until trade unionism and popular pressures gradually wrested a measure of liberty from the capitalist system. In other words, if we are in a position today to fight for a just society in a capitalist environment, our ability to do so has not been bestowed on us by a benevolent capitalism.

Now—to your contention that 'the spectre haunting Eurocommunism is the spectre of Communism, Soviet-style'. Yes, you can put it like that, but perhaps it would be closer to the truth to say that we are trying to fight off [an oppressive 'father-complex'] the heritage of Stalinism. We adopted a resolution at our recent Congress which expresses satisfaction over the repudiation and defeat of Stalinism while also stressing that certain residues of Stalinism are still alive in our ranks and must be fought until we are absolutely free from them, both in our institutions and in our thinking. This, we contend, is the precondition of building socialism in the spirit of Eurocommunism.

Urban I am intrigued by your conception of a bloc-free international order. Your scenario, if I understand you correctly, is broadly speaking as follows. A Eurocommunist type of 'socialism' advances to the point of taking power in Western Europe. The same mixture undermines the Soviet type of 'socialism' in Eastern Europe. Eurocommunism in Western Europe causes the North Atlantic Alliance to disintegrate; Eurocommunism in Eastern Europe does the same to the Warsaw Pact and Soviet hegemony. With bipolarity gone, Europe—and perhaps the world—advances to a shared 'socialist' order.

Now I can well conceive of the collapse of NATO if Italy or France should embrace Eurocommunism. It is entirely possible, indeed it is probable, that the American people would not understand why they should go on supporting an alliance that was originally set up to defend the West against Communism but has now admitted Communists into its ranks. But I cannot see the Soviet Union packing its bags in Eastern Europe on the parallel argument that 'if the East Europeans no longer believe in our system, let them look after their own interests! . . .'

The net effect, therefore, of the progress of Eurocommunism would be the collapse of NATO and the survival—and probably the enormous extension—of Soviet hegemony.

Azcárate The socialist transformation of society is a broadly desired objective in Western Europe: the Communists want it, the Socialists and Social Democrats want it, and several parties of Christian inclination want it too. I am, therefore, not foreseeing *Communist* governments installing socialism in Western Europe, but broad coalitions in which the Communists—and, as I hope, the Eurocommunists—would play a part. The political and ideological overspill of such a development would reach far beyond Europe, rendering the world's bipolar preoccupations increasingly irrelevant.

Would the Americans have reason to worry? I don't think they would. They would hardly want to 'do a Czechoslovakia' to the Italians or French to keep them in line. The NATO alliance would fall apart, but this would be a gradual process and would not happen in a vacuum. It would give Europeans and Americans a chance to rethink the whole American/West European relationship and put it on a new and sounder footing. There is room here for entirely new forms of cooperation.

Eastern Europe would also change [as the libertarian strand in socialism got the better of the Soviet variety and the economic strains between Moscow and the East European capitals began to weaken Soviet control]. How would it change? Frankly I don't know—what I do believe strongly, though, is that the days of Soviet military intervention are over. The last ten years have seen some of the East-Central European countries [notably Hungary, Poland and in a different sense Rumania] carving out for themselves considerable areas of relative freedom from Soviet cultural, economic and political pressure.

Urban Visiting Hungary, for example, one senses that the Iron Curtain is more tightly drawn between the Soviet Union and Hungary than between Hungary and the West.

Azcárate All in all, then, I would venture the opinion

that the advance of Eastern Europe to a democratic and free type of socialism, of which we can, here and there, already see some evidence, would be unlikely to result in Soviet repression. In other words, the military blocs would eventually disappear and the bipolar relationship give way to multi-polar relationships in which the Third World and China, as well as the Soviet Union, the US and Europe, would play their parts. I foresee a new world equilibrium.

Urban But don't you think that the Eurocommunists would be the chief victims if 'socialist' governments came to power in Western Europe and the Americans lost interest in maintaining West European security? For what, in fact, would happen? With NATO in ruins, the Americans gone, but the Warsaw Pact (as I assume) intact, the 'self-Finlandisation' of Western Europe would be inevitable.

Your 'socialist' governments would, then, come under severe pressure, either directly from the Soviet Union, or, as an act of pre-emptive surrender, from their own ranks, to get rid of their Eurocommunist members as the principal obstacles to good relations with the Soviet Union. If there is any lesson to be learned from Soviet history it is that Moscow is always more willing to collaborate with suitably cooperative Christian Democrats and even Social Democrats than with heretics inside the Communist movement. In other words, for Eurocommunism to survive, you need American protection.

Azcárate Here is where we differ. You see the world in incorrigibly bipolar terms. Your scenario assumes that Soviet hegemony will continue to exist and be forcefully exercised. In my conception there will be a strong Third World, a strong non-aligned movement, a strong China to throw their weight into the scales and change the world balance of power. I see a pluralisation and democratisation of international relations where you see the old pattern persisting.

Urban But, surely, yours is at best a very long-range forecast?

Azcárate Long-range, or possibly not so long-range. There is nothing fanciful about imagining a Western Europe in which Eurocommunism contributes to the erosion of rivalry between the superpowers, in which the importance of the military blocs is diminished, in which every country, emphatically including the small ones, is fully independent and free from crippling entanglements. I can see such a broadly socialist Western Europe conducting fruitful cooperation—in economic relations, technology, culture, and so on—with the United States *and* the Soviet Union: a dynamic kind of coexistence rather than one merely based on the absence of war; one in which the whole problem of disarmament, too, could at long last be squarely tackled.

We have to bear in mind that the concentration of nuclear weapons in the hands of the two superpowers—the nuclear terror—has to some extent immobilised them; but this stalemate is also creating fresh opportunities for the rest of the world to make its weight felt. We intend to use these opportunities.

Urban You have stated that the Spanish Communist Party stands for common European defence—

Azcárate —Yes, we do—

Urban —against all-comers?

Azcárate Against all-comers.

Urban I suppose your plea for a common European defence has to be seen in the context of Carrillo's observation:

> What I cannot understand is how the USSR can prefer Western Europe to be in NATO—in a certain manner under the control of the United States—to an independent and autonomous Europe such as we propose. This forces me to think that the existence of NATO Europe, controlled by the United States, justifies a second Europe on the other side, controlled by the Soviet Union.

Would I be right in thinking that your common European defence would be facing eastwards—towards the USSR?

Azcárate It would be facing in all directions, including the east.

Urban I am still curious to know whether you would agree that a Eurocommunist party in office would be more in need of the protection of the Western alliance than other parties. This is certainly what many Italo-Communists think, and I am assuming that you agree with them even though you have, so far in this conversation, not said so. If your answer is a tacit 'Yes', I wonder why your Party is opposed to Spain joining NATO?

Azcárate NATO was created more than thirty years ago under the conditions of the Cold War. No country has joined it since its inception. If Spain joined now, the whole concept of the world divided into military blocs would be reinforced, which is not our objective. Also, if NATO were strengthened, the Soviet bloc would have to react in some way, and that could spell a new crisis—in Yugoslavia, for example. Our interest is not to provoke a sharpening of the role of the military blocs but rather to defuse it.

Clearly, Spain, stretching as it does from the Pyrenees to the Balearic Islands, occupies a strategically key position. But we are satisfied that our national security is sufficiently guaranteed by our own armed forces—and so, in fact, are the armed forces themselves. Entering NATO would be giving unnecessary hostages to fortune. In any case, we have already a number of major US bases on our territory, and we have an agreement with the US covering military [cooperation] matters. The Spanish Communist Party does not question either—we accept them. We propose to do nothing to weaken America's strategic position. We do not want to change the existing balance between the United States and the Soviet Union.

[Coming to the crux of your question: we do not, of course, like the military division of Europe but, in an imperfect world, it undoubtedly carries certain helpful features. NATO has created a zone of security in Western Europe which shields those countries too which are not members of the alliance. We do therefore enjoy indirect protection against the possibility of Soviet intervention. This is a positive fact about NATO.]

Urban We began this conversation with the impact of the Czechoslovak events on Eurocommunism. What would you, as a Spanish Eurocommunist, say to the Czech people on the tenth anniversary of the suppression of the Prague Reform Movement?

Azcárate We had this anniversary very much in mind

when we recently invited Frantisek Kriegel[1] to join us at a meeting specially arranged in his honour in Madrid. He was not allowed to leave Czechoslovakia, but he sent us a message explaining his situation. The final speech at this meeting was made by myself, and I said in the name of the Spanish Communist Party that we were looking forward to the establishment of liberty and justice for the Czech people.

The destiny of Czechoslovakia runs parallel with our own. We both suffered from the evils of Fascism—both the Czech and the Spanish Communists were cruelly deceived by the bureaucratic misrule of Stalinism. In 1968 we hoped with the Czech people that the Prague Spring would result in the sweeping democratisation of [the Soviet type of] socialism, and we are deeply indebted to them for their example. We want to repay this debt by not losing sight of our solidarity with them in their struggle for democracy and national independence.

[1] A prominent, Jewish-born, member of the Dubcek leadership and a special thorn in the flesh for the Soviet Union in August 1968.

Eugene V. Rostow

The View from Washington

Urban How did the Johnson Administration read and react to the crisis of the Czechoslovak Communist Party between January and August 1968? Was it seen as an internal matter—Communists quarrelling with Communists—or as one that might affect the whole Soviet system and indeed the Soviet-American relationship?

Rostow There were two views, as there always are in America about Soviet affairs. There were those who thought that Czechoslovakia was in real danger of being taken over by the Russians, and those who pooh-poohed the idea and insisted that the Czechs were going too far too fast and that the Russians, with their military exercises and the pressure they exerted on the Czechoslovak leadership at Dresden, Cierna and Bratislava, were simply trying to calm them down or, at worst, to intimidate them.

There was a big argument in the Administration about these rival evaluations—until, early in August 1968, a telegram came from Tommy Thompson, our ambassador in Moscow and doyen of our Sovietological establishment, indicating that there was in his view an imminent danger of the military suppression of the Czechoslovak Government. That decided the debate—the more optimistic Sovietologists changed tack and admitted that the threat of a Soviet invasion had to be taken seriously. But, as I say, right up to August the view was strongly held in some quarters that the Russians were merely mounting a demonstration and that the threat would not be carried out.

Mind you, the Sovietological lobby was not easily persuaded. I remember having arguments with Ambassador

'Chip' Bohlen on the meaning of the Czech events and the likely Soviet reaction. He, too, poured cold water on the idea that the Czech threat to the Soviet system was real and that the Russians would interfere—until Thompson's cable came through. But it is an almost permanent characteristic of a considerable part of the American Sovietological establishment (today my friend Marshall Shulman is the best known among their number) that Soviet action must always be given the benefit of the doubt.

To cite a typical example: the first time 'Egyptian' MIG fighters appeared over our 6th Fleet shortly after the 1967 Six Day War, our monitoring sources reported that the pilots of these 'Egyptian' planes were talking Russian to each other. Well, for two weeks our Soviet experts were explaining this away for us: first, they said the whole thing was of insignificant proportions; then came other explanations—that these were training flights; that the pilots were Egyptians who had been instructed in Russian by Russian personnel; that the whole business was an experiment, and so on. Of course, it soon transpired that the pilots were Russian and these arguments collapsed. But for two weeks they were stubbornly held by a persuasive and indeed technically knowledgeable lobby of official Washington Sovietologists.

Urban Where did you personally stand on the Prague events?

Rostow I saw them as part of a process of an increasingly profound political change—almost of revolution—which would sooner or later transcend the boundaries of the Czechoslovak Party and indeed of Czechoslovakia.

We saw a significant connection between the Six Day War of June 1967 and the eruption of unrest in the Czechoslovak Communist Party. That war, and the Soviet defeat it implied, sent an electric shock throughout the world, but it proved to be a particularly vivid shock in the Soviet Union and Eastern Europe where popular opinion—among Jews and non-Jews alike—was uniformly on the side of Israel while the Communist Parties and Governments supported the Arabs. Israel's spectacular victory was a stimulus to political protest in Russia itself and throughout Eastern Europe, and we trace the Prague Spring to the impulses that began to gain momentum during and after the Six Day War. After

January 1968 the process was continuous and cumulative, and we felt that it began to pose a danger to Soviet and indeed Communist control throughout Eastern Europe. For the Soviet leaders Prague was a cancer which could spread into Russia itself—as indeed it did to some extent.

The Soviet leaders take a long view—they were extremely conscious of the coup that had brought the Czechoslovak Communist Party to power (with camouflaged Soviet backing) in February 1948, and decided that they could not afford to take risks.

Urban You were a senior member of the Johnson Administration—did you give any thought to the possibility of protecting, if not directly aiding, the Prague Reform Movement? Was the leverage of NATO to be brought into play? Were you thinking of making Moscow conscious of certain penalties they might draw upon themselves if they suppressed Czechoslovakia in terms of the impending SALT negotiations and détente generally?

Rostow Czechoslovakia and the 'penalty-areas' you have mentioned represented two different contexts. We were certainly informed of what was going on in Prague and the repercussions that were beginning to take shape. We were in close touch, not only with our own intelligence people but also with British and French intelligence which were pooled for all practical purposes. Also, the Yugoslav and Rumanian ambassadors took a very active part in our discussions—they were immensely concerned from the very beginning that the Soviet military preparations, which were deployed in a wide arc, might be aimed at both Yugoslavia and Rumania, and there were even rumours that the Russians might aim a blow at Yugoslavia from the west, violating Austrian neutrality (I am referring to General Sejna's revelations and the Polarka file).

So while we knew the facts and the fears they inspired, we did nothing about the Czechs themselves. Indeed we tried very hard not to take any position encouraging or even commenting on what the Czech Government and the Party were doing. Equally we made it clear that NATO would not contemplate taking action whatever happened in Czechoslovakia—we were acutely conscious of the Hungarian events of 1956 and did not want to see them repeated. The only time we called in the Russians was when their propaganda began to claim that the Czechs were being aided by Germany and NATO. Dobrynin was sent for and Rusk told him: 'This is not true, and you know that it isn't true—you must stop saying it', and they did stop saying it.

Our concern was: did the Soviet military exercises on the borders of Czechoslovakia signify a general threat to south-eastern Europe? We recognised, and it was a very painful and hateful thing to recognise, that under the standing rules of the Cold War there was nothing we could do about Czechoslovakia, but if the Soviet moves represented something wider than an 'internal' response to the Prague reforms—that was going to be treated as a very different matter.

Urban But if the defensive nature of NATO demanded an absence of any action on Czechoslovakia, would it not have demanded non-interference in Yugoslavia too?

Rostow We took the view that a threat to Yugoslavia, and to a lesser extent to Rumania, would immediately affect us. Our concern to maintain the independence of Yugoslavia was very great in terms of defending Western interests in Italy, Greece and the Eastern Mediterranean, and it may surprise you to hear that we were strongly supported in this by the *French*. Michel Debré had just become Foreign Minister, and I remember vividly talking to him at a small lunch on the 8th floor of the State Department: Debré, Rusk, myself and a few senior officials. What do we do if Yugoslavia's anxieties prove to be well founded? Well, Debré agreed that if a threat to Yugoslavia developed we would have to fight, and he pledged full French cooperation—

Urban —in terms of fighting on the American side—

Rostow —that is right. When, therefore, Czechoslovakia was invaded, our statements and warnings closely reflected our concern to protect Yugoslavia and Rumania. President Johnson warned the Russians in his speech at San Antonio, Texas, and then again in September in Washington. 'Don't unleash the dogs of war, for no one can predict or control the outcome.' I advised those warnings myself.

Urban Were the Rumanians and Yugoslavs reassured?

Rostow They thought that the President's public warnings had some effect. They still believed that the Russians were about to attack them but at least they knew that they were being taken very seriously, as indeed their situation deserved. The Yugoslavs were certainly assured that we were not prepared to see Yugoslavia knocked off. What we would have done about Rumania, I don't know, because we were intent on respecting the basic rule of the Cold War: 'Don't cross the East/West demarcation line'—but it was Yugoslavia that was chiefly on our minds.

On the night of the invasion—it was a most depressing night because we knew that we could do nothing—a statement had to be prepared for the President for the next day. One draft was written by Chip Bohlen and another by myself. President Johnson chose mine, which was more fierce, expressing our protest against the aggression which the Soviet Union had committed, its violation of the United Nations Charter, and so on.

An extensive discussion then followed on the instructions which George Ball (by then our ambassador at the UN) should be given in representing the American position at the United Nations. After a great deal of careful consideration the President decided that we should take the line of protesting in the name of the UN Charter. And George's orders were: 'Go and give the Russians hell'.

Urban Not having given them hell in Prague and Bratislava, did the President consider that his instructions to Ball were an act of courage and statesmanship?

Rostow No—but they were, and are, important politically, and in the long run, because they gave evidence of our commitment to uphold international order in the name of *international law* (and I shall have more to say about this in a moment). It presents an interesting contrast to the position taken by Henry Kissinger in 1973—when exactly the opposite decision was made. The Yom Kippur war was a violation of the UN Charter, but Kissinger took the line that our only interest was to get a settlement—never mind the Charter. And, in fact, no protest was made in the United Nations against the invasion of Israel; we never named the aggressor and never spoke of the nature and significance of this act of aggression.

Urban Did the Czechs seek any form of help or reassurance?

Rostow No; so far as I know, they never said a word about military aid. The advice we received from the Czechs and—more important—from the Yugoslavs and Rumanians was: 'Don't rock the boat; don't say anything provocative because there are hawks and doves in the Soviet firmament and we don't want to give the hawks any excuse to act'. After the Soviet invasion a joint American and British intelligence assessment concluded that there had been *no* hawks and doves in the Soviet leadership! *All* were hawkish when they saw their rule threatened.

The Czechs *did* talk to us, but they had to watch their step *vis-à-vis* the Russians very carefully and we, of course, respected their caution. Two small vignettes to give you the feel of things in Washington at the time. Shortly before the Soviet invasion the Russian Embassy gave a party. At one point the Czechs, Rumanians, Yugoslavs and ourselves were talking together in a corner, but it soon became clear that it was impossible to conduct a serious conversation because we were constantly looking over our shoulders to see whether Dobrynin or one of his troops was approaching our group. As soon as they did, we switched the subject of our conversation. This tells you something about the position of the Czechs in Washington in 1968.

The Czechoslovak Ambassador was a fellow called Karel Duda. He was a very buttoned-up man so that we did not know a great deal about him. But he was not too buttoned-up to let it be known in Washington soon after the occupation of Czechoslovakia that the Russians had approached him to head a Czechoslovak 'government' to furnish them with the invitation they were so anxiously seeking. Duda said he had turned them down, and his explanation to his friends in Washington was: 'I have been a prostitute long enough—this time I will stand with my people'.

Urban The Czechs sought, as you say, no military assistance; were the lessons of the invasion of any military assistance *to us*? Technically, the occupation has been rated as a first-class piece of work—

Rostow No doubt about it—but then the Russians were invading their 'own' country, one whose armed forces and their day-to-day deployment were entirely under Soviet control. If you cannot perform *that* kind of task properly then there must be something gravely wrong with your military.

But there were other and more significant lessons to be learned from the invasion. We concluded after the examination of all the evidence that the Soviet leaders used Central Asian crack troops to do the job and that these were taken out of Czechoslovakia a few days after the invasion. This meant two things: first, we knew that it took four months to mobilise these troops—therefore we concluded that Moscow was getting ready for some kind of action in Central Europe early in the spring of 1968. Second, it was clear that the Soviet high command, having learned the lessons of Hungary, where men of the Soviet forces either did not fight with any enthusiasm or in some cases directly joined the Hungarian freedom fighters, decided to deploy troops in Czechoslovakia who spoke no European language and could therefore not easily be contaminated. Not only that, but the speedy removal of these Central Asian troops and their replacement by others meant, in our view, that the Soviet leaders' confidence in the loyalty of their troops left a lot to be desired. These were important lessons. They gave us an insight into Soviet weakness behind the façade of Soviet power and self-confidence.

Urban Was there any link between the date of the invasion and the 1968 Democratic Congress?

Rostow I think there was, and the story is fascinating. On the Monday night of that week (18–25 August 1968) Rusk was giving a party on the presidential yacht. I was talking to Dobrynin when Rusk tapped me on the shoulder and said that he wanted to have a word with me. So I got up and Rusk asked me in a whisper to do the honours when the party broke up because Dobrynin had just given him a message that the Soviet side had agreed to the SALT talks, in which the President was very much interested, and that he, Rusk, wanted to convey the message personally to the President.

So it was arranged that on Wednesday morning there was going to be a joint announcement in Washington and Moscow that SALT talks were to be held, and that in

October, a month before the elections, the President was to visit Moscow. On Tuesday night Dobrynin came with his message that the Soviet Union had invaded Czechoslovakia. It reached the Democrats under dramatic circumstances: Rusk was testifying to the Platform Committee of the Democratic Party (which was shown on television) when someone came up to him and handed him a piece of paper, whereupon Rusk excused himself, explaining that he had just had word that Czechoslovakia had been invaded by the Russians and the President wanted him in the White House.

At midnight, Dobrynin was called in and Rusk told him that the President's visit was off. Dobrynin was (or showed himself to be) astounded: 'What do you mean, the President's visit is off? It is being announced first thing in the morning!' But Rusk repeated that the visit was off. Dobrynin tried to frustrate the decision by a technicality—he could not, he insisted, get a message back in time—but Rusk assured him that he would help out by sending a 'flashed' message for the Russians on our own network (a type of message reserved for international emergencies)—and he did.

In other words, the Russians thought that the President would be so attracted *politically* by the notion of an announcement of his Moscow visit a few days before the opening of the Democratic Convention on Monday, 26 August, that he would acquiesce in the occupation of Czechoslovakia without so much as a protest. Imagine what we would have looked like if the President had *not* cancelled his visit and the Democratic Convention would have been blanketed by news of détente at a time when Russian tanks were occupying Prague!

Urban You are implying that the Soviet move was deliberately timed so as to reduce American reaction to a minimum?

Rostow Absolutely—although I have no evidence for it except the fact that it happened.

Urban President Johnson had the reputation of being an impulsive man who attracted strong hatreds and inspired strong loyalties. Did he cancel his visit in a state of anger?

Rostow He was not at all impulsive. He did have strong feelings, but he always took a long view—everything was decided in terms of what would happen ten years from now. He was vitally concerned with American-Soviet relations, but he had no illusions about the nature of the animal he was facing in Moscow. 'In dealing with the Russians,' he once said, 'you must always have your right hand out and your left hand up.' Nothing the Russians did, therefore, surprised him. His preparations for the Glassboro meeting of 1967 give one an insight into the patient circumspection with which he handled the Soviet problem.

The Russians had moved to put the Middle Eastern question into the General Assembly of the UN. We were opposing this because we felt that the Security Council had by no means exhausted its jurisdiction. But then rumour got around that Kosygin was coming, and as a consequence of that other world leaders also let it be known that they would address the United Nations. So the question arose: should Johnson go too to show his respect for the United Nations?

Everybody advised him to do it, and I too went along to say—Yes, he should go. But Johnson never decided anything instantly. 'If you want No for an answer I'll decide now,' he used to tell us, 'but if you wait until tomorrow it may be Yes.' So he thought about it overnight and told us the next day that he would not go. 'If I go,' he said, 'de Gaulle and Wilson will come too—then there will be no way of preventing a Four Power meeting, and I'll be one against three, and I don't want that.'

Eventually he made his major speech on Middle Eastern policy in Washington to an absolutely astonished group of school teachers, and that was that.

Urban Who, then, represented the Administration in the Middle Eastern debate of the United Nations?

Rostow The President made an amusing decision. He said to us: 'If Kosygin speaks, tell Arthur Goldberg not to answer for the United States—leave it to Eban: it will be David against Goliath and Eban can take care of himself.' This is the way he thought; he was a shrewd man and a realist.

Now Johnson was very conscious of the possible aftermath of the occupation of Czechoslovakia—so he had no hesitation about giving the San Antonio warning. But before the invasion he was concerned to make sure that we could not be accused of stirring up trouble in Czechoslovakia. He remembered Hungary vividly and the charges which had, rightly or wrongly, been levelled against Dulles in the wake of Hungary.

Urban So American inactivity was carefully calculated?

Rostow The inactivity was calculated; NATO was instructed not to go on the alert, and no threats of any kind were made. The President *hated* all this, but he accepted it as a fact of life. He was a man of strong passions but he was at the same time a most disciplined fellow. He recognised that on Czechoslovakia our hands were tied if we did not want to have a world war on our hands.

Urban Nevertheless I should have thought there was more room for action than the Administration made use of. President Johnson's memorable speech in October 1966, of which Zbigniew Brzezinski was the main author—

Rostow —Brzezinski and Henry Owen had sketched out the first draft of that speech but I actually wrote the speech, and changed the draft fundamentally.

Urban —President Johnson's speech was an offer to 'build bridges' between the Soviet Union and the West, and the thinking behind this exercise in 'peaceful engagement' (to use Brzezinski's phrase) was to change the nature of Soviet hegemony in Eastern Europe by treating Russia's client states as independent. Although nothing in this programme set out to encourage defection from the Soviet camp, it was nevertheless implied that liberalisation in the satellite states would be rewarded by American incentives and these incentives, in turn, would encourage the governments concerned gradually to detach themselves from the Soviet Union and pursue their national interests.

If this interpretation is correct, then it is surprising that so little thought should have been given, between 1966 and 1968, to making use of the Prague Reform Movement as the first potent opportunity for 'building bridges' with a liberalising satellite state. The Prague Spring did not start in the spring of 1968—it went back to 1966 and before. There was time enough to say to the Soviet leaders that the United States and NATO were interested in seeing a more humane and politically less strident type of 'socialism' establish itself in the centre of Europe. If the Soviet Union would not agree that peaceful reform in Czechoslovakia would lower the temperature in the whole East–West relationship and decided not to tolerate it, then (so one might have argued) the United States would have no incentive to ship grain to Russia, permit the transfer of technology, or indeed talk about the limitation of strategic arms. What I am saying is that the United States had important cards to play without challenging the post-war division of Europe.

Rostow I very much doubt that we had really effective cards to play—it is possible; maybe something *could* have been done—but remembering the Dulles experience, Johnson was reluctant to make threats that could or would not be carried out. The only truly effective hand we might have played was a military one—and that we were not prepared to play against the background of Yalta, Potsdam and the whole of post-war history. Maybe we should have tried to do more than we have done, but we always hesitated to go to the point where a threat was implied. Concern about Czechoslovakia—yes. Sympathy with the developments in Czechoslovakia—yes. Encouragement to the Germans to talk with the Czechs and the Poles—of course. All this was time and again conveyed to the Russians and became part and parcel of our posture *vis-à-vis* the Soviet Union; but the linkage between Czechoslovakia, technological transfers and the prospect of SALT was not made. As for food—food simply is not a weapon, because we could not refuse help to starving people.

There was also another important factor: we scrupulously avoided doing anything in Eastern Europe that would have upset Germany's then incipient *Ostpolitik*. This was a German initiative with Willy Brandt as Foreign Minister and Kiesinger as Chancellor. We supported it, as indeed we had supported the Hallstein doctrine, as long as the Germans themselves kept it alive. (So much indeed did we support it that when, before Johnson's presidency, the Russians approached us with a package deal which would have put both Germanies, both Koreas and both Vietnams into the UN, we turned it down out of loyalty to the Hallstein doctrine. It is an interesting question whether Vietnam would have happened if both Vietnams had been admitted to the United Nations.)

The German attitude was the key to our approach to Czechoslovakia. The Germans were building, certainly with our encouragement, bilateral relations with the Czechs, Rumanians and (with much greater difficulty) with the Poles, and it was widely felt both by the Germans and by ourselves that any initiative of the kind you have just mentioned would have cut across *Ostpolitik* and would, in any case, probably have proved futile. Occupying the geopolitical position it did, and does, Czechoslovakia, we felt, could not be put through internal reforms, much less taken out of the Soviet glacis, without full Soviet agreement. *If* there was any chance of obtaining that agreement it was through *Ostpolitik* rather than any other policy that was open to us. And, of course, Willy Brandt was anxious to avoid creating any impression that no sooner was *Ostpolitik* launched than the Soviet Union's post-war position became threatened at one of its most sensitive points in the centre of Europe. (The Germans were subsequently accused of working for this in any case, and Brandt eventually had to re-direct the course of *Ostpolitik* and approach the satellites via Moscow rather than influence Moscow via the satellites.)

Urban One knows from diplomatic memoirs and other sources that President Johnson took a rather narrow view of the Czechoslovak phenomenon. According to one reliable account, his practical dealings with Czechoslovakia during the Prague Spring were restricted to two issues: first, he was angered by reports that small arms made in Czechoslovakia were still being supplied to Vietnam (which betrayed a poor understanding of the control of the armaments industry in any East European country) and tried to get the supply stopped; second, he wanted to extract compensation from the Dubcek leadership for American property nationalised in the late 1940s—not a very helpful step at a time when Czechoslovakia was in the grip of a profound economic crisis on the solution of which the Reform Movement largely depended—or so it was thought in Prague.

Might it have been the case that the President, Dean Rusk and yourself took a historically rather unbending view of the whole Czechoslovak experiment: 'We do not want to see Communism reformed—we want to see it destroyed. A Communism that has shown its ability to assume a human face while still being Communism is, in the long term, *more* dangerous to the cohesion of the West than the undisguised Soviet article. Hence we have no interest in aiding the Prague reform Communists.' This is the 'the worse the better' kind of attitude which has a respectable constituency and corresponds to a matching view which certain leading Marxists (with Georges Sorel as their nineteenth-century example) have taken of *capitalism*.

Rostow No, I don't recall any such attitude; we were as helpful to the Prague reformers as we could be, and we were sincerely hoping that in Czechoslovakia, as elsewhere in Eastern Europe, the reforms would move broadly in the Yugoslav direction—toward economic decentralisation, self-management, greater respect for individual rights, a certain pluralism of interests and equality for the constituent nations and nationalities. We realised that, short of launching a world war, we could not restore the freedom of Eastern Europe; therefore the Yugoslav type of evolution struck us as realistic and acceptable. We could see that once Yugoslavia had detached herself from Soviet tutelage she also stopped being an aggressive neighbour, she no longer supported so-called wars of national liberation, she opened up her frontiers in both directions and behaved like a responsible and predictable member of the international community. These, we thought, were desirable ends to work for, even though we knew that the Yugoslav system was very far from what Poles, Czechs and Hungarians would choose if other alternatives existed.

Urban Ten years have now passed since the Prague Spring and the invasion of Czechoslovakia—long enough for us to take a broad look at the American scene and ponder what if anything has changed in it in relation to Soviet behaviour in the world.

Rostow As you know, the Committee on the Present Danger, of which I am Executive Chairman, was, and is, critical of what seems to us to be the irresolute leadership of both the Nixon–Ford–Kissinger Administrations and the

Carter Administration. The reasons underlying this weakness are complex; let me try to depict some of the more important ones.

The first general factor we have to remember is that American foreign policy has always had to struggle with a fundamental inhibition: the tradition and memory of isolation. The ordinary American still feels (a bizarre thought when you put it in the context of jet travel, communications satellites and the rest) that the normal posture for us in world politics is to be isolated, neutral and exempt from entangling alliances in distant parts of the world. The NATO treaty was the first military alliance we made since our alliance with France in 1778. Hence every American step abroad has to be argued for and justified, and is exposed to attack and to the risk of being discredited. This is a normal thing to happen in a democracy, but it does not make for strength or continuity.

The second element accounting for the weakness of American foreign policy is Vietnam—and the misinterpretation by both the Ford and Carter Administrations of the public mood generated by it. We have now had three presidents—Nixon, Ford and Carter—who were or are afraid of the legacy of Vietnam, afraid of the American public and afraid to lead American public opinion. Yet the after-effect of Vietnam is not, in my opinion, repugnance to use force if one has to—it is the humiliation of *defeat*, which is a very different thing.

The American public is way ahead of the Administration in its willingness to reassert the primacy of the United States in its encounter with the Soviet Union. This is supported by every poll and the manifest determination of Congress not only to pass but in fact to *increase* various defence appropriations which the President has asked for. The American people—and Congress expressing the will of the American people—do not want to be Number Two in the world. They do not trust the Soviets; they feel it is important to have all-round military superiority and to be able to use it if and when the need arises. Why has even the self-styled 'liberal' group in Congress stopped trying to cut defence appropriations? Because Congressmen and Senators read their mail and realise that the feelings of their electors are running strongly against knuckling under. Congress's great and prolonged reluctance to carry the Panama Treaty was a clear reflection of popular sentiment: 'God—do we have to *give up again*?!'

The crux of the problem is that American presidents and political leaders are very conscious of what happened to the men who led the United States before them and are anxious to avoid their fate. They remember how Truman and Johnson left office, and they are apprehensive. Truman and Johnson, whatever their faults, had the courage and patriotism to say: 'We will do whatever has to be done—we will walk the plank, if need be with our political careers, to do it.' Not so Nixon, or Ford, or Carter.

There is a remarkable passage in Admiral Zumwalt's book which illustrates my point. Zumwalt had a conversation with Nixon in 1970 on the 6th Fleet in which they were reviewing America's military difficulties with Soviet power in the Eastern Mediterranean after Nixon successfully faced down the Syrian threat to Jordan and Israel. 'Mr. President, why don't you tell the American people about Soviet power and policy?' Zumwalt asks Nixon. '*After* the 1972 election, when the Vietnam thing is finished', Nixon answers.

In other words, with the business of Vietnam unfinished, President Nixon did not think that he would get re-elected if he confronted the American people with yet another problem in yet another distant part of the world; hence his decision to keep the public in the dark about the situation in the Eastern Mediterranean and about the growing Soviet military threat generally.

But, of course, presidents are elected to give the people a clear lead—not to lead them from *behind*—and to explain to them again and again the realities of the world. That is what leadership means; that is what presidents are for. And that is what the American people have not been getting for a decade.

Urban We are being treated to a bizarre and unfamiliar spectacle: the world's strongest country not being willing to use its power. There are many examples in history of states of modest size and modest means trying to behave like world powers through some combination of aggressiveness, delusions of grandeur and sheer luck. But I can think of no example, except for Great Britain in this century, where a genuine world power shied away from the opportunities presented to it by history. The irony of seeing America's own conception of 'manifest destiny' thrust upon a reluctant America by her weaker allies (some of them yesterday's enemies) will not be lost on future historians.

You have mentioned America's innate isolationism as one factor accounting for this strange behaviour—and one accepts this up to a point as a psychological inhibition we will have to live with for some time to come. But what accounts for the American failure of imagination—the failure to understand that Soviet society is not like American society; that the motivations of the Soviet leaders are not those of United States politicians; that the Soviet interpretation of détente is totally different from what Americans think it is; that the Soviet eagerness to trade with the West and talk about strategic arms limitation goes side by side with a considered long-term strategy to outflank and conquer the world's non-Communist areas of influence—whether in the Middle East or Africa? Surely the American people are not short of a sense of realism—surely they would understand, if their leaders cared to explain it to them, that the Soviet Union is not just another power which one can tackle on a case-by-case basis, but a combination of *a cause and a power* which has to be dealt with using the same instrumentalities of military strength, economic, political, diplomatic, cultural and ideological means as the Soviet Union is using in its dealings with us?

Rostow Why indeed are we so anxious to reach an accommodation with the Russians? Why these inhibitions? Why the appeasement?

The answer is: fear. The American political class is afraid of living with the evidence of reality, because if you accept that the Russians are embarked on an imperialist course for the indefinite future; if you accept that their military, economic, educational and cultural policies are all geared to the reduction and eventually the destruction of the ability of the United States and its allies to resist, then you have to do something about it. Then you have to stop believing the notion that the Soviet military build-up is an over-reaction to the memories of the Second World War, or a defensive reaction to China, or any of the other delusions which the American Sovietological establishment and part of the East Coast opinion-making intelligentsia keep offering us. You then have to face up to the needs of rearmament, of having mobile troops, of having an effective world-wide military deployment, of restoring the genuine solidarity of your alliances, of building a positive relationship with China, of allowing your President to make a set of strategic decisions, and of releasing him from various restrictions with which Congress rendered him politically ineffective in the wake of Vietnam.

The easy way out is to turn your eyes away and convince yourself that these uncomfortable facts do not exist. It takes a very courageous politician to tell the public that our defeat in Vietnam cannot be permitted to paralyse our ability to recognise what the real world is about and to act on that information. The paralysis of the American political will reminds me very much of the 1930s. The Carter Administration is showing signs of a response, especially since the second invasion of Zaire, but it has not yet really recognised what the American public has been sensing for a long time—that Soviet action, wherever it may occur, has to be met by counter-action. It does not always have to be *military* action, but it does have to be a response that fits in with the pattern of our general relationship with the Soviet Union—linkage, overall strategy, call it what you will.

Nor would one have to be inflammatory about getting the message across to the Soviet leadership. One would simply have to say that we welcome the agreements which Mr Brezhnev signed with President Nixon; we had high hopes for them but we are now disappointed in those hopes on account of Soviet action in the Far East, the Middle East and Africa, the non-observation of the Indochina Peace Agreement and the Helsinki Agreement, the Soviet military build-up in Europe and so on. In view of all this one would then go to Congress for higher military appropriations. This, to my mind, would be the best diplomatic signal we could give the Soviet leadership. I am certain that a low-key, measured but unambiguously businesslike warning of this kind would be understood by Moscow in the same spirit in which it was given.

Urban Is it your impression that the Carter Administration may sooner or later be provoked into giving a warning of that kind—if indeed it has not quietly done so already?

Rostow I am going on the assumption that a measure of rationality will soon return to the conduct of United States foreign policy, and, as we have both said, there are signs that the process is at work, although it is still far from reaching a decisive turning-point. If we do not assume that, there is nothing to talk about.

Urban In the days of Henry Kissinger the American people found it extremely difficult to understand what power politics was about—why they should send men and money to prop up a corrupt dictatorship somewhere in Africa as part of America's over-all relationship with Moscow. My impression is that their comprehension of a crisis in Eastern Europe would be only marginally better. Would the man in Denville, Kentucky, risk his skin to push the gobbledegook of restive Krakow intellectuals against the gobbledegook of the Warsaw government?

Have you any answer to this problem—for it is all very well to suggest that American politicians should tell the people the facts of international life, but how should they go about it?

Rostow The American people do understand power very well indeed. Our society and constitutional system are preoccupied with the issue. But you are quite right—people do not readily rally behind the idea of the world balance of power. However, the notion of the Charter of the United Nations—the old notion that peace is indivisible—*has* an appeal in America. One would have to ask the question whether the Charter is going the way of the Covenant of the League of Nations, and if it is, what is it one should do to prevent it? One would have to point out that since 1971 or so the violation of the United Nations Charter has become an everyday occurrence. Since the beginning of the end in Vietnam there has been a steady increase in the boldness, scale and importance of aggression. The violation of the Indochina agreements, the Bangladesh affair, and the 1973 war in the Middle East are only some of the worst examples—no attempt to justify them in terms of international law, no explanation, just naked aggression. All over the world states and statelets undermine one another, invade one another and slaughter one another with total immunity and total disregard of their obligations under the United Nations Charter. Therefore at a given moment we would have to say: 'We cannot go on like this. Unless everyone returns to the norms of the Charter, we—the United States—will declare that we have a free hand to stop international lawlessness, and if that involves us in going into Cuba or Libya or wherever, we will do so.'

In other words, it is the context of these events in world politics that determines one's reaction to them, and the art of statesmanship is to create the right context.

Urban Wouldn't this be looked upon and resisted as a form of neo-colonialism—America becoming, certainly in Soviet propaganda, the world's—and especially the Third World's—gendarme?

Rostow The permanent members of the Security Council are supposed to be the world's gendarmes. Certainly the course of action I have suggested would lend itself to abuse by propaganda (we are, of course, being abused anyway), and it would also be resisted by our official experts in various departments of government. However, the latter can be overcome. To give you an example (and I have already mentioned our official Sovietologists' reluctant recognition of the nature of the 1968 Czechoslovak crisis): our policy in 1967 in the Middle East was based on an independent appraisal of Soviet intentions from Morocco to Iran. It was conducted by a retired ambassador, Julius Holmes, in whom Rusk and I had very great confidence. Now the official departmental experts hated to see their favourite subject taken away from them and drawn into the 'cold war'. But this inter-departmental survey was completed, and what came out of it was a clear picture of Soviet imperialism knocking at every door, taking advantage of every opportunity, and moving not just against Israel, but against Europe, against Western oil supplies and Western interests in Africa. That appraisal, too, was resisted by our experts but was later accepted under the weight of evidence and written into our policy.

It is possible that we may have to take another knock or two on the head in Africa and elsewhere before we can drive home the point that the United States should make a principled stand in support of the United Nations Charter. The American public is certainly ready for such a reappraisal. Nobody could interpret the 1972 or 1976 elections as a victory for pacifism or American inactivity.

Urban But couldn't a man of common sense—not necessarily a pacifist or an apologist for Soviet behaviour—reasonably argue that no number of Mobutus or Ogadens or even Yugoslavs would make the threat of nuclear destruction a risk worth taking? Would one want to see Washington exposed to the danger of annihilation to prove the Cubans wrong in Ethiopia?

Rostow There would be no such danger. The fact of the matter is that the Soviets learned a long time ago that we would not use our nuclear weapons unless we were severely pressed in areas that are central to our interests, and we have reason to believe that Soviet policy *vis-à-vis* ourselves is similar to our own. One might of course argue that an informal or implied nuclear threat helped to precipitate the Korean negotiations, and later to bring the Korean war to an end; but that was only after a long and costly war, after the talks at Panmunjon had dragged on and on, we had suffered massive casualties, and took the position on the war-prisoners which we did. But the Soviets have learned, and we have learned, that there is nothing in the notion of massive retaliation. *We* wouldn't use it—*they* wouldn't use it, at least so long as we maintain our second strike capability. The 'nuclear terror'—the uncertainty about the use of nuclear weapons—concerns extreme provocation in the defence of vital interests on both sides, and not peripheral ones. Even the Cuban missile crisis did not pose a threat of nuclear war of any kind. If it had gone on, the alternative for us would have been to invade Cuba with *conventional* forces. Berlin, Iran, Suez and all the other crises took place without a serious nuclear dimension—even when we had a monopoly or great superiority of nuclear weapons.

In other words, it has become very clear that whatever deterrent effect nuclear weapons may have, they do not affect the 'border wars' in Asia and Africa. President Johnson once observed that for centuries the British had got used to the fact that frontier wars were a permanent feature of life. The Americans, he said, would have to get used to it, too.

Urban But would a critical tension in the centre of Europe—perhaps over unrest of one kind or another in Eastern Europe—be a candidate for your 'frontier war'?

Rostow No—but neither should one give a hostage to fortune by declaring, as President Carter did in his election campaign, that America would not fight for Yugoslavia. Much concern was caused by that statement. It has by now been explained, although there is still a great deal of sensitivity about it in the Administration, and it is still not clear whether the President has backed out of it. Gerald Ford, who is a graduate of this school [Law School, Yale University] came here soon after his retirement from the presidency, and sitting in this room where we are now sitting we had a long talk about the state of the world in the late 1970s. Ford struck me as being very conscious of the risk the United States was running by appearing to be undecided. He was concerned about Yugoslavia, and he remarked that it would be a great mistake to leave Moscow with the impression that we would not assist Yugoslavia if she was in trouble or, more important, that we would not be prepared to take whatever action the situation called for to *prevent* a threat to Yugoslavia.

Urban Taking a large view of American-Soviet relations in 1968 and 1978—where would you see the main differences?

Rostow The post-Vietnam paralysis of American policy has made it possible for the Soviet Union to make significant gains in Asia and Africa. But even though this has to some extent weakened our global position, and even though the pretence of détente is being unilaterally exploited by the Soviet Union (with our misguided willingness to serve as technological and financial milch-cows)—one big and absolutely decisive factor has emerged since 1968 which is in our favour: China. The Johnson Administration was working for a *rapprochement* with China, and when the matter was finally clinched by Nixon and Kissinger and the Carter Administration, the constellation of power in the world underwent a dramatic change. The Soviet Union has now to attend to its security both in Europe and along its long frontier with

China. This should be an immense opportunity for us. Europe, America, Japan and China have more than enough power to stabilise world politics.

Urban What you are basically saying is that the American-Soviet relationship is well manageable if America regains her self-confidence. Without going into the vexed question of what makes for a society's morale and what makes for demoralisation—would you say that the American political class is slowly emerging from its ten-year-old loss of political will and psychological disorientation?

Rostow The American political class, especially as it is represented in the present Administration, is, as I have already pointed out, way behind the mood of the American public. However, politicians in a democracy—and particularly in the kind of instant-democracy we have in the United States—are highly conscious of what goes on in the minds of the people who have voted for or against them, and whose vote they are hoping to keep or to gain. There is no doubt that there is a groundswell for a more realistic, more self-confident, no-nonsense kind of attitude toward the Soviet Union. The American people are tired of being told that the world's strongest nation is unable to cope with what are really mini-problems by the standards of United States power—the Horn of Africa, Rhodesia and the like. They are tired of being the victims of circumstances—of being time and again on the passive and losing side—and of being asked to believe, as Kissinger rightly put it, that while tiny *Cuba* is in a position to conduct a global policy, the *United States* is *not*!

The American political class has its ears to the ground—it is aware of these feelings, and I am confident that the nation's recovery from the trauma of Vietnam will soon be translated into policies that will stop the drift and set limits to Soviet expansionism.

Claiborne Pell

Limits of Solidarity

Urban The tenth anniversary of the 1968 Prague Spring and its suppression by the Soviet Union and its allies provides us with a convenient opportunity to look at the lessons of Communism in Czechoslovakia, both in the form in which it left the stage in 1968 and as it had entered it in 1948. You were an American Foreign Service officer in Czechoslovakia at the time of the 1948 Prague coup—

Pell —Yes, I first served as Third Secretary and Vice Consul in Prague in 1946; in 1947 I was transferred to Bratislava where I established the US Consulate General. From both places I could observe the events that led up to the Communist take-over. It was clear by 1947 that Communist strength was declining and that the Party was going to do worse at the 1948 elections than it had done in 1946 when it had captured (in the Czech lands) 38 per cent of the vote as against Benes's National Socialist Party, which had received only 18 per cent, and Fierlinger's Social Democrats who had scored a mere 13 per cent. I remember predicting at the time that the Communists were highly conscious of the impending change in their fortunes and that they would probably stage some kind of a coup to prevent the 1948 elections from taking place.

Urban Did you make this point in your reports to Ambassador Steinhardt?

Pell Yes, I did. Ambassador Steinhardt was an activist diplomat who strongly supported Benes's National Socialists and did not believe that a coup would be attempted or that it could be successful. Years later I went through some State Department files to see how my particular emphases in the

Ambassador's report looked to us in retrospect. I would say they stood the test of time.

Urban Steinhardt had a reputation of being rather strongly involved in the country's internal politics—

Pell Well, he was, as I say, in favour of the Benes people and made no secret of his dislike of the Communists.

Urban There was surely nothing reprehensible in that, considering that the Russians had been using, through the National Committees and the Czechoslovak Communists and, earlier, through the Soviet Army, especially in Slovakia and Subcarpathian Ruthenia, every trick in the book to draw Czechoslovakia into their sphere of influence.

Pell The Soviets had, in 1944–45, undoubtedly used their muscle in Czechoslovakia in the ways you describe. Yet the surprising thing in 1948 was that at the time of the coup there wasn't a single Russian soldier in the country. It is a real reflection on the Communist system that whereas the Communists took power in 1948 without the help of Soviet troops and with scarcely anything one could describe as violence, after twenty years of Communist rule it took hundreds of thousands of Russian and Warsaw Pact troops, and a good many deaths, to *keep* Czechoslovakia Communist.

Urban Did you regard the 1948 coup as the destruction of the country's legitimate order?

Pell The Communist take-over was a *putsch*—no less. Czechoslovakia had exemplary democratic traditions, going back to the foundation of the Republic, which the Communist minority subverted and destroyed.

Urban Would you attribute some of the responsibility for Czechoslovakia's destruction to the credulity of Benes? Was he naive in thinking that a treaty with Stalin would protect him? Was he right in trusting Gottwald? As late as 16 July 1944, Benes expressed the view that the Soviet Union was so badly devastated and needing American aid so much that 'the Soviets will not interfere in our internal conditions any more than in those of other countries'.

Pell I should not like to apportion blame to Benes or anyone else. The geopolitical situation of Czechoslovakia was such that the Soviet Union felt that she was essential to Soviet security. I do think, though, that Czechoslovakia might have offered more resistance in 1948 than she did.

After all, even observing matters from Bratislava, it was obvious enough that, well before the 1948 *putsch*, the Ministry of the Interior, to name one example, was under heavy Communist influence, and large numbers of political prisoners under its authority were being treated with great brutality. The warnings were there—you could choose to read them or not to read them.

Urban Was there anything the US could have done and ought to have done before the Prague *putsch* or at the time of the *putsch*? After all, Czechoslovakia was, unlike Rumania and Hungary, an allied nation, and the US, unlike the Soviet Union, was in possession of nuclear weapons. Moreover, the Czechoslovak-Soviet Treaty of Friendship, Mutual Aid and Postwar Cooperation of 12 December 1943 stipulated, under article 4, that the contracting parties would 'regulate their actions according to the principles of mutual respect of their independence and sovereignty and non-interference in the internal affairs of the other signatory'. Would the US, as the senior nation among the United Nations, not have done well to flex its then considerable muscle and stand up for its ally? Ambassador Steinhardt's belated offer of an American loan of $25 million to help the forces of democracy was no match for the powers Ambassador Zorin brought with him from Moscow.

Pell I don't think there is anything we could have done. We probably backed one particular party, Benes's National Socialists, a shade too energetically—it seems in retrospect that we would have been better off if we had stayed further removed from them than we did. But there is a more general point here. So many countries in the world fall into the error of saying: 'Couldn't the US have helped?' The plain fact is that basically every country has to help itself. Czechoslovakia was, and is, a victim of its geographic location and shape: it is a long and narrow country which would have represented, in the Soviet view, a Western wedge running deep into Soviet-controlled territory. The Russians first snipped off Subcarpathian Ruthenia and then took control, through the 1948 *putsch*, of the entire country. Their worry of vulnerability drove the Soviet leaders to use utterly illegal methods.

Urban The Churchill–Stalin agreement, such as it was,

foresaw a fifty-fifty balance of influence both in Czechoslovakia and in Hungary; therefore the rape of Czechoslovakia was not a foregone conclusion.

Pell No, it wasn't. The Russians took over by virtue of the fact of their geographic dominance—assisted, as I say, by the lack of Czechoslovak resistance of any sort. This was truly amazing.

Urban The Czechoslovaks didn't fight in 1948 any more than they had fought Hitler in 1938 or were to fight Moscow in 1968. What is your explanation of this apparent lack of a fighting spirit?

Pell The relative apathy of 1968 (it was relative because there was no lack of an effective *passive* resistance) was, I think, due to a sense of fatalism. First, Czechoslovakia's desertion by its French and British allies, followed by German occupation in 1939, drained the spirit of the country. But earlier, under Habsburg rule, the spirit of dependence was deeply embedded. For centuries the Czechs had their decisions made for them in Vienna as the Slovaks had in Budapest. Traditions of this kind are not wiped out overnight. Except for those wonderful years between the two world wars, the peoples of Czechoslovakia acquiesced in the habit of being led.

Urban Czechoslovakia was born in Pittsburgh, on American soil, and the founding fathers of Czechoslovakia, Masaryk in particular, enjoyed profound American support. Woodrow Wilson's Fourteen Points were in some part responsible for the dissolution of the Austro-Hungarian Monarchy and for the success of the Czechs' and Slovaks' drive for self-determination. Are the American people—are you as a US Senator—conscious of any sense of responsibility for the survival of a state you have helped to create? I do not, of course, mean responsibility in the legal sense, but rather as a self-imposed moral obligation to stand up for Czechoslovakia simply because it is an outpost of liberal, parliamentary democracy in an inhospitable environment?

Pell That would be like saying that we have a responsibility to North Vietnam because it originally copied the American Constitution—which it then didn't follow. The fact that the Czechoslovak Government was formed in Pittsburgh and that Wilson's policy of self-determination provided a political rationale for the creation of the successor states—which, mind you, would have been created anyhow because the Austro-Hungarian Monarchy was falling apart under the twin blows of a lost war and internal dissension—does not mean that the US is responsible for the eventual health of the Czechoslovak Government. It is perfectly true that America did play a part—American Czechs and Slovaks were, in those early days after the First World War, extremely active in putting Czechoslovakia on its feet both economically and in determining its political institutions. But I cannot conceive of this as implying American responsiblity any more than British or French responsibility—except for the responsibility every man has to prevent the slaughter and torture and suppression of his brother, wherever he may be.

Urban But isn't there in the US a greater cultural and emotional identification with the Czechs than with the North Vietnamese? No one would claim that North Vietnamese history, culture or religion are part and parcel of Western civilisation—but Czech culture *is*.

Pell I think the American public has a feeling of solidarity towards all countries that have been free but are free no longer. But it is not more of a feeling toward Czechoslovakia than it would be to France or Belgium or other countries if they, too, were under the Communist heel.

Urban Czechoslovakia was founded on the principle of self-determination. Did the forcible expulsion of the Sudeten Germans accord with this principle?

Pell We are faced here with the dreadful business of *quid pro quo*—paying off old scores, to call it by its proper name—in history; the Nazis had maltreated many Czechs, therefore, when their turn came, the Czechs maltreated a great many Germans. I must, however, say this: when you examine the record of Nazi behaviour in Czechoslovakia, both before the occupation and after, you can understand the natural anger of the Czechs. There is a degree of brutality in that part of the world which shocks *us* but appears to be almost part of a way of political life in Eastern Europe. I remember once talking to the president of the Slovak National Council—his name was Smidke—and asking him apropos the Slovak maltreatment of political prisoners:

'How can you permit your people to be abused in this way?' He ripped open his shirt and showed me the scars left from where he had himself been abused thirty years earlier by the Hungarians at the time of the Bela Kun regime. It is all very shocking and hard for us in America to understand.

Urban It is worth recalling that the original idea for the expulsion of the Sudeten Germans and Hungarians came neither from the Czech Communists nor from the Russians, but from Benes's Government in Exile in London, and was limited to Germans and Hungarians of proven Fascist behaviour. It is true that already in 1942 Benes cast the net wide: he spoke of the expulsion of 'all the German bourgeoisie, the pan-German intelligentsia and those workers who have gone over to Fascism', and in another instance he estimated that this would involve 80 per cent of Czechoslovak Germans. Yet he made it very clear that 'decent Germans who had fought as brothers on our side for democracy' should not be 'forced into a tragic situation'. But when the transfer was actually put into effect—with American, Soviet and British approval—it was very hard to distinguish it from a brutal exercise in racism. One can argue that the Germans were being paid back in their own coin—but if so, they were being paid back by *us*, in defiance of all *our* principles.

Pell I do not quite understand the point of this interview. Are you trying to create anger?

Urban No—the Soviet and Czech Communist record in this matter is, if anything, less open to question than is the American, for example. In fact, until 1944, the Czechoslovak Communist Party leadership abroad opposed the idea of the transfer of the German and Hungarian populations. And in May 1968, Milan Hübl, Jan Prochazka and Vladimir Blazek, in a celebrated trialogue in *Host do Domu*, condemned the indiscriminate expulsion of the Germans as 'a crime'. They were, of course, promptly rebuked by the Soviets.

Pell There were very few Germans at the end of the war in Czechoslovakia whom you could point a finger at and say: 'these were not Nazi Germans, they stood up to Hitler and remained loyal to the Czechoslovak state'. There *were* some—I had German friends there, Austrians, who identified themselves with the Czechs as Czechs. But when the chips were down even they were expelled, as was more or less the entire German population.

Of course we cannot say, in retrospect, that the blanket expulsion of three million people was in keeping with our principles, but it is very hard to turn back history. At the time of the collapse of Poland in 1939 many Poles were expelled from the eastern provinces. This too was an enormous injustice, and so was the expulsion of the Germans from Silesia who were then replaced by Polish settlers from the eastern provinces. It is very difficult to unravel history, and if you do try to unravel it and unduly extend the range of collective memory, you usually end up in disaster. Today these things are best forgotten to the extent that individual suffering permits us to forget, and the wise thing to do is to leave the post-war boundaries where they are.

Urban Do you feel that the Prague Spring marked the beginnings of a type of Communism significantly different from the Soviet variety—of Eurocommunism?

Pell Yes, I do. The Czechoslovak Communists were perfectly sincere in trying to create Communism 'with a human face', as they put it, and I have cherished memories of being in Prague in that glorious spring, talking to some of the political leaders, seeing the new vitality in literary life, in the theatre, on television and in the press. The excitement was unforgettable. At the same time I remember talking with a very wise, conservative European head of state who believed that Soviet intervention was inevitable because, he said, if the Czechs were allowed to get away with their alternative Communism the end-result would be the removal of Czechoslovakia from the Soviet sphere of influence, which the Soviets would not and could not permit. My personal view is that the pace in Prague was too fast, and more might have been achieved with less haste.

Communism as a system of government goes against human nature: once a man can fill his belly, obtains some consumer goods and becomes literate, he very soon acquires the same desires to work freely, travel freely, think freely, talk freely and worship freely as any of us has in our own societies, and any system of government that denies him these things is sooner or later bound to go down to defeat. The nemesis of Communism may take time, but it is inevitable.

I have been going behind the Iron Curtain now just about every year for many years, and my impression is that Communism, even in the Soviet Union, is less harsh today—still harsh, still brutal, and I wouldn't want to live under it—but less harsh than it was in 1948 when I first saw it in action. What happened in Czechoslovakia in the spring of 1968 is going to develop in other East European countries stretched over a longer period of time, and my prediction would be that fifty years from now the brutality and totalitarian character of the Soviet system will be greatly dissipated.

Now the link between Prague and Eurocommunism is clear to me though I cannot see a linear relationship. The Italian Communist leaders are certainly close to some of the Czech reform Communists, but this is little consolation to those Italians who fear that perhaps within six months of its arrival in the corridors of power, an Italian Eurocommunist government would be replaced by a much harsher and more orthodox Communist regime—as it well might.

Urban Did you feel at the time that if the Czech and Slovak reform Communists had succeeded in institutionalising their ideas, the country would eventually have slipped back into a bourgeois type of multi-party system?

Pell I just didn't know—there was no precedent to go on. I knew that the Reform Movement could not stay as it was because Czechoslovak society was in a flux and had to move on—in what direction, nobody could say. My hope was that the reforms would create an alternative socialist society providing a nice bridge between the West and the Soviet Union. Again, geography was the villain, causing the Czechoslovak revolution to be aborted. But, as I say, the last chapters in that story yet remain to be written.

Urban Is your idea of a 'bridge' another way of saying that the two social orders will eventually converge?

Pell There will probably be some convergence—but I don't think we should measure all the world's possible political systems against ours on the principle that American democracy offers some kind of a gold-standard. I am not at all sure that the American type of democracy would fit in with the character and requirements of quite a few countries in the world. Many need and desire a degree of authoritarianism, and as long as authoritarianism meets with the approval of the majority of the people, I don't think we should quarrel with it.

Urban Do you feel that NATO, or the US acting alone, could and ought to have done anything to prevent the suppression of the Prague Reform Movement? I am not thinking of warlike intervention but of putting political incentives and disincentives in the way of the Soviet Government.

Pell I don't see what we could have done. We did what we could, but the Russians moved in because they considered the 'corruption' of the Soviet model of Communism in Czechoslovakia to be a question of national survival. They feared that the contagion would quickly spread and undermine Soviet power throughout Eastern Europe and indeed within the Soviet Union.

Urban How would the Russians have reacted if two or three satellite rebellions had coincided under the impact of a successful renewal of Communism in Czechoslovakia?

Pell They would have made an enormous effort to put them down, and I still think, speaking in 1978, that they would have had, and still have, the strength to put them *all* down. But in another twenty years from now it might be a different story.

Urban Would you agree that NATO ought to look upon the coincidence of two or three such rebellions as qualitatively different, both in the political and military sense, from a single rebellion, and that it ought to think of ways of exploiting it?

Pell I do not want to start the Third World War, because in a new war there would be no winners. If we intervened with force, the Third World War would be quickly upon us.

Urban Using a large enough historical canvas, wouldn't you say the Czechs were possibly right not to have fought—in 1938, 1948 or 1968? Prague with its magnificent monuments of the European past survived the war intact, and the Czech population as a whole, and especially the working class, got away rather lightly under German rule. The Yugoslavs, on the other hand, fought with great determination—one another as well as the Germans and Italians—but the end of the war found their country in ruins and large parts of it almost depopulated. In other words: aren't perhaps a nation's values ultimately better protected if the emphasis in its philosophy is on survival rather than costly and irreversible acts of heroism?

Pell I would hate to be pushed into giving a yes-or-no type of answer to that question. This is a highly personal matter which everyone has to sort out for himself. I used to come up against this problem when people asked me in 1948: shall we flee Czechoslovakia? Shall we become refugees in the free world?

My answer would always be: 'Don't leave unless you are in actual danger of life or limb. It is better to stay and survive in your own country if you possibly can because the national character will win out in the end.' But whether I would applaud the Czechs' lack of a fighting spirit for the reasons you have given and deplore the spirit of the Serbs and Montenegrins—I would not want to get into a position of applauding or not applauding.

Urban What would you say if Czechoslovak people in trouble asked for your advice in 1978 whether they should leave their country or play the system from within?

Pell I would again tell them that, unless they were greatly threatened, they should hang on because Communism as a system of government cannot last. I would advise them to inculcate in their children the spirit of freedom and Christianity and try to live within the system. I would remind them that the life of a refugee is an unhappy one and that the long-term survival of decency and democracy in Czechoslovakia depends on the staying power of decent people and democrats.

Jacob D. Beam

Ambassador in Prague

Urban Professor Eduard Goldstücker has told us that the Communist take-over in February 1948 was in reality only a reflection of the disintegration of the war-time alliance between the Western powers and the Soviet Union. That would seem to imply that the alliance was in tolerable working order during the war and for some time after the war.

Beam Oh no, our troubles with the Soviet Union were almost continuous during the war despite our alliance and the common enemy. There were endless recriminations between Churchill and Stalin. I had first-hand experience of some of these as I was private secretary to Ambassador Winant in London from 1941 to 1944. I remember one notable occasion when Maisky, the Soviet Ambassador to the Court of St James, had been sent instructions to complain to the British Government about the non-arrival of certain supplies from Britain to Murmansk. As you will recall, the British had sent a huge convoy of arms and supplies to Murmansk under the most difficult conditions and under permanent and successful German U-boat attack, so much so that they lost 60 per cent of their ships and men. Yet Maisky had the nerve to complain. Well, Churchill threw him out of his office. But incidents of this kind, misinterpretations, bad faith were daily occurrences in our relationship with Stalin. Books have been written about them—I have very little to add to the sad tale.

Urban Was the Czechoslovak Government in Exile one of the causes of these tensions and misunderstandings?

Beam No, it wasn't, but our relations with Benes were

not very good. He made an alliance with Stalin in 1943. We had told him not to, but he went ahead all the same. Benes was a difficult man. He was despondent during the war and completely lost heart after the war.

Urban But weren't Benes's pessimism and his policy of mending fences with Moscow dictated by prudence? In 1938 Czechoslovakia had been sacrificed by Britain and France in an unsuccessful attempt to achieve détente with Hitler, and Benes could, in 1941 or 1942, see no guarantee that the Western allies would make a more determined stand on behalf of Czechoslovakia *after* the war, risking their precarious alliance with the Soviet Union. That his realism did not pay dividends is another matter. But his forebodings of Western passivity were borne out in February 1948, when the West turned out to be even less prepared to risk a confrontation on behalf of Czechoslovakia than it had been in 1938.

Beam Benes was certainly disillusioned with the West and feared Germany. This induced him to play the Russian card. Also, the Czechs and Slovaks displayed, and had displayed for a long time, strong Pan-Slavic sympathies, so that playing the Russian card was popular. Nevertheless, if Benes had listened to our advice and not signed up with Stalin we might have been able and willing to give him better support in 1948 than we did. But Benes did not heed our advice. He made concession after concession to the Communists and accepted Gottwald as prime minister. By February 1948 he was in no position to resist. Consequently there was not much we could do to help him. On the personal level, Benes was profoundly prejudiced against the West. By contrast, our own attitude to him and his country was, originally, extremely friendly. After the Moscow treaty, however, we began to suspect both Benes and his policies. In the post-war period there was virtually no frank and easy communication between Prague and Washington.

Urban Was there any feeling in the State Department that the fate of Czechoslovakia was of immediate concern to the US? Or was it thought that the Yalta agreement and the post-war military balance in Central Europe made Czechoslovakia's slide into the Soviet camp inevitable?

Beam It was more or less the latter. We got no

encouragement from Benes, no requests for aid—nothing. We were sympathetic to his plight, and Ambassador Steinhardt and his staff did what they could to be of assistance. The British and French, on their part, showed even less interest and were inclined to write off Czechoslovakia. World affairs also interfered. The Berlin crisis was upon us, there was trouble in the Middle East—it was, therefore, very difficult to catch the ears of the Secretary of State or of Mr Lovett, the Undersecretary, who was then responsible for Czechoslovakia.

Urban It is not quite clear to me for what precise reasons Czechoslovakia was thought to be defenceless against Soviet machinations in 1948. The Yalta agreement had not put the country in the Soviet sphere of influence; Czechoslovakia was an ally, and Benes's treaty with Stalin contained iron guarantees that Czechoslovakia's integrity would be respected. So, unlike Hungary, Rumania, and even Poland (which is a special case), Czechoslovakia stood a good chance of staying outside the Soviet glacis.

Beam The Czechs did not have close ties with the West—neither during the war, much less after the war. The British, who carried the ball for the West in most things concerning the Benes Government, discouraged us from taking too much interest in Czechoslovakia. And Benes himself was, as I say, an awkward man to deal with. He really declined to deal with us, and I think he did so on the calculation that this would keep his lines open to Moscow. My feeling was that Benes was *inhibited* from being an ally.

Urban In other words, in 1938 the Czechs expected help but got none—in 1948 they asked for none and got none.

Beam Yes, they didn't ask for it any more than they did in 1968. We let it be known in 1968 that we might be willing to help them, but the answer we drew was: leave us alone; we can handle this—we are good Communists.

Urban But you were, in 1948, also in close touch with the non-Communists, who were, after all, the majority. Did they not seek American support—moral support if no other?

Beam They were frightened and despondent—almost paralysed. To give you one example: after the November–December 1947 Foreign Ministers' conference in

London, the State Department sent me on a consultative trip to Prague a week before Christmas. The Ambassador was in Washington, but Mrs Steinhardt had me to dinner with Jan Masaryk, the Foreign Minister, who had just returned from the UN meeting in New York. Masaryk was not popular with the State Department which thought him frivolous. Our conversation accordingly was brief. I asked if I might see him the following day, but his direct response was, 'It's no use your talking to me—go and see Clementis who knows more about what is going on than I do'. This was about four months before his suicide.

Urban Masaryk was, in fact, saying that he was powerless?

Beam Yes, he was.

Urban Did he utter any views about foreign policy?

Beam None, except to thank me for keeping the Czech delegation well informed at the London conference. We had gone out of our way to keep the Poles and Czechs well in the picture in London; but, I must say, the Czech delegation were a rum crew, most of them Stalinists.

Urban What was your impression of Clementis? You met him some five years before his trial and execution.

Beam I was pleasantly surprised. He was, of course, a Communist, and sympathetic towards the Russians, but at the same time he wanted to have good relations with us. He seemed knowledgeable, balanced and objective. That is probably why he had to perish with Slansky and others.

Urban To move on to 1968, I was surprised to read in your memoirs that in the critical months of the Prague Spring American-Czech relations were limited to some very odd problems: the supply of Czech rifles to Vietnam; the return of the Czech gold, and the indemnities you were hoping to obtain from the Czechs for American property nationalised after the Communist take-over. I would have thought none of this was terribly relevant to what was happening in Prague.

Beam Ah, but you have to see our relationship with the Czech Government in a larger perspective. When I was sent to Prague as US Ambassador in August 1966 we all realised that Czechoslovakia had not been de-Stalinised and therefore there was little room for American action. Nevertheless Dean

Rusk, then US Secretary of State, thought that we should try to interest the Prague Government in an independent approach to the war in Vietnam. 'Your mission,' Mr Rusk told me, 'is practically hopeless, but you arrive there with clean hands, and even if you can't get the Czechs to cooperate with us, perhaps they will give you a fair opinion. It's worth the effort, anyway.'

Urban What was your new approach to Vietnam?

Beam The position I was to ask the Czechs to consider was roughly this: we were willing to enter into discussions with Hanoi without condition; we were not seeking the destruction of the North Vietnamese government; we would not oppose reunification but insisted that it must come about by free elections; we would stop the bombing of the North in return for reciprocal action; we were not attacking Communism itself but we did support resistance to aggression. I was to point out that a small nation such as the Czechs had a stake in our cause.

Urban No doubt you hoped that the Czechs might be lured away from the Soviet position?

Beam No, we had no hope of that. We simply thought somebody in Prague would wish to enter into a dialogue with us, answer some questions about our plan and possibly make some suggestions.

Urban The Johnson Administration must have been rather desperate to seek the resolution of its Vietnam troubles through the good offices of Stalinist Czechoslovakia, of all governments.

Beam Yes, dismay over the war in Vietnam was growing ever deeper in the Johnson Administration, and the nation was more and more divided. The US was heading for the 1968 campus rebellions, mass demonstrations and the virtual collapse of the hinterland.

Urban How were your proposals received by the Czech Government?

Beam I first called on Foreign Minister David who spent the best part of half an hour denouncing our bombing of Vietnam, berating us as the principal disturbers of international peace and for failing to follow the 'socialist' example of both advocating and practising peaceful coexistence.

I left our Vietnam document with him. A couple of days later I was received by President Novotny.

Urban What sort of an impression did he make on you?

Beam Not a favourable one. He was a primitive man—a locksmith by training.

Urban How did he respond to your plan for tackling the war in Vietnam?

Beam He was extremely frank with me, even if he was nothing else. He strongly disapproved of our proposals. He said it was quite out of the question that his government should change its position on Vietnam and fully endorsed the stand of the Soviet Union. He stressed that his country was no satellite of Moscow and decided independently that this was the right course. He rejected any attempt to drive a wedge between his country and the Russians. I denied that this was our intention and expressed the hope that his government would come up with new suggestions.

Novotny then complained bitterly about our refusal to return the Czech gold. He said that if his country were a great power he would come over to the US and *get* it. I pretended not to understand the translation of this remark so I asked the interpreter to repeat it for me—which visibly set Novotny back a bit.

Urban Obviously, Novotny was still very self-confident.

Beam Yes, this was in mid-1966. The nemesis of Novotny's power started only with the 1967 writers' conference. In August 1966 he was firmly in the saddle. He was cocky and offensive towards us.

Urban You were, in the spring and summer of 1968, the Ambassador in Prague of the world's most important power. What was your brief for dealing with the Prague ferment? Did you feel the US had a stake in seeing the Reform Movement succeed, or were you spectators rather than supporters?

Beam The Czechs had given us a lot of trouble both with the virulence of their Vietnam propaganda and their supply of small arms to Hanoi. I made a trip to Washington in May 1968 and President Johnson sent for me to express his anxiety over the support which the Czechs were giving the North Vietnamese. I was also invited to meet the Joint

Chiefs of Staff who expressed great anger over the same issue—the continuing supply of the Czech AK 47 automatic rifle to the Vietnamese.

Our interest in Czechoslovak domestic developments was, therefore, qualified from the very beginning. And as we received absolutely no indication from the reform Communists that they wanted our help, we gave none. The American press, radio and television did, of course, deal sympathetically with the Prague events, but it was not at all clear that even this distinctly unofficial support was to the reform Communists' liking. After the Cierna and Bratislava meetings senior officials of the Czech Foreign Ministry complained to us that the US press was far too optimistic and doing the Reform Movement a disservice by alleging that at Cierna and Bratislava the Czechs had won a victory over the Soviet side. This, we were told, was not true and would create ill-will in Moscow. We could, of course, not judge how representative this line was of reform Communist thinking because it was unfailingly conveyed to us by officials of the Foreign Ministry, and these were, alas, the old crew—many of them Stalinists and deplorable individuals.

Urban Was it their intention to show the Soviet leaders that reform Communism was a family affair from which the Americans would not be allowed to benefit?

Beam I think it was, but we, too, at first tended to look upon reform Communism as an internal squabble which had only a secondary bearing on our concerns.

Urban How did all this affect your reporting? There was, as you say, a strongly held view in Washington that these Prague Communists had fallen to quarrelling among themselves over the definition of words rather than fundamentals, and that, from the American point of view, there was not much to choose between them.

Beam Our reporting was highly sympathetic to the reform Communists, many of whom we knew personally. And as the movement advanced we repeatedly pointed out in our reports that a fundamental type of change was being enacted in Prague. We devoted increasing attention to the importance of the Reform Movement, even though we often felt that these enthusiastic reformers were too gullible and naive. Mind you, the Rumanians and Yugoslavs also believed that the reformers had a touch of political innocence about them—but went on supporting them all the same.

Urban Did you at any time tell Washington: the reforms have reached a phase where a clash with Moscow seems inevitable?

Beam We got worried in July. The reformers began to talk of a multi-party system, they put up political clubs and re-wrote the Party statutes. All this was bound to drive the Russians up the wall, and we said so in our reports. Similar advice reached the State Department from Ambassador Thompson in Moscow.

Urban Did the reform Communists share your feeling that they were on a collision course?

Beam No. They were exuberant. They sensed no danger at all. We wished them luck and we said we hoped that they would win. We had no reason to say more and we couldn't say less. The Soviet Embassy in Prague was unapproachable and we had no idea how they were reacting. But for those of us who had some experience of Soviet affairs it was not difficult to surmise that the breaking-point was near. The Warsaw Pact's five-party letter made the danger crystal clear, for it contained a warning that the Russians would tolerate no erosion of the 'achievements of socialism'. This was another way of telling the Czechs, and the world, that the Soviet leaders regarded any change in Czechoslovakia's internal *status quo* as a domestic concern of their own and would act accordingly.

Urban Did you feel at the time that the invasion of Czechoslovakia was primarily due to Soviet power-political considerations? Or was the ideological disease implicit in the Czech example the prime mover?

Beam Probably the latter, although the two were, and are, interrelated: loss of hegemony reduces the estate of 'socialism'—the erosion of 'socialism', Soviet-style, reduces Soviet hegemony. But the ideological danger was paramount. The Soviets knew that if they lost the battle over ideology and party organisation, then Czechoslovakia would no longer be either an ally or an asset. Worse, the Czech type of reforms would have spread elsewhere and undermined the entire Soviet system.

Urban Professor Eduard Goldstücker, himself an important architect of the 1968 reforms, told us that this danger of proliferation did not exist. Moscow's repressive apparatus was strong enough, he argued, to prevent unwanted repercussions—whether in Eastern Europe or in the Soviet Union.

Beam This was a risk the Soviets were *not* prepared to take. The Czech example *would* have spread. In any case, we shall never know *what* precisely the Czech example would have implied, as it was not allowed to run its course.

Dubcek and Smrkovsky lost control of the Party. Day after day, the most extraordinary statements were made, and it was clear that the Russians could not tolerate any of this. If you put yourself in the shoes of the Soviet leaders you will at once sense that their worries were justified.

Urban Did this rather sympathetic appreciation of the Soviet position colour the reports you were sending back to Washington?

Beam No, it didn't. We reported punctiliously what the reformers were doing and they had our full sympathy. At the same time we felt that they were taking very grave chances and the time would come when they would be silenced. With the Cierna meeting we shared the feeling of the reformists that a confrontation with the Soviet leaders *had* taken place, and a trial accommodation had been reached.

Urban How strong was the Administration's interest in the success of the Reform Movement after Cierna and Bratislava? I would have thought these critical meetings at the highest level—and Moscow's grave discomfiture which they revealed—would have alerted the Administration to the possibility of *some* action.

Beam The US Government seemed not to have given the matter its concentrated attention. The Administration felt that this was an internal Communist disagreement, and the best we could do was to stay out of it. But, right up to the last moment, it was not believed that the Russians would take military action. They had moved up their troops very artfully under the cover of summer manoeuvres. It was a beautiful piece of deception. When the Russians struck they had perfect cover.

At a reception given for the visiting Rumanian President three days before the invasion, a leading official from the Czech Presidium came up to tell us in a great state of dismay that the Soviets were demanding the stationing of troops in Czechoslovakia and that 'the city is filling up with Soviet agents'. In retrospect, what he really meant was that the Soviets were making new demands which the Czechs knew they would have to meet in a re-opening of negotiations. I doubt whether he or his colleagues contemplated an imminent attack.

Urban American spy satellites apparently had the troop movements fully recorded but the delivery of their pictures was delayed. By the time they reached the President, the US was faced with a *fait accompli*.

Beam In 1968 the pictures used to be dropped, which took time. Nowadays they are transmitted direct.

Urban Would it have made any difference if the photographs *had* arrived in time?

Beam It might have made *some* difference. We would have mounted a campaign to let the world know what the Russians were planning. The President might have expressed serious warnings. A week's notice might have been useful. We would have made it more costly for the Russians to strike.

Urban Was there any sinister reason for the delay of the satellite photographs?

Beam No—it was just bad luck.

Urban Do you think that either the President or Secretary Rusk would have gone beyond making a number of gestures expressing American indignation?

Beam We would not have gone to war over Czechoslovakia. The President was anxious to get a SALT agreement. But we had really given up our ability to offer military help to the Czechs, or the Hungarians for that matter, when we signed the Austrian state treaty: first, by destroying the Austrian side of a possible Bavarian-Austrian-US military pincer; second, by guaranteeing Austrian neutrality. Any US move to aid the Czechs would have resulted in the immediate reoccupation of Austria by Soviet troops. Therefore—quite apart from the larger considerations of world peace and the future of East-West relations—military intervention was not a practical possibility.

Urban You have said that a war over Czechoslovakia was ruled out, and this is also what I learned from former Secretary Rusk, Mr Eugene Rostow and Senator Pell. Yet when, in April 1969, you presented your credentials to President Podgorny as US Ambassador to the Soviet Union, Podgorny said to you: 'Soviet action in Czechoslovakia prevented the beginning of another war'. Were the Soviet leaders completely misreading American intentions (a rather difficult thing to imagine, as NATO hadn't been so much as put on the alert), or was Podgorny giving you *ex post facto* propaganda?

Beam Podgorny, an uncultured, rustic type of a man heartily disliked by all and sundry, claimed that the West had been inciting the Czechs with political overtures—which I don't for a moment believe we had—and that the loss of Czechoslovakia would have upset the East-West balance in Germany. This appears to have been the chief Soviet worry. The Germans were invariably depicted as the leading troublemakers, not only in Podgorny's words to myself but in a number of similar utterances both by him and by Kosygin, the Prime Minister. Needless to say, the Germans were unfairly accused. True, they had a smart man in charge of their Trade Mission in Prague (no formal diplomatic relations had been established) who got along with the Czechs very well. Economic ties were being picked up, lucrative business deals for both sides were being hammered out—the Germans knew their way about Czechoslovakia much better than the Americans or the French. But Soviet stories about a coming German take-over were the grossest fabrication. I don't think the Russian leaders believed it themselves—but some excuse had to be manufactured for their heavy-handed action. Their principal concern was to keep the *status quo* intact. They feared that a loosening up of 'socialism' in Czechoslovakia would, in one form or another, take away from their overall estate and increase Western power in central Europe.

Urban And in this they were, I suppose, right. An ideologically emasculated Czechoslovakia would have been, 'objectively speaking', a net gain for the West even if NATO had never recalled a single soldier from his weekend leave.

Beam I think it would. We may not approve of this view, but this was the Soviet perception.

Urban Eduard Goldstücker told us that future upheavals in Eastern Europe would give the Soviet leaders a great deal more to worry about than did either Hungary or Czechoslovakia because they would coincide or might indeed be coordinated. The people of Eastern Europe, he said, learn from experience; trouble in one spot would automatically lead to trouble elsewhere. Suppose this were true—is there any reason to assume that Moscow could not cope?

Beam No, there isn't. The present leadership is certainly determined to maintain complete control over these countries. They *will* make concessions, as they did in Poland when they got rid of Gomulka, but they will permit no change that would undermine the system. And they have the power to suppress, not one but two or three simultaneous rebellions. Their police agents are everywhere; their whole empire is, in one way or another, under the control of the KGB.

Now if Brezhnev leaves and a new man takes over, there may, or may not, be a period of uncertainty in the Soviet leadership which might create an opening in Eastern Europe. But this is crystal-gazing.

I would say that Eurocommunism as a long-term influence offers *some* hope of change. But so far at least the impact of Eurocommunism has been nil, and I cannot see it making any headway in the near future.

The nations of Eastern Europe do not really want Eurocommunism in preference to Soviet Communism—they want *no* Communism. This is the basic fact about Eastern Europe which we must always bear in mind if we don't want to fall into the trap of thinking that what Eurocommunists claim is good for Eastern Europe is, in fact, what the Eastern Europeans themselves think is good for them.

Urban You wouldn't envisage a post-Brezhnev leadership *itself* taking the lead in shedding some of the baneful heritage of the Soviet type of 'socialism'?

Beam I would not rule it out completely. After all, Malenkov was a liberal of sorts in relation to Stalin, and Khrushchev in relation to both Malenkov and Stalin. Yet the limits of their, and especially Khrushchev's, reforms were narrow, and Khrushchev's adventurism in foreign affairs was much in excess of anything Stalin in his wily but cautious wisdom would have contemplated. We just don't know.

Urban Ten years have passed since the Prague Spring. Would it be fair to assume that the American people and the American Administration are now more conscious than they were in 1968 of the leverage that would be handed to them if the nations of Central and Eastern Europe made another bid, or a number of linked bids, for their independence? Would the Americans want to use it?

Beam I don't know. The American people—to be completely frank with you—have about written off the possibility that these nations can regain their independence so long as the present correlation of world forces exists. It isn't that we don't care or that we have lost interest. But having seen the pattern of Soviet reaction in Poland, Hungary and Czechoslovakia, we have lost hope that anything can substantially change in Eastern Europe in the foreseeable future. My impression is that Brezhnev will be with us for quite some time to come despite his failing health. It would, therefore, be rather foolish to speculate about what will come after him.

Urban I can sense behind your guarded answers a rather depressing reading not only of the immobilism of the Soviet system but of the immobilism of the Russian people too. Is it really unreasonable to hope that in this age of electronic communications and jet travel the Soviet Union will somehow emerge from its unnatural isolation and the self-induced traumas and phobias which flow from isolation? In Britain, it has been said, we treat our prisoners better than the Soviet system treats its ordinary citizens. Can two such disparate systems continue to coexist?

Beam The Soviet leaders are firmly in the saddle because they know the ropes. They have their little satrapies, their little and not so little islands of support which they have built up over the years and which they can rely on with the confidence of feudal landlords.

The system is, of course, a despotism, but it is politically efficient. And the Russian people don't care. Their standard of comparison is not Switzerland—not even Hungary, where the standard of living is much higher than in the Soviet Union—but their own former and much more wretched condition. Life in Moscow has undoubtedly improved; indeed I would say that life in most of the Russian parts of the country is tolerable. And it isn't a distinctly unpleasant life either. There is no great rush, no killing competition or nervous tension.

The Russians don't like to work, so they don't. They do perhaps six hours a day—and that slowly and badly. The rest of the time they devote to idleness and cultivating a refined sense of despondency and self-pity. But indolence and lack of method offer a certain human comfort.

Urban Not an overwhelmingly attractive picture . . .

Beam No—I would, if I were a Central or East European, certainly be a little hesitant to base my hopes for any improvement in my condition on the reforming zeal of either the Soviet system or the Russian people.

Vladimir Maximov

The Russian People and the West

Urban Our topic is: Russian popular reactions to the 1968 Prague Spring and, more generally, to libertarian reform in socialist societies of the Soviet type.

Two contrasting attitudes come to mind. One is a rather self-righteous condemnation of any attempt to question Soviet hegemony as rank ingratitude for Soviet sacrifices in the Second World War. This stance expresses itself not only in response to such major challenges to Soviet interests as the 1956 Hungarian Revolution and the 1968 Prague Reform Movement. Rather is it a visceral assertion of the power of the newly-arrived toward all-comers—a shared platform on which members of the Party apparat, Stalinists, bureaucrats, leaders of the military caste, Slavophile nationalists and men of no reasoned views but a good deal of ordinary bloody-mindedness ('if we can't have a better life why should they?') mix and mingle without embarrassment. I would, for want of a better word, call it a national-socialist attitude, because its nationalism is as irrational and its 'socialism' as phony as were those of the earlier, German variety.

The second attitude—very much a minority affair—stresses the guilt of the Russian individual who has come to realise the criminality of the Soviet moloch state, but has himself inescapably become an instrument and accomplice of it. Admirable character portraits of this type of man are given in your own novel *The Seven Days of Creation*. In Budapest, one of your characters says, 'we were sweeping those . . . barricades off the face of the earth. . . . We killed the wounded on the spot . . . including little boys . . . some of them were hardly fifteen.'

My interest in these reactions is twofold: do they, in fact, continue to exist thirty-three years after the war, twenty-two years after Hungary, and ten years after the Prague events? And if they do, has there been a perceptible shift from the hubris of Russian national-socialism to the equally Russian but soul-searching, self-mortifying and contrite attitude of those who would, if they could, make amends in their personal lives for the misdeeds of the Soviet system?

My own impression is—not least from what I have gathered from Andrei Amalrik in another series of discussions[1]—that the dominant strain in Soviet life is still, and some would say increasingly, the first type of attitude I have tried to describe.

Maximov Amalrik is entitled to his opinions, but the thought-processes of Soviet society are by no means as simple as Amalrik makes out. Even at the time of the 1956 Hungarian uprising, when Soviet opinion on matters concerning the outside world had hardly emerged from Stalinism, many ordinary Russian soldiers, and in some cases entire units, refused to fight the Hungarians and indeed passed over to the revolutionaries. Between 1956 and the 1968 Czechoslovak events, popular attitudes underwent further change and, more significantly, by 1968 the Russian intelligentsia, including the Party intellectuals, were strongly in favour of Czech reform Communism.

Let me give you some personal impressions. About a month after the Soviet occupation of Czechoslovakia a propaganda film was shown in the Soviet cinemas. I saw it in one of Moscow's biggest film theatres; the house was full and I especially remember shots of Antonin Liehm giving an interview. Somebody sitting next to me remarked in a loud voice: 'Just look at the face of that gangster!' I turned to him and said: 'You'd better look at your own face first.' Well, a heated exchange followed, but what was (for Soviet conditions) remarkable was that no one spoke up in support of my neighbour. If this had happened ten years earlier he would have had the whole audience loudly on his side, and I would most probably have ended up in prison. But not in 1968. This tells you something.

[1] *Eurocommunism*, pp. 236–54.

The great mistake Western people make, supported in many cases by our own emigrés, is to think of the Russian people as a nation born to be slaves or, at any rate, born without the guts to oppose oppression. This is historically and intellectually untenable. The Russians have protest in their blood—protest at the injustices of human institutions and the inadequacies of the human condition. Men like Solzhenitsyn, Sakharov, Bukovsky and all the other known and unknown representatives of the feelings of our people could not have arisen had it not been for the tensions generated by the Russian people's innate and perennial protest.

Urban I don't think I have ascribed any form of inborn slavishness to the Russian people—

Maximov No, but the Western belief that lack of freedom and lack of democracy are good enough for the Russians because they know no better, is a highly mistaken evaluation which leads to the misjudgment of the strengths of the Russian people and their potential for libertarian influence on the world stage at the right moment.

Urban But, to come back to our immediate problem, you would agree, would you not, that the kind of primitive envy which animated a great many ordinary Russians against Czechoslovakia in 1968—why should *they* have internal liberties if we can't?; why should *they* live better if we can't? etc.—was, and probably is, a widely shared Russian feeling? In your own novel we hear one of your characters, Osip, say: 'In Russia anyone who lives better than the rest is hated in his own way.' It would be surprising if this feeling did not also express itself on a national level, adding an unpleasant slant to traditional Russian xenophobia. Indeed, at another point in your novel you do yourself say: 'The Russian peasant . . . lives like a pig, so everybody else has got to live that way, too. That's why he hates Europe and despises the whole world.'

Maximov My novel is a polyphonic affair. It addresses itself to the condition of *man* rather than Russian man. It may be truthfully said of every country that you are envied and hated if your standard of living is grossly in excess of the majority's. France provides a good example.

The West is very eloquent about the sins of racial

prejudice, but it is precisely the Western intelligentsia that is guilty of something very close to racial prejudice *vis-à-vis* the Russian people. The intellectual presumption of thinking that something the French or British people would regard as outrageously demeaning is good enough for the *Russians* is a form of racism. A British Labour Party delegation recently visited Poland, and after their return to London one of their number was asked what he thought of conditions in Poland. 'Well,' he said, 'it is a mess, and *we* wouldn't for a moment put up with their system here in England, but I suppose it's all right for the Poles—they have different traditions.' Now, if this can be said of the *Poles*, you can imagine how much worse the Russians come out of any comparison.

It is illiberal and most mischievous, as well as historically inaccurate, to speak of nations as though there was a rank-order among them in respect of their dedication to liberty. No nation is born with congenital political defects any more than with qualities of superior intelligence. We saw between 1933 and 1945 how one of the most civilised nations in the heart of Europe was reduced to behaving with the morality of pigs! Yet it would be entirely wrong to say that the German people were somehow predestined to be ruled by Hitler.

Urban I don't think one has to posit a genetic typology of nations in order to allow the point that national characteristics, typical attitudes, thought-patterns, tastes, preferences and the like exist. One of these would appear to be the Russian people's extremely generous love of Mother Russia—and the abuses which it willingly suffers in the service of the motherland. Let me quote the words of yet another character from your novel—Mark Frantsevich, discussing the fortunes of a Soviet air force general:

> A full general . . . in a lunatic asylum. . . . Just look at him—he is contented. Yes, contented! This awful Russian nostalgia! He doesn't mind what he is—slave, or beggar, or homeless dog—as long as it's in his homeland. 'The homeland', he calls it! The fact that this very homeland has first disowned him, then made him run the gauntlet of its prison camps from Kolyma to Pot'ma, and finally, as a special favour, graciously permitted him to draw

rations in a madhouse till his grave is dug—none of that counts.

Maximov Well, arguments of this kind *must* be found in a Russian novel of our time simply because a large section of the Russian people has no experience of democracy. But this is a matter of education and historical background—not of any inborn imperfection.

Opposition to totalitarianism is daily growing in the Soviet Union. The Soviet occupation forces in Czechoslovakia had to be changed four times, and some 80 per cent of the troops now there come from the minority nations and nationalities. Why had this to be done? Because it took Soviet troops of *Russian* nationality only a few days to understand that there was no counter-revolution in Czechoslovakia and that the threat by NATO was Soviet make-believe. One of the staple charges against the Russian people consists of quotations taken from the Marquis de Custine's description of Russian servility in the 1830s, and to say that nothing has changed. Well, I could quote you several Russian publications which attribute the same sort of characteristics to the *French* people. Does that make them true? Of course not.

You have mentioned Amalrik as one source of your information. Well Andrei Amalrik suffers from a typical disease which tends to afflict certain members of the Russian emigration—the inclination to say what Western liberal thinkers and scholars *expect* them to say of the Soviet Union. If you want to be 'in' with these people, especially in England and the US, you have to be prepared to serve their intellectual and spiritual comfort by reinforcing their preconceptions about the Russian character and Russian psychology. Unless you agree, and indeed unless you advocate the idea that the Russian people deserve nothing better than Stalin and the KGB, your position in the Western intellectual community is precarious.

Urban You have recently participated, together with other distinguished French and Russian emigré intellectuals, in a round-table discussion organised by *Kontinent* of which you are the Editor. One of the most surprising but, to my mind, unmistakably Russian, statements came from the sculptor

Ernst Neizvestny. Discussing the question of what precisely constitutes personal happiness, this is what he said:

> I believe that happiness is evenly distributed in a person. One half sleeps in the happiness of the slave and the other half in the happiness of liberty. I myself experienced the happiness of the slave. Maybe that was the most delightful feeling in my life. I graduated from a military school where the discipline was strict, but where there was a problem of choice anyway. For instance, I could go to the latrine when I wanted to. But when they put me on a train and did not say where it was going, I lay down on the bench, and the train left, and I realised that they had liberated me from my will. They were taking me somewhere and they would feed me in time. There is a Russian proverb: 'The soldier sleeps, but duty goes on.' And I experienced a real feeling of happiness. I was totally free. I had obtained the freedom of the slave. That is why I know that the freedom of a slave is equal to the freedom of a free man.

Now, I would not argue that this sort of feeling is *inevitably* Russian, but I *would* say that it is more likely to come from the pen of a Russian than an Englishman or American. And I would, like you, not say so on biological grounds, but simply on grounds of historical and cultural experience.

Maximov The subject of our discussion at *Kontinent* was general and international: how is totalitarian thinking born and why do totalitarian societies exist? Neizvestny's point was that there is a totalitarian personality lurking in every one of us irrespective of nationality. We are, all of us, part slaves, part free men. Given the right historical conditions, the totalitarian side asserts itself and becomes dominant—

Urban —which is Jean-François Revel's thesis in *The Totalitarian Temptation*, and I noticed with interest that he contributed to your discussion.

Maximov Yes, he did, and he made the remarkable point—remarkable especially in the context of our present argument—that it was *after* Soviet tanks had appeared in Prague that the Italian and French Communist Parties experienced their greatest upswing since they had been founded. This does not strike me as a resounding confirmation of the Italian and French people's love of liberty or of their natural resistance to totalitarian political philosophies!

Let me give you a small example from my editorial experience. An article was recently offered to *Kontinent* by a Russian emigré living in the US on condition that it was printed under a pen-name. Almost simultaneously with the arrival of this contribution we received another, from the Soviet Union, signed by the author giving his full name. I telephoned the first man and told him:

> You claim to be a free person living in a free society—the US. You want me to print your article, but only under a pseudonym because you fear that using your real name might get you into some sort of unpleasantness. Yet here is this other man who lives in the Soviet Union, appending his full name to his article even though he knows well enough that he may have to pay for it with his life. Which of the two of you, then, is a *free* man? You or the other chap?

Let me say it again: bravery and cowardice, love of liberty and servility are not peculiar to any nation. They are warring elements in the minds of human beings. As Dostoyevsky says: 'Man's heart is a battleground.'

Urban I do, of course, understand that a novel, especially a *Bildungsroman* of the Soviet-Russian type, is a polyphonic creation. Yet you would not be a significant novelist if you failed to identify with some of your characters more than with others, and if the words of these characters did not convey themselves to the reader with complete conviction as your own 'message'. You must have had some such purpose in mind or else you would not have written the book you have.

For example, you stress time and again that the Russian people, through their great trials and sufferings, have rendered the rest of mankind a kind of premonitory service: Look at our fate and be redeemed by our crucifixion. 'The whole world curses us!' Kreps says to Vadim; 'Yet the world ought to bless Russia from now till doomsday, because with her own experience of Hell she's shown all the rest what not to do!' This is a Dostoyevskian idea which also occurs in Solzhenitsyn—an indelibly *Russian* idea in your novel, because it depicts the Russian people under Bolshevism as a sacrificial victim offered in an act of atonement by the rest of mankind. Am I misreading you?

Maximov Well, to deal with your parallel with Dostoyevsky first, Dostoyevsky spoke from a strictly Orthodox point of view which I do not share. Nor do I believe that the Russian people alone have put, as it were, an advance payment of suffering into the bank on which other nations may draw. *All* nations have done that at one time or another, and even if we were to restrict ourselves to the sufferings caused by Communism in Europe, the sacrifices of the East European peoples ought also to be included.

When Kreps says: 'the world ought to bless Russia from now till doomsday, because with her own experience of Hell she's shown all the rest what not to do', he is expressing a univeral truth about human suffering. We have, regrettably, learnt very little from his warning.

That said, it is of course true that the time and life of my central character, Pyotr Vasilievich, reflect my own life. His blind faith in the Party is *my* blind faith, his disillusionment is *my* disillusionment, his penance is *my* penance. I, too, denounced my father, who was arrested because I had spied on him. I, too, repudiated my errors only after the damage had been done. The only difference between Pyotr Vasilievich and myself is that in his case the curve of 'ideology–disillusion–guilt–and–redemption–through–faith' stretches over a long life, whereas I went through the same sequence of experiences in a much shorter period.

Urban I respect your courage to admit all this, but, to return to our principal theme, can it possibly be denied that Kreps's words, 'why did the Creator allow one particular people to become the sacrificial victim in an act of atonement?' do, in fact, refer to Russia, seeing that Kreps makes a point of telling us so at every turn?

Maximov Maybe so, but I can see nothing very dangerous in that.

Urban Well, if you are the Creator's 'one particular people' destined to redeem the rest of mankind, you are, in fact, the chosen race: a nation appointed by destiny to be the 'Godbearer', as Dostoyevsky puts it—and that is a dangerous notion.

Maximov Ah, it is a dangerous notion *if* you equate nationalism with totalitarianism and aggression. But contemporary Russian nationalism runs in precisely the opposite direction: it is a force *against* totalitarianism, *against* the expansionism of the Communist state, *against* the suppression of the independence of Poles, Czechs, Hungarians, Latvians and so on. The whole message of Solzhenitsyn's 'nationalism' (if that is the right word) is directed *against* Soviet hegemony. He pleads for the rapid curtailment of Soviet commitments abroad, for the withdrawal of Soviet troops and the concentration of Russian energies on the peaceful cultivation of the home country. This is, indeed, a unique phenomenon—the first time in modern history that the edge of nationalism is directed *against* aggrandisement and any sense of primacy among nations. What we have here is a nationalism which is, in effect, another word for self-preservation—a defensive and peaceful reaction to the depredations of ideology and totalitarianism. And that is why *Kontinent* is an organ of Russian national consciousness, Russian culture and the reconciliation and symbiosis of all nations within the Soviet state.

Urban A replay of 1848? Of *libertarian* nationalism?

Maximov The process is in some ways similar. Our nationalism is a response to the destruction of Russian culture, to the erosion of the identity of the Russian nation. We want to remain Russians—that is the meaning of our nationalism.

Urban But how much support is there for this anti-totalitarian sense of nationhood? I am perfectly prepared to acknowledge the importance of the wavering and disloyalty of Soviet forces in 1956 and 1968—but these happened under very special conditions: in the case of Hungary, the original garrison forces had been in the country for many years and were contaminated; in Czechoslovakia the complete lack of armed resistance must have driven *some* doubt into the skull of the most bone-headed Russian foot-slogger. But there is no evidence that I have heard of that the Soviet

Government has difficulty in harnessing Russian national pride to Soviet ambitions nationally or internationally.

Indeed, most of the evidence points the other way: dissidents, human rights activists, Helsinki watchers, people wishing to emigrate are either not understood or, more often, distinctly unpopular. Russian national sentiment seems to be carried on the surge of the spectacular advance of the Soviet state as a superpower.

Maximov Well, Czechoslovakia was invaded in the name of international—not national—slogans. The legitimation of putting Soviet troops into Czechoslovakia was NATO's alleged threat to the achievements of international socialism—

Urban —but would Soviet troops want to stand up for *those*? If it is true that Russian national feeling is strongly running against the Soviet system, why should Soviet troops prove reliable guardians of 'international socialism' seeing that 'international socialism' is, of course, only another name for Soviet hegemony?

Maximov First, as I've already said, minority troops had to be repeatedly brought to Czechoslovakia to stand up for 'international socialism'. The Russians had little stomach for it. Second, we must bear in mind the nature of totalitarianism. We are faced here with an all-encompassing, repressive machinery. Nothing and nobody can escape being drawn into it and serving it. In the last war we witnessed the efficiency with which totalitarianism entirely dominated the lives of Germans and Italians. They fought where they were sent to and carried out orders whatever their private thoughts. The Soviet system constitutes a similar, but much older, very much larger and totally inescapable net. I am as certain as can be that if Vlassov and his fifteen Soviet generals had not fallen into German hands but carried on fighting in the Red Army, Vlassov would have been one of those Soviet marshals who advocated and carried out with great glee the occupation of Czechoslovakia in 1968. The system tolerates no half-measures in thought or action.

The Politburo and members of the Central Committee are prisoners of it no less than the man in the street is. The powers of a man like Brezhnev himself are strictly limited. He may give the appearance of possessing unlimited might, but his ability to use power in the political sense is, in fact, not much greater than that of the humblest dustman in the streets of Moscow. Brezhnev may be wealthier, he may live more comfortably, and he may even be able to order the dustman to be put to death with impunity—*but he cannot say that there is no bread in the Soviet Union*! The machine would immediately get rid of him if he did. Khrushchev, you will remember, was dismissed for that kind of offence. Ideology sets a limit to what *any* Soviet leader can do and say. This is also the reason why the Western world is so dangerously mistaken in thinking that the Soviet Union can extend détente from American-Soviet relations to the international struggle for power and influence. The moment the Soviet leaders did that they would forfeit their title to legitimacy.

Urban In one sense, the Soviet system may be weak because it is repressive, but in another it does, precisely because it is repressive, guarantee a form of disciplined and readily available power 'on the set' as it were—armies of enormous might which are inextricably tied into the totalitarian network and do, therefore, constitute a threat to us no matter what the Russian private soldier may think when he is off duty. *On* duty he will carry out orders.

Maximov Well, in the first phase of the Nazi-Soviet war this was not at all what was happening. Millions of our men put up their hands very gladly and went into German captivity because they thought the Germans had come as liberators. But Hitler made the ghastly mistake of treating the Russians as inferiors, and this eventually saw to it that the Russian people fought him with the bitter resistance his methods so richly deserved.

But—lo and behold, the unimaginable is happening: the Western countries are repeating Hitler's ghastly error in the 1970s! They, too, are thinking of the Russians as a nation not really up to their own standards, not fully civilised, not quite deserving of human rights, not mature enough to be thought of as a member of the comity of democratic, free nations—and therefore not worth making sacrifices for!

The lesson is clear: the war was won by Hitler, not Stalin—or, if you like, by Hitler *for* Stalin—because the prejudices which governed Hitler's attitude to Russia now govern the policies of the Western nations.

Urban I'm a little puzzled. You are saying that in Czechoslovakia the Soviet troops were misled into believing that they were acting in the defence of the achievements of 'international socialism'—not Russian national interests—and that is why they could be more or less held in line. But this is not at all what we have learned about the springs of Russian behaviour. Indeed the contrary has always been assumed—not least during the war by Stalin himself—viz. that the ordinary Russian would readily fight for Russian *national* interests but not for the Soviet system. Are you in fact saying that, if it came to a serious crisis between the Soviet Union and the West, the Soviet Government would have a better chance of winning popular support if it said that it was fighting for 'international socialism' rather than the defence of the fatherland?

Maximov Whether the slogan would be socialism or nationalism would not be all that important. What *would* matter would be the attitude of the West. Napoleon's invasion of Russia was a success so long as he carried with him the message of the French Revolution. He proclaimed, in the first stages of his campaign, the brotherhood of men, freedom and equality, and the Russian people embraced him as their liberator. Later, however, all this went by the board, and he treated the Russian people as a nation of slaves: the Russians closed ranks and the invader was defeated. Hitler, as I've said, made a similar mistake but on an even larger scale.

The West has been warned. In a warlike situation it must make an unequivocal distinction between the Soviet system and the Russian people and avoid taking a superior 'I'll teach you democracy' type of attitude. If the West falls into Napoleon's and Hitler's error, the Soviet apparat will find it easy enough to activate the masses in the name of self-preservation.

Urban I don't know if there is a tendency in the Western countries to think of the Russian people as inferior—there is certainly none in the racist sense. But there is a fairly strongly-held opinion that whereas in a warlike situation the peoples of Poland, Hungary, Czechoslovakia and Rumania might not support Moscow, the Russian people would. It is the lack, or seeming lack, of any internal resistance to a despotic regime which has now lasted sixty years that translates itself into the opinion that a nation which has put up with all *that* cannot have an overpowering desire for freedom and democracy. This, of course, leaves open the question of whether freedom and democracy are always and everywhere a more desirable form of government than authoritarian rule. But whatever the answer to that question may be, the Western view of the matter has long been settled.

Maximov If what you say is true—and I can well believe that it is—I can only conclude that the Western world has a grossly mistaken idea of what the Russian people are about. I do not want to sound critical of the nations of Eastern Europe whose freedom-loving inclinations are in one way or another always assumed as proven, but it is an odd fact, is it not, that the Nobel prizes for resistance to tyranny have gone to Pasternak and Solzhenitsyn; that virtually all the great names in the civil rights movement are Russian (Sakharov, Plyushch, Bukovsky, Shafarevich, Orlov, Shcharansky and any number of others); and that even the occupation of Czechoslovakia evoked no public protest in any of the Central and East European countries, whereas it did in the Soviet Union, and arrests had to be made.

Or take the matter of trade unionism. Although daily life in the satellite countries is much freer in every respect than it is in the Soviet Union, it was a few dozen *Russian* workers who recently started a free trade union movement at great risk to themselves. Sakharov, with his international reputation, is (so far, at least) protected; but these unknown people are not. They knew well enough that they would come up against the full rigour of the Soviet law and persecution by the Soviet authorities. Yet they did it.

I am not at all sure that the West is right in thinking that whereas the Poles, Hungarians and Czechs might not fight for Moscow, the Russians would. My personal conviction is that, given the appropriate Western attitude—and this goes for the current cold-peace as much as for a warlike emergency—the Russian people would not support the Soviet system. In any case, who are the Russians? Would the Ukrainians put their lives on the line for Moscow? Would the Georgians? I doubt it. Western students of Soviet affairs should take a closer look at the lessons of the occupation of Czechoslovakia.

Urban You are, Mr Maximov, a man of profound historical knowledge. Your training as a Communist first equipped you with one set of keys to history, and, as we gather from your magnificent *The Seven Days of Creation*, your anti-Communist and religious outlook on life have now equipped you with another. You would, then, surely not quarrel with the proposition that a country's past is part of its historical (not biological) personality; and if you accepted this I would put it to you that a country which abolished serfdom only as late as 1861 is in some, admittedly ill-defined but nevertheless real, ways closer to the habit of tolerating unfreedom and authoritarian rule than, say, Holland or England.

Maximov The United States freed *its* slaves two years *after* the abolition of serfdom in Russia—in 1863—yet no one would suggest that we should today regard the Americans as a nation of slave-holders! It is fallacious and improper to draw historical judgments from one period and impose them lock, stock and barrel on another. The hunt for precedents and analogies can be as misleading as ignoring them altogether.

Also, let me remind you that according to the 1858–59 census, the number of serfs in Russia ran to no more than 37 per cent of the empire's population of about 60 million; and that side by side with serfdom one of the world's great literatures was being born.

Western ignorance of these matters is astounding. I was talking to a so-called expert on Russian affairs at the US Department of State the other day, and I expected him to be armed with at least *some* knowledge of the subject for which he drew a specialist's salary. Well, in the course of our conversation he insisted on dilating on Russia's historical backwardness. I told him to pick up any of the encyclopaedias on his shelves, look up the entry on Russia, and convince himself by statistical evidence that Tsarist Russia was in the 1900–1914 period *the* world leader in economic growth and modernisation, and that the Soviet Union has in many respects never caught up with Russia as she was in 1914. Alas, the extraordinary backwardness of the *Soviet system*—not Russia—had to be paid for with 50 million lives!

Urban I never cease marvelling at the pride with which many of the old White Russian emigrés now living in France and England look upon the new-found might of the Soviet Union and the respect it commands. These people appear to have long forgotten why they had fled Russia. They now identify with the Soviet state on the reasoning that, highly objectionable though the Soviet regime may be, it *has* turned Russia into a force which has drawn level with the Western world and is powerful enough to keep mighty America as well as Germany, France and Britain in a state of permanent anxiety.

Wouldn't this kind of psychology ('it is a wicked system, but has muscle and is *ours*') operate *a fortiori* inside the Soviet Union and secure the loyalty of otherwise reluctant Russians and Ukrainians? The success of the Nazi war effort was arguably based on a like sentiment.

Maximov It is certainly odd that the old emigrés and the new Soviet bureaucracy should share a platform on this question. But the fact is that neither group matters. These are dead people—the old emigrés because they are old emigrés, and the Soviet bureaucrats because they are Soviet bureaucrats. They represent no one—East or West.

Urban It seems to me that whatever the real strengths and weaknesses of the Soviet system may be, the regime is assumed to be immensely powerful and secure both by the Western Left and by the Western Right for psychological reasons of their own. The Left—and especially the far Left—has a deep-seated need to believe that the Soviet system, whatever its shortcomings, enjoys popular support; and the Conservatives, projecting *their* psychology onto the Soviet scene, tend to believe that the Russian people take nationalistic pride in the fear and respect their country inspires—never mind disappointments in the supply of fresh vegetables.

Maximov Rationalisation and wish-fulfilment are powerful agents in shaping our attitudes. The trouble is that they tend to have a very threadbare contact with reality. Given the right psychological bias we can prove that the Khmer

Rouge in Cambodia are, 'objectively speaking', the world's foremost fighters for civil liberties; that the 'Protocols of the Elders of Zion' is the action-programme of world Jewry to enslave the world's gentiles; that three persons praying for ten minutes each stand a better chance of being heard by God than one person praying for thirty minutes (a bone of serious contention in mediaeval theology)—you can prove anything. To stay nearer home, take the case of M. Peyrefitte, French Minister of Justice, of all things. He has recently written a book on China in which the Communist regime is described in very favourable terms—it is certainly good enough for the *Chinese*, opines the Minister of Justice!

Well, what the Western Left and Right think and say of the Soviet system tells us something about the Western Left and Right, but nothing at all about the Soviet Union. For that we have to look at the state of the Soviet system as it really is, and that is what we are trying to do in the modest framework of this conversation.

Urban Your principal characters in *The Seven Days of Creation* have an apocalyptic vision of the collapse of the Soviet system and indeed of the future of the Russian nation: 'Rage is stifling Russia. If it ever breaks its bonds, blood will be held cheaper than water.'

What sort of a catastrophe do you foresee?

Maximov The moment of truth may come when the Soviet Government has exhausted its stock of lies and has no more to say to the people. That may be the time for the final *dénouement*. It might, one fears, take the form of a multiple conflict between the various nations and nationalities. But this must be prevented.

The Democratic Movement has long set itself the task of preparing a framework for the free coexistence of the various nations and nationalities if and when Soviet rule comes to an end. We have already made a great deal of headway—Georgian democrats helping Armenians, Ukrainians taking up the cause of the Crimean Tatars, and so on. For more than six decades, national feeling has been denied an outlet. We must do everything in our power to prevent the rise of mindless, runaway and mutually destructive nationalisms by filling out each nation's consciousness with democratic meaning, and doing it *now*.

Urban I can see this working well enough as long as the totalitarian state provides a common adversary. But should that disappear—would the various nations and nationalities not fall out among themselves and submerge Russia in chaos? My impression is that you are anxious to preserve the integrity of the Russian state, that is, of the *Soviet* state as it exists at present.

Maximov It is an absolutely universal interest to preserve the peace and promote cooperation on the basis of equality among the various nations that now make up the Soviet Union. The West can do a great deal by supporting the Democratic Movement and by stressing in its general attitude, and especially in its broadcasts to the various nations and nationalities, that any post-Soviet *dénouement* must be democratic, collaborative and libertarian.

The enlightened self-interest of the West, too, would seem to militate for a policy of that kind, because chaos or civil war in a state of the size of the Soviet Union could not be contained within Soviet borders, any more than the upheavals of 1917 could.

Urban If the collapse of Soviet power threatens to bring such awesome consequences in its wake for the peace of Europe and possibly for the peace of the world, aren't we better off with the *status quo*? This may fall short of what we would ideally wish, but it does secure a recognisable order; it keeps Ukrainians and Russians, Rumanians and Hungarians, Czechs and Slovaks from flying at each other's throats and—more important—we have thirty-three years' evidence on hand to show that our understanding with the Soviet state has kept the peace in Europe. It is, indeed, a seriously held view in some Western capitals that the present Pax Sovietica over the traditionally most quarrelsome and ethnically most mixed parts of Europe is something we ought willingly to accept even though we may find it politically embarrassing to praise it.

Maximov If this is a moot to provoke me, I shall ignore it, but if your view is seriously held, I will counter with an even more provocative scenario. If the Pax Sovietica is good enough for Russians and East Europeans and if, therefore, nothing is to be done to roll it back or even to contain it effectively (and *I* can see nothing that is being done on either score), then the West will no doubt also welcome the extension of the Pax Sovietica to Britain, for example, where it would immediately put paid to the troubles in Northern Ireland, or to France where the arrival of Soviet tanks in the streets of Paris would at once take care of Corsican nationalism. Indeed, a Pax Sovietica over the whole of Europe would be the perfect answer to European security: 'Why spend hard cash on self-defence when Soviet power can guarantee *your* security too?!'

There is, alas, no remedy for stupidity. Has the West learned nothing from the Nuremberg trials? From Hitler's Pax Germanica? After all, that, too, established a 'recognisable order'—but it was the order of the cemetery. Peace under Soviet suzerainty is no better.

Urban I infer from what you have told me about the internal weaknesses of the Soviet system that Czechoslovak armed resistance in August 1968 might have set off a chain reaction. Is this, in fact, what you think?

Maximov No one can be certain what the consequences would have been. But I do know that armed resistance was what the Soviet leaders feared most. For three whole days the Central Committee was in continuous session because there was a presumption that the Czechs might fight, and that this would provoke further trouble elsewhere in Eastern Europe and indeed in the Soviet Union. I don't think it is very important for us to assess what prospects of success simultaneous rebellions in different parts of Eastern Europe would have had—the thing to remember is that the danger of internal disintegration was foremost in the minds of the Soviet leadership. As one official connected with the Central Committee put it to me, 'All we need for this big house to be brought down around our ears is a small incident.'

Urban But if the system is so weak—why is it so strong? Why do we go around thinking that we wouldn't last one week in a military conflict with the Soviet Union? That self-Finlandisation is the better part of virtue? That we should not sell military aircraft to the Chinese in case the Russians should take offence? Have we got *everything* wrong about the Soviet Union?

Maximov The Soviet leaders have long memories. They

know perfectly well that now, as earlier in Russian history, a meat-queue in Poland or a bread-queue in Kiev could be the signal for intense trouble.

How did the February Revolution set Russia on fire? Precisely in that fashion: discontented housewives queuing for bread in short supply, reinforced by a demonstration of women celebrating International Women's days; a false statement by the authorities that there *were* ample supplies of bread in the shops; a general strike in Petrograd; an ukase by the Tsar to the city commandant to restore order; an ineffective threat to mobilise all workers who refused to return to their jobs; clashes with the soldiers and mutiny by the Pavlovsky regiment who refused to fire into the demonstrators.

That's how it started. That's how the Bolsheviks eventually came to power—and that's how they may one day be catapulted *out* of power. And well they know it. This is why internal security is the overriding concern of the Soviet leadership. They are not afraid of trouble abroad—it is the spectre of internal disintegration that has haunted them since the days of the October Revolution.

But why then is it, you rightly ask, that the Western world lives in mortal fear of this clay-footed giant?

Western societies are democratic societies. They are, by definition, peacable societies; indeed, when set against the militancy of Soviet behaviour, they are *capitulationist* societies. The Soviet Union, on the other hand, is governed by ideological militancy *and* a psychological attitude of great self-confidence which stems from victory in the last war—the belief that the Soviet Union is and will remain a natural victor. Add to all this Moscow's vast conventional power ready in place along its Western border, and you will agree that the West has reason to worry.

But the Soviet leaders themselves take a very calm view of the chances of international conflict. Time and again they have discovered—and Czechoslovakia was only the latest flagrant example—that the Western countries have neither the will nor perhaps the power to put the Kremlin under critical pressure.

Urban I'm still slightly puzzled. You have now argued two points which seem to me contradictory: first, that the

Soviet machine is immensely strong by virtue of the totalitarian and militant character of the system and, second, that the Soviet Union is extremely weak because it enjoys no popular support.

Can it be strong and weak at the same time?

Maximov It can. The two operate on different levels. Once you have been sucked into the machine you are a prisoner of the machine: you march with it, you identify with it, you serve it because there is no alternative. So, at the level of the apparat in the broadest sense, the system feeds on the solidarity of men who have committed so many crimes and errors together and have exploited their privileged positions to such disproportionate advantage that they must hang together if they don't want to hang separately. And as long as the system exists, the machine operates with impressive force.

But, on an entirely different level, the system is up against the silent resistance of the whole population *and* the centrifugal pressures of the various nations and nationalities, and the whole of Eastern Europe. It is here that the Soviet Union is most vulnerable. Any accident in Poland or Yugoslavia, for example, might set off a chain-reaction. I have heard it said by people very close to the Central Committee that if in an armed conflict with the Soviet Union the Yugoslavs sustained organised resistance for a bare two weeks, the entire Soviet system might begin to shake.

Urban You have said that your Democratic Movement is based on the recognition of the complete freedom of all nations and nationalities in the Soviet state, and that you don't want to see the Soviet state disintegrate. Would I be right in thinking that what you really want is the preservation of a large *Russian* state along the present borders of the Soviet Union but removed from Soviet rule? A 'Holy Roman Empire of the *Russian* nation'?

Maximov You would be entirely wrong to think that. The purpose of the Democratic Movement is to provide the various nations and nationalities of the Soviet Union with a philosophy which will hold them together in a cooperative framework—*now*, as well as if and when Soviet power has ceased to exist. We are, as I have said, Russian nationalists only in the defensive sense of the word. We don't stand for Russian hegemony; we stand for its opposite. We are, indeed, anxious to provide that very cement between the nations constituting the Soviet Union which Marxism, with its abysmally faulty analysis, has always and everywhere failed to provide. Soviet rule has not resolved the conflict of nations: it has suppressed it, bottled it up, swept it under the carpet—pick your metaphor. Only liberty, tolerance, the spirit of compromise and forgiveness can resolve it—and these do not occur in the Marxist-Leninist blueprint. Indeed, in Marx's philosophy of social hatred and Manichaeism there *can* be no room for liberty, tolerance and the spirit of forgiveness.

Hugh Seton-Watson

The Fall of Multi-national Empires in Our Time

National consciousness and nationalism

Urban I suppose it is uttering a platitude, but one which is necessary to my argument, that no need in human affairs clamours more persistently for our attention than the need to assign meaning to our personal existence by appointing it a place and function in some seamless explanation of the human adventure. In other words: man is a worshipping animal and a system-building animal.

Hegel defined this need rather tellingly in the words *bey sich selbst seyn*—to be at home and at peace with one's universe, to refuse to become driftwood in some heterogeneous mix of races, cultures and languages. Anthropologists, psychologists and sociologists have shown in their different ways how religions, utopias and ideologies all minister to our desire for philosophic certainty and attempt to allay our fear of the contingency of human life and achievement.

All that need concern us in the present context is the capacity of nationalism to provide one such framework of philosophic certainty, bearing in mind that nationalism, as it has been known to us in this century, has often been a far cry from that earlier nationalism of libertarian provenance which swept Europe in the wake of the French Revolution and resulted in the momentous upheavals of 1848–49.

Today the prevailing attitude to nationalism—certainly the white man's nationalism—among Western intellectuals of liberal or socialist inclinations is to berate it as a deplorable regression. And one can quite see that a perspective of history which has made it possible for nineteenth-century Poles to claim, with Mickiewicz, that *they* are the 'Christ-nation' after whose resurrection 'wars shall cease in all Christendom'; for nineteenth-century Russians that in *them* has been vested the privilege of embodying God's special message on earth; for nineteenth-century Italians to make an almost identical claim in support of the *Risorgimento*; and for twentieth-century Germans to demand world leadership in the name of a Teutonic destiny—one can, as I say, quite see that a *Weltanschauung* of this kind has not much appeal to the liberal mind, and is indeed an invitation for it to be dismissed as harmful and nonsensical.

It may well be both—but rightly or wrongly the world is not what intellectuals would like it to be. It is irrational as much as it is rational, and nationalism shows no signs of weakening, much less of disappearing. Indeed, deep down in the heart of every one of us there is, I suspect, a 'nationalism' of sorts, if perhaps only in the most benign sense of Hegel's *bey sich selbst seyn*—as a search for community, a common language and protection.

My question, then, is: what is your reading of the political and cultural significance of contemporary nationalism? Does it contain elements that might balance its proven ability to disrupt and to destroy? Is it in some ways the residuary legatee of 1848? Has it any merit as a substitute for religion, seeing that religion has a diminishing influence on our culture?

Seton-Watson I would begin with a distinction between nationalism and national culture. Nationalism—by which I mean either a doctrine about the rights of a nation, or a movement which pursues certain objectives in the name of that doctrine—has created a series of ghastly international crises in the last hundred years. Appalling crimes have been and are still being committed in its name so that one has no hesitation in saying: nationalism is a pest. But national consciousness, the individual person's conviction that he is part of a nation and of a national culture in which he has grown up and in which his parents grew up before him, is perfectly right and natural. It provides a necessary framework for most people's desire to 'belong', and, certainly in Europe and the US, it frequently went together with a commitment to religion.

The danger arises when loyalty to the nation takes the place of religious beliefs and the nation becomes God. That is the point where national consciousness grows into a mortally dangerous nationalism. The classic example is the story of German nationalism: German national consciousness around 1800 was a rather admirable, mild, culture-based patriotism which became perverted in Hitler's Third Reich, until the German *Volk* was elevated to divine status and crimes on an unparalleled scale were committed in its name. One would hope today, after all those horrors, that nations which have achieved a high level of national culture, and whose status is more or less assured, might at last prove able to combine with one another for practical purposes. The European Community is an association of that kind, though it has great inadequacies. Still, we must not expect a community of that sort to evoke in individual men and women the same emotional loyalties as nations and religions do.

Urban But how difficult was it to make the jump from national consciousness to nationalism? If we agree, as I think we do, that modern nationalism is rooted in Herder, then the jump was, in certain circumstances, rather easy to make and perhaps inevitable. For what did Herder say? He believed that each nation is a self-contained microcosm grouped around its language and its linguistic culture. Each nation differs from every other according to its inner character. Each has its intellectual and spiritual *Gestalt* which makes it incommensurate with other nations. Each is a manifestation of the Divine and therefore sacred.

Now Herder surrounded these assertions with a number of important caveats: each nation, he said, is only *one* element—different but equal—in the concert of nations in which history unfolds its great wealth. Each has its unique contribution to make to the splendour and variety of human existence. And although all nations are different, they obey one rule: only moderation and reciprocity make them happy. 'The human race is one whole,' he wrote; 'we work and suffer, sow and harvest, each for all.'

But, as so often in history, Herder's message was soon

bent to the designs of men whose purpose was not always disinterested enquiry. Herder's emphasis on the uniqueness and divinity of nations was heard to the *exclusion* of his emphasis on their equality and their shared duty to unfold through civilisation the potentialities of mankind.

I will not pursue the distortions which Herder's idea of the nation underwent at the hands of Pan-German and Pan-Slavic nationalists, for the story is well known. Let me simply quote a famous Slavophile passage from Dostoyevsky's *The Possessed*, not only because it is symptomatic of the degeneration of Herder's idea into Slavic messianism, but also because it prefigures the twentieth-century German variety:

> The people is the body of God. Every people is only a people so long as it has its own god and excludes all other gods on earth irreconcilably; so long as it believes that by its god it will conquer and drive out of the world all other gods. . . . A nation which loses this belief ceases to be a nation. But there is only one truth, and therefore only a single one of the nations can have the true God. . . . Only one nation is 'god-bearing', that's the Russian people . . .

I would, therefore, cautiously conclude that there was, in Herder's writings, enough emphasis on national exclusiveness, national self-glorification and the divine nature of nationhood to make the jump from national culture to a rabid nationalism a fairly easy one, particularly when, as in the German case, occupation by the Napoleonic armies and, a century later, a lost world war, offered incentives to hurt national sentiment and made nationalism a handy tool of state policy.

Seton-Watson The jump was not inevitable. Let us look at the conditions under which nationalism most easily arises. This is when an elite group of a community with a common culture believe themselves to be prevented from developing their culture by foreign rule. This causes them to react against foreign rule and seek national independence; or if they happen to be divided among different states, to seek national unity. How either is brought about depends on a number of unpredictable factors, such as the quality of leadership in the national movement and among the alien rulers, and the influence of a number of extraneous forces independent of either the alien rulers or the national leaders.

The First World War offers good examples. Its immediate cause was a number of frustrated national aspirations in Austria, Hungary and the Balkans as well as in the Russian empire. But, of course, other factors were also important in causing the war to happen, and causing it to be fought in the way in which it was. These created passions of their own, so that the eventual collapse of Austria-Hungary was only loosely connected with the original national aspirations. This did not prevent a great many people from feeling and saying at the time that the rulers of Austria had been wicked men who were defeated and punished for their crimes—and that the leaders of the Czechs and Yugoslavs were virtuous men who received their just award. We can now see that this was nonsense: there were good men and bad men, merit and demerit, all round.

If you say that Hitler was derived from the German national idea of the nineteenth century, Fichte for example, this is true up to a point; what you cannot say is that the national aspirations of Germans for unity, as they were worked out at the beginning of the nineteenth century under the first impact of Herder's wide influence, could *only* have ended in Hitler. They could have ended in many different ways. National consciousness does not *have* to lead to nationalist movements and conflict. National consciousness *may* lead to nationalism and conflict if it is frustrated, but even nationalist conflicts can end up as a beneficent force, provided that there is statesmanship, wisdom and moderation.

It would, therefore, be very wrong to argue as follows: 'Nationalism is a destructive force, therefore let's suppress national consciousness.' That is what many governments have tried to do; they justify their repression of the national consciousness of their subjects on the grounds that they themselves stand for a higher civilisation—could there be anything wrong, they argue, in freeing these recalcitrant minorities from the beastly distemper of nationalism? Well, if history teaches us anything it is this, that the attempt to repress national consciousness is almost always self-defeating. This does not, of course, mean that people who make national claims on the basis of national consciousness are always right—but that is another story.

Urban Can we look at some examples?

Seton-Watson One is obviously Hungary in the second half of the nineteenth century, after the 1867 Compromise. The rulers of late nineteenth-century Hungary were men of a rather broad European outlook. They had genuinely liberal convictions, and they were justly proud of Hungarian culture which had made great progress in the preceding decades and went on making progress right up to 1914. These men genuinely believed that Slovaks, Rumanians and others who had been brought into this culture had benefited, and that Slovak and Rumanian nationalism was a reactionary phenomenon which ought not to be tolerated. The result was that although there were, and had been for some time, Rumanians and Slovaks who were attracted by Hungarian culture and did enter into it to the extent of becoming Hungarians, more and more they found themselves put off by an arrogant 'Magyarisation' and became bitterly nationalistic. Thus the Hungarian policy of repressing national consciousness ended up by strengthening minority nationalism and eventually destroying Hungary herself.

Another example: Canada under the Governor-Generalship of Lord Durham in the 1840s. Faced with the divisions between English- and French-speaking Canadians (there had been two rebellions before his appointment), Lord Durham put forward various proposals for constitutional reform. These were extremely well thought out, so much so that to this day Canadian democracy derives largely from his initiative. But in his famous report, on which these reforms were founded, he said categorically that the French-speaking people of Quebec were a primitive people, speaking an antiquated and bad French, that their priest-ridden parochial outlook (he didn't even think it deserved to be described as a culture) was bound to disappear, and that French-speaking Canadians would be happily absorbed into the much more civilised English culture. And now look what has happened a hundred years later! The Quebec French are more fervently nationalistic than ever, and they are talking of seceding from

Canada. Durham completely failed to appreciate the problem of national consciousness.

It is extremely dangerous for members of one national culture to say to another that it is inferior and should accept assimilation. On the other hand, it is certainly true that some national cultures are more advanced and more attractive than others. In Spain, for example, over the centuries millions of Basques and Catalans have become Castilian Spaniards and have been absorbed into the Castilian Spanish nation. Nevertheless many others have stuck to their identity and have become Basque and Catalan nationalists.

Urban The paradox is that the belittlement and absorption of 'inferior' minority cultures was part and parcel of the typically nineteenth-century faith in progress, the educability of man and the democratic duty of the more highly educated to lead those who need their guidance. This may strike us, with hindsight, as an insufferable paternalism, but in the nineteenth century it was an important plank in an enlightened man's philosophy.

Seton-Watson That is true. What is interesting to observe is the way in which this ideology of a superior culture—liberalism, to call it by its shorthand name—was identified by these admirably liberal politicians of the nineteenth century with their *own* nationality—for example, with English (or British, if you like) nationality, as in the case of Canada.

Now something similar has happened in our own time in the Soviet Union. There, rapid industrial and economic progress combined with the ideology of international communism has been identified by the rulers of the Soviet Union with an essentially crude Russian nationalism: the Soviet rulers are forcing Russian nationalism down the throats of Uzbeks, Latvians, Ukrainians and others, while at the same time telling them and the world that they are simply 'building socialism'. Abstractly considered, socialism may be defended as an advanced form of human society, but what these Uzbeks and Ukrainians and Latvians are getting is Russification. The same is true of the Polish experience of Soviet-Russian nationalism. As a result of Russian pressure, the people of Poland are now compelled to rewrite their history in such a way as to show that throughout Polish history the best friends of the Polish people have been the noble Russians. This creates immense rage in Poland—not just among history professors, but among ordinary Polish working people. It is, of course, entirely counter-productive.

Urban I must confess I find something attractive about the nineteenth-century liberal approach to the problem of nationhood—for on what ground can we fault the idea that a backward culture has a great deal to learn from, and indeed should aspire to the condition of, a more advanced culture? If that is nonsense, then the whole idea of education, of passing knowledge and experience and wisdom from one generation to the next, is nonsense too. If all cultures are of equal merit, or should be treated as if they were, I cannot see what right we have to make a fuss over Beethoven while failing to hold high the aesthetic significance of the liturgy of head-shrinking in Papua.

Your mention of Basque nationalism reminds me of something that John Stuart Mill says about the Basques' place in French civilisation:

> Experience proves that it is possible for one nationality to merge and be absorbed in another: and when it was originally an inferior and more backward portion of the human race the absorption is greatly to its advantage. Nobody can suppose that it is not more beneficial to a Breton, or a Basque of French Navarre, to be brought into the current of the ideas and feelings of a highly civilized and cultivated people—to be a member of the French nationality, admitted on equal terms to all the privileges of French citizenship, sharing the advantages of French protection, and the dignity and prestige of French power—than to sulk on his own rocks, the half-savage relic of past times, revolving in his little mental orbit, without participation or interest in the general movement of the world.

Surely as a university professor you would approve of a brighter and more advanced student exerting his influence on a less bright or less experienced one; and surely a younger or intellectually less well endowed student would take no offence (indeed he would relish the opportunity) if he were tutored and assimilated by a student with a better reading record, a more cultivated home and a greater intellectual curiosity than he himself possesses. By the same token, I cannot see why it should have been wrong for nineteenth-century Slovaks, Rumanians, Slovenes or Croats to be assimilated into Austrian and Hungarian culture, seeing that the latter were quite clearly, and had been for centuries, superior in their music and literature and learning. And it wasn't that the leading spokesmen of Hungarian cultural nationalism were satisfied that Hungarian culture was all *that* highly advanced—if anything, they spent an excessive part of their time brooding over and attacking Hungary's own backwardness and idealising the 'cultured' West, especially England and France.

I don't want to lend support to any Soviet policy of Russification, but it would be unreasonable to deny that the kind of cultural superiority which, for example, Lermontov's characters enjoy, in *A Hero of our Time,* over semi-savage Circassians in the Caucasus had some tangible justification, and it is at least arguable that even today Circassian culture stands to benefit from Russian influence. The real problem with the Soviet Russians arises when they try to Russify cultures which are superior to their own, running counter not only to nineteenth-century liberalism (they would hardly mind that) but also to Lenin's warning that a superior culture always comes out on top of a less developed culture even if the former is militarily conquered by a nation of inferior culture (and Lenin was, of course, echoing Marx).

Seton-Watson To stick to my Austro-Hungarian example: Austrian culture had many admirable qualities, and when the Austrian empire was destroyed something very valuable was lost (fortunately not completely lost, for it has left its traces), because the Austro-Hungarian monarchy was, potentially at least, the most promising association of numerous nations in one state. But why was it destroyed? Because its rulers were unable to find an arrangement whereby the growing national cultures of its constituent nationalities could be satisfied.

Take the Slovaks, who were probably the most primitive. From the time of the Hungarian conquest, about a thousand years ago, the Slovaks were peasants; they spoke a different language from the Hungarian peasants. Their rulers were big landlords, some of them spoke Slovak, some Hungarian, but whatever their language, they were the upper class of the kingdom of Hungary and the Slovaks were their serfs and lived the sort of life serfs lived in mediaeval Europe—not always utterly miserable but essentially unfree and poor. Then, in the eighteenth century, schools were introduced, and the bright sons of Slovak peasant families began to get an education. There had already been a small number of Slovak children who had gone to theological training colleges to become pastors and Catholic priests—to these was now added a broader stratum of young Slovaks who began to mix with Hungarian and German children and to read Hungarian and German books, thus becoming aware of modern ideas of popular sovereignty, democracy and so on. Above all, they became aware of their own language and eventually applied their knowledge to working out a literary Slovak to replace a number of loosely connected Slavic dialects.

This process was immensely exciting. The discovery of Slovak as a national language, the scientific development of the language, the use of the language for poetry, thrilled these young Slovaks, and, of course, it was not long before they began to feel that it was their duty to speak up for the people who spoke the Slovak language. Until this time it would have been quite absurd to say, and nobody did say, that because there were about a million people who spoke Slovak dialects, there was a Slovak nation. But after some thousands of Slovaks had acquired a modern European education, such at any rate as was available in 1790 or 1830, they began to demand for their people the same kind of liberties as other peoples in Europe were asking for. More and more they thought of the Slovaks as a nation, and the claims of Slovaks were put forward as the claims of a nation. This worried the Hungarian rulers who were perfectly willing to encourage individual Slovaks to better themselves, but would never admit the idea of a Slovak nation. Here lay the beginnings of the conflict between Hungarians and Slovaks.

Now the governments in Vienna tried their best (whether

their task was possible or not we shall never know) to find a solution to the problem of minority cultures growing into nationhood, followed by claims for the recognition of nationhood. They did not succeed. There *were* people in Austria, particularly Austrian socialists like Karl Renner and Otto Bauer, who put forward—admittedly, late in the day—a number of highly intelligent ideas for the reorganisation of the monarchy in such a way that, while the central government's policies would be binding on all citizens, each community with a distinct national culture—each 'nationality', to use the word which was current in Austria—would enjoy complete cultural autonomy, which would cover not only every nationality as a compact body but also all its members individually wherever they lived. (For example, a Slovak living in Trieste would have the same right to have his culture respected, to have his children educated in his own language, and so on, as a Slovak living in Presov.) However, these ideas could not be put into practice because the Socialists did not get into office, and it was probably too late anyhow: by the time the First World War broke out the different 'nationalities' had thrown up bitter nationalist movements which could not be contained.

Urban We may observe a similar process in the British and French empires: the rulers of the empire extend education to their colonies, the colonies, in turn, produce intellectual and later nationalist elites, who then demand sovereign rights for their newly emerged nations and ultimately destroy the empire.

Seton-Watson Yes—what we have to remember is the novelty of this exercise in nationalism. Going back to the Habsburg monarchy again: until the mid-nineteenth century, Slovaks, Hungarians, Rumanians, Ruthenians lived and quarrelled together, but their quarrels had not been national quarrels—they had been conflicts between landlords and tenants; between rival landlords or rival princes; or else they occurred in the backwash of wars between the Habsburg monarchy and neighbouring states. Nationalism had not been a factor. But once the idea of popular sovereignty, from which all democracy has descended, had taken root among the educated, national aspirations began to appear and somehow they had to be satisfied. We are back at our original problem: how does one satisfy national consciousness and national aspirations—which are essentially cultural phenomena—without disrupting the state? By definition, *nationalism* aims at a state the borders of which are coextensive with the nation. *National consciousness* does not require anything of the sort, but if national consciousness is repressed by attempts to denationalise the group in question, then you *create* a demand for an independent nation state.

Urban One good illustration of your point is the change in Frantisek Palacky's attitude to the Austrian empire between 1848 and the late 1860s: when the Czechs were invited by the 1848 Frankfurt Assembly to join the German confederation as a German nation, Palacky rejected the offer in the famous words: 'if the Austrian state had not existed for ages, we would be obliged in the interests of Europe and even of mankind to endeavour to create it as fast as possible'. His argument was that a united German national state would weaken Austria and thus undermine the chances of the small nations within the Austrian empire withstanding Pan-Slavic Russian expansionism and Hungarian intransigence. Palacky saw the growth of Russian power as 'an infinite and inexpressible evil, a misfortune without measure or bound which I, though heart and soul a Slav, would nonetheless deeply regret for the good of mankind even though that monarchy proclaimed itself a Slav one', and he believed that only a strong, just, multi-national Austria could contain the ambitions of the Tsar's dreaded 'universal monarchy' ('totalitarian state' would be our word for it). But when, after the 1867 Hungarian Compromise, Palacky saw his hopes frustrated for the equal treatment of the Czechs as a nation, he joined the Pan-Slavists and turned on Austria as a Czech nationalist. It was then that he said of the Czechs: 'Before Austria existed, we existed; and we shall still be there when Austria has ceased to exist.'

Seton-Watson The practical problems of satisfying claims of national autonomy are immensely complicated. It is not just a straightforward matter of a national group making a claim and a supranational government accepting or not accepting that claim: third-party interests have to be taken into account, constitutional difficulties arise, and there are always large economic interests involved for or against promoting the claims of a particular nationalist movement.

I'm coming back to my basic generalisation that national consciousness is a reality. All over the world there are millions of people who accept and take for granted their national culture because it answers the questions: Who am I? Where do I belong? There are, of course, many other people, especially in the advanced industrial countries, who just don't care, which is lamentable, and yet others who suffer from an identity crisis and are looking for some new loyalty—liberal internationalism, Communism, the United Nations, and so on. But national culture is the framework in which the vast majority of people live and want to go on living. And as it does by and large satisfy the human need of giving individual men and women a role in life, a common language, and a sense of being protected—and this takes us back to the original theme of your questioning—we are perfectly entitled to say that national consciousness is a good thing—indeed it is vital to our moral and psychological welfare.

The problem we cannot answer with any certainty is: how do we design a state organisation which both guarantees the effectiveness of central government and permits the unhindered development of national cultures? For it is clear to me that it may often be far better to preserve large states in so far as they have shown their ability to permit and to promote the symbiosis of a variety of national cultures, than to break them up into a lot of small states whose liberalism, even *vis-à-vis* their own people and culture, is most questionable. It is in this sense that we can, I think, rightly regret the disappearance of the Austrian empire as well as of the British empire. Palacky writing in 1848 was right—a look at the map of Europe in 1978 gives us a measure of his prescience.

Lessons from Austria-Hungary

Urban I cannot let slip this opportunity of asking you as a distinguished son of a distinguished father what you think of the part which R. W. Seton-Watson and Wickham Steed, his close friend and associate, played in destroying or, at any rate, accelerating the destruction of the Austro-Hungarian monarchy. As you know much better than perhaps anyone else, your father's and Steed's names are not among the most popular in Austria and Hungary. In the successor states, on the other hand, their names were, especially in the 1920s and 1930s, among the most celebrated. The question is interesting on many grounds, but it interests me most because the destruction of the Habsburg Monarchy has absolutely borne out Palacky's prophecy: the Austrian multi-national state has disappeared and, after a spell of ephemeral national independence, both its successors and the two halves of the mother-country itself came under the domination, first of an expansionist German state, and then of an equally expansionist and even more powerful Soviet Russia. And there, with the exception of Austria and the partial exception of Yugoslavia, they remain.

It would seem to me, to take the problem on broader ground, that R. W. Seton-Watson—like Woodrow Wilson—was drawing on the Anglo-American experience. What they were basically both saying was this: 'We are persuaded from our own history that only people who are self-governing are well governed, therefore we support every people's right to self-determination.' But what the nations (nationalities) in the Habsburg Monarchy were claiming was something quite different: 'Only a people which lives within its own state is a free nation, therefore we demand self-determination.' The first implies that self-government equals a just, free and compassionate society, while the second simply asserts that the attainment of national independence *is* freedom. Soon it was to be attested by history that this arrogant identification of liberty with nationalism degenerated into the freedom to be *ill*-governed and indeed to be *despotically* governed.

Seton-Watson It is quite true that my father made friends and enemies as a result of what he wrote about Austria-Hungary, particularly during the Great War. He travelled there as a young man, made acquaintances and friendships among the different nations of the Monarchy and became convinced that the Hungarians' Magyarisation policy was a menace to peace because it provoked fierce nationalist reactions and made it impossible to hold the Monarchy together.

As for the rest of the Monarchy outside Hungary, he was rather more hopeful, yet as time went on it became more and more clear to him that the deep conflict between the Vienna Government and the South Slavs was going to be extremely hard to resolve. All the same, right up to the assassination of Franz Ferdinand in 1914, he hoped that the Monarchy could be reformed and saved. He was acutely aware of the value of this great, multi-national state in the middle of Europe acting as a sort of buffer between German imperialism and Russian imperialism.

The war, which was brought about largely by the insoluble problems of the Monarchy, finished Austria off, and the successor states made a dreadful mess of their affairs. My father was very much aware of that, too, in the twenty years that followed. Yet he thought and repeatedly said to the end of his life that, with all its faults, the peace settlement of 1919, by rearranging the frontiers more in accordance with nationality than they had been before, did more good than harm. It did at least make it possible for Slovaks, Rumanians and Croats to go ahead—as they did. And there has, indeed, been a trend discernible throughout this century right up to the present time for these emancipated peoples to develop their distinctive national cultures and enter fully into the heritage of the modern world.

Urban The 1919 peace settlement was indeed a highly imperfect affair. If politicians of unsophisticated or irrelevant credentials—a Lloyd George, for example, or a Chamberlain, or a Woodrow Wilson whose knowledge of Europe was based on book-learning—try to make sense of the world's complicated problems in terms of their own parochial experiences—that is bad enough but understandable. But should we make similar allowances for the cream of our intellectual elite (keepers, as I like to think, of the public conscience) who have gone into politics from Oxford and Ivy League universities only to acquire similar blinkers? And this raises the even broader question: are a scholar's wartime judgements and activities excused by his country's involvement in war?

Seton-Watson Perhaps you are right to say that that is how people of Anglo-Saxon or Central European background thought. But still the fact remains that when whole cultural communities become disaffected, and their 'foreign'—that is, their multi-national or supranational—rulers fail to satisfy them, they become explosive human material, and the multi-national empires sooner or later blow up. I don't think more expertise in Ivy League or Oxbridge colleges would have affected that.

As for scholars' judgments in wartime, I don't think I can give you any answer to that. Scholars in both world wars were affected by what they felt to be their countries' danger and their countries' need. Austria-Hungary in fact was harnessed to the Pan-German war chariot—even if people like my father's friends, Professors Joseph Redlich and Oszkar Jaszi, were unhappy about that. I myself a quarter-century later wanted my country to win. I wasn't anti-Hungarian—I had no reason to be—but I was anti-German for a long time, though I have ceased to be by now. Should I have condemned Stalin, my country's ally, whose men were dying on the German front? Should I have believed the Polish story of Katyn? I didn't believe then, I couldn't, but today I know it is true. How near to omniscience is it reasonable to expect scholars to come? Frankly, I don't know.

Now, to come back to my father, his thinking was not modelled on exclusively Anglo-Saxon examples. He was steeped in nineteenth-century German literature; the libertarian period of the German movement for unity was a formative influence in his life. He probably overrated the importance of liberalism in Germany (as did many others), but his ideas for the future of the Habsburg monarchy were strongly influenced by both German and Anglo-Saxon variants of liberalism and self-determination. Steed's plans for democracy in Central Europe drew on French rather than English models. Of course, all this planning failed, but I doubt whether the Anglo-Saxon distortion in my father's thinking can be considered the main reason for the discrepancy between hope and reality in Central Europe. In short: there was an Anglo-Saxon model which was irrelevant, there was a French model which was irrelevant, and there was a German model which was not so much irrelevant as too weak.

Urban Sixty years after the collapse of the Austro-Hungarian state, would you say that your father and Wickham Steed did the right thing in 1914–18?

Seton-Watson When I think about this question nowadays, I see it in the perspective of an entirely different world situation from the one which formed my father's opinions. My father's views took shape against the background of a stable and immensely strong British empire, and although he was no naive imperialist, he certainly believed that the empire, and particularly the white Anglo-Saxon dominions, was there to stay. The Habsburg Monarchy was, as we now know, the first of the big empires of the last few centuries to collapse. There were no precedents for it, unless you count the Ottoman empire as a precedent—and in those times, only sixty years ago, few Europeans would think of a Muslim and a Christian empire in the same terms. No one really knew what the destruction of a large Christian empire was going to mean either for its constituent elements or for the rest of the world. If you look at the world as it is in 1978—the British empire has disintegrated, in a different way from the Austrian, but just as completely; the French empire has gone; the smaller colonial empires have vanished, and the Russian empire began to disintegrate but was saved from disintegration by the Bolsheviks, who actually made it into a more rigid and oppressive empire than the one they had inherited from the Tsars.

One has, therefore, to think of the collapse of the Habsburg Monarchy not as an isolated case but as the first in a series of break-ups of empires which have transformed the world. And if one asks: what did the world lose by Austria-Hungary and, conversely, what kind of success did the Monarchy's successors make of their opportunity, one has to ask the same questions about the British empire and the French empire, and the only answer we can come up with is severe: everywhere nationalistic and chauvinistic states with artificial boundaries and highly inequitable internal political systems have come to replace the empires they have destroyed in the name of self-government, equity and justice. The phenomenon of *Kleinstaaterei*, which one saw in Central Europe in the 1920s, has been exceeded by what has happened in southern Asia and Africa in the last twenty-five years.

Nevertheless, if I were to answer your question whether my father's policies were the right ones, I would probably say 'Yes', not because I believe that these policies led to a happy state of affairs—I know all too well that they didn't; I myself first got to know Central Europe when Fascism was at its height—but because one can only evaluate a policy in relation to the possibilities of the time. Granted that Austria was at war with Britain, and granted that the nationalist movements were as strong as they were and burst the dykes of the Monarchy in the last few weeks of the war—nothing else could have happened. There might have been changes in detail if the British, French and American governments had been able to keep their men under the colours long enough after the cessation of hostilities to *impose* a settlement. For example, they might have seen to it that certain territories beyond the river Tisza, which had been taken away from Hungary, should be restored, or that Bulgaria got juster frontiers. But it is an unprofitable exercise to speculate about these possibilities because the one factor which determined the policies of the British, French and American governments was their absolute determination to get their men out of uniform and to let their population have their brothers and fathers back home again.

Urban A rather dismal comment on the quality of Western statesmanship, repeated, *mutatis mutandis*, after the Second World War—

Seton-Watson Yes, but it is also a ghastly comment on democracy. One can't help feeling that, given the unstable condition of world order, democracy is a bad form of government. Churchill said as much, but he added that other forms of government were even worse. I am not so sure that that is always true. I am not convinced that *no* type of autocracy or oligarchy could *ever* be better than mass democracy. At least autocrats and oligarchs are able to take their decisions and stick to them. Anybody aspiring to a career in a mass democracy, on the other hand, has to do what is immediately acceptable to the vote-givers—what is interesting, or pleasurable, or has novelty—and that is certainly no prescription for statesmanship.

Urban At times of war the Western democracies have shown a remarkable ability to impose on themselves an almost all-embracing discipline. Why have they repeatedly thrown away the fruits of war by failing to prolong the discipline of war to tide them over the first few years of peace? The defeat of Churchill before the Second World War was concluded, contains, I suppose, the answer to my question.

Seton-Watson Yes—Churchill was not a typical product of democracy. He came from an aristocratic family; his entire habit of thinking of the state was untypical of British thinking in the mid-1940s; the things he considered to be meritorious or lacking in merit were not those of the ordinary man or woman. But most politicians who make our history for us, in Britain no less than in other Western democracies, are thrown up by electoral politics. The men who led us after the First World War did not believe very deeply that bequeathing a just and workable peace in Central Europe really mattered, and the voters cared even less. Exhaustion by war, ignorance, and lack of leadership saw to it that a disastrous war was followed by an ill-conceived peace which carried within it the seeds of another and even more disastrous conflict. Incidentally, my father spent two months or so in Paris during the peace conference, and absolutely loathed the whole atmosphere. He often used to tell me that it was one of the unhappiest periods in his life. This is also confirmed by some of the letters which he wrote to my mother at the time.

Urban The Soviet state in the 1970s may be approaching a period when its unity can be just as threatened by disaffected nations and nationalities as was the Habsburg Monarchy in its last years. You said: granted that Britain was at war with Austria and the nationalities within Austria were anxious to obtain independence, it was inevitable that the Entente powers should have supported the enemies of their enemy. Now I am assuming that, though we are not at war with the Soviet Union, the Soviet state and the Soviet Communist Party are our adversaries. This strikes me as a safe assumption, partly because the Soviet Union never stops telling us so, and partly because our governments make that assumption in their daily political thinking and predicate on it our military preparations.

Given all this, and given the Soviet leaders' extreme (and justified) fear that the nationalities problem will prove the Achilles heel of their country's unity, should we not support the claims of disaffected Latvians, Estonians, Ukrainians and Uzbeks?

Count Witte notes in his *Memoirs* with considerable anxiety that at the time of his premiership, in 1905, the number of non-Russians in the Russian empire was as high as 35 per cent (counting Ukrainians as Russians but excluding Poles). 'It is impossible to rule such a country,' he wrote, 'and ignore the national aspirations of its varied non-Russian groups, which largely make up the population of the Great Empire. . . . It might be better for us Russians, I concede, if Russia were a nationally uniform country. . . . To achieve that goal there is but one way, namely to give up our border provinces, for these will never put up with the policy of ruthless Russification.

According to the latest Soviet census, the ratio of Russians in the Soviet population has fallen to about 50 per cent, and is still falling. In other words, the balance of nationalities in the Soviet Union is approaching that of the Austro-Hungarian Monarchy shortly before its dismemberment (about 40 per cent Austrian-Germans and Hungarians, and 60 per cent nationalities).

Seton-Watson First of all, let me point out an important difference between the Russian empire and the Austrian empire. The existence of a huge Russian empire is a *menace* to the human race and has been for centuries in a sense in which the Austrian empire never was. Certainly the Habsburg empire was at various times the scene of religious persecutions, and certainly crimes were committed under various Habsburg rulers—but the Habsburg state in Austria (as opposed to Spain) was never a menace to the rest of Europe. The Russian empire is. It has grown like a cancer from the little state of Muscovy into a monstrous superpower which now stretches from the Elbe to Kamchatka and spreads darkness wherever it goes.

I simply cannot see that the maintenance of this vast

moloch state should be regarded as some sort of sacred doctrine in international politics. If this empire should collapse from within, by the breaking away of its constituent nations, as Austria did, that would be a blessing for all humanity.

But I should like to say a little more about the problems of subject nations. I believe very deeply that a nation's culture inherently deserves respect. The right of a national culture to exist, and the right of the people who belong to that national culture to cultivate and develop it, is as fundamental as the citizen's right to his personal liberty. Therefore it is axiomatic that nations like the Ukrainians or Volga Tatars, whose culture goes back a long time in history, are fully entitled to preserve and to enhance it.

The Soviet Government's imperialist policy, its attempt to bring all national cultures, including the Russian, under the uniformising and all-pervasive control of the moloch state with its capital in Moscow, is doing two things, both of which we ought to resist.

First, it is depriving more than half the Soviet population of their right to a national existence. If we believe in our principles, this is a right we ought to uphold. Second, in attempting to deprive them of this right—which has nowhere yet succeeded unless the carriers of national consciousness were physically exterminated—the Soviet Government is creating centres of unrest and conflict which make Soviet society unstable and dangerous to itself as well as to the world.

What should be our attitude to this? Should we feel, and express, sympathy for the non-Russian subject nations, or should we reserve our sympathy for the Soviet rulers and Russian imperialist officials, and strive to maintain the Soviet empire intact, and reinforce the hold of Russians over other nations? I myself would answer: the first. I have two reasons for this. One is that these nations deserve the respect and sympathy of free nations. The second is that the Soviet leaders act always and everywhere as if they were our enemies, and so we have to accept it as a fact that they are our enemies. This does not mean that we should wish to go to war with them, or even that it is at all likely that we ever shall; but it does mean that we should not try to strengthen them, and that we should welcome those developments which weaken them.

To support forces which weaken a hostile state is a natural act of policy. The Soviet Union does it to us: all over the world, openly and in secret, Soviet spokesmen and Soviet agents try to exploit against us any nationalism and any feelings of hostility they can find, whether it be the hostility of some primitive tribe in Mozambique which can be involved in guerilla warfare in Rhodesia, or that of highly sophisticated French intellectuals whose resentment of the US works on an entirely different level but provides an equally useful leverage. Any and every feeling of hostility is being used as ammunition against us—it is absurd not to do it in reverse.

It has become a kind of dogma in the United Nations, especially as expressed by the 'third world' countries, that self-government is more important than good government (a point we have already touched upon). Therefore the people of Upper Volta (or whatever) are said to have a right to national independence. All right. I am not sure whether there *is* an Upper Volta national culture, but if there is, undoubtedly Upper Volta has a right to its national life.

On what principle, then, are the Uzbeks denied their national rights? They have a culture going back at least 3,000 years—Turkistan was the centre of a highly developed civilisation when our ancestors were naked savages running around in the West European forests—but this is never said in the United Nations. Nobody on our side ever gets up there to repudiate Soviet imperialism and demand national independence for the Uzbeks.

Urban In our international relations with the Soviet Union we recognise the integrity of the Soviet state, but we are also saying that no country that has signed the Charter of the United Nations with its various instruments on human rights can claim that its internal affairs are exempt from the scrutiny of other signatories. Since the Helsinki agreement we have reinforced this by claiming that there are, strictly speaking, no internal affairs left in the world. How can our politicians and propagandists do justice to these conflicting assumptions?

Seton-Watson I'm not sure that there *is* a conflict. The

Soviet Union does, after all, say *of itself* that it is a state containing many nationalities. The Soviet leaders admit that Ukrainians are different from White Russians or the Cheremiss—so why should *we* not say it? Obviously the American Government in its international relations with the Soviet Government is a state negotiating with another state and accepts, as all states do unless they are at war with each other, the frontiers of the Soviet state as they are. But, then, nobody is suggesting that the Soviet state should give up a piece of territory that belongs to it. If the minority nations want to secede, that is another matter, but it is simply not true that by talking to them and encouraging them to maintain their national culture in a way they *cannot* under present conditions, we are also inciting them to rebellion and secession. Heaven knows, the Soviets are past masters at encouraging every kind of disloyalty in our parts of the world—think of the Irish situation which is being exploited 100 per cent, openly and covertly, by the Soviet state machine—so if we remind the suppressed Soviet nationalities of their rights, the Soviet leaders have no right to say that they are being unfairly treated.

Urban The Soviet Union has three representatives in the United Nations on behalf of three of its fifteen republics. Might it not give our nationalities policy a good start if we took the Soviets up on that claim and proposed to have each of our countries represented in the Soviet Union, not by one but by three embassies and three ambassadors: one in Moscow, one in Minsk and one in Kiev?

Seton-Watson Oh, it would be highly legitimate—and some more embassies would make sense, too, in Uzbekistan, for example, which is a large republic. A suggestion of this kind was made in the 1940s but was refused and then forgotten. But it is a perfectly legitimate request and it would be interesting to see how the Russians reacted.

Let me try to summarise what we have said so far on the question of nationality. The right of a nation to go on being a nation seems to me unchallengeable. Not so the right of a nation to make an independent state of its own. That is a function of the power-relationship between that nation and other nations with which it shares a common state. If they cannot agree and one wants to exercise its right to secede, that nation may or may not be able to put up house as an independent state. To say that every nation has a right to go on being a nation does not mean that it has a right to be a separate state even if that state has to be brought about by force. These are two different points, and I would not accept the second as a doctrine. I would merely say that secession by violent means, resulting in separate statehood, does sometimes happen, and when it does the outside world has to take it into account, but it is not something that should be proclaimed as a right, whereas the right to nationhood is.

Urban If I were a Soviet leader arguing with you in front of an *Anglo-American* audience, intent of course on capturing the goodwill of that audience, I would keep very quiet about Lenin's theory of nationality and say something like this: nineteenth-century liberals like Acton saw very clearly the difference between the individual's connection with his race, or nation, as merely physical, and his connection with the state, or political nation, as moral. The biological link between the individual and the nation was dominant in savage life, so I would argue, but lost its predominance in civilised communities.

Civilisation emphasises the individual's recognition of the superior authority of the state, or political nation, because it is only in the cauldron of the state that the divergent and selfish interests of nations (or nationalities, as Acton liked to call them) are harmonised for the good of the political nation and ultimately of mankind. It was in this sense that nineteenth-century liberals believed that the coexistence of several nations in one state was the best guarantee of their freedom. At this point, my hypothetical Soviet leader might throw at you a quotation from Acton: 'Where political and national boundaries coincide, societies cease to advance, and nations relapse into a condition corresponding to that of men who renounce intercourse with their fellow men. . . . A State may in course of time produce a nationality; but that a nationality should constitute a State is contrary to the nature of modern civilization. . . .'

With his case (as it would seem to him) half won, my Soviet leader would then proceed as follows: scientific socialism is only a higher form of bourgeois liberalism; the

Soviet state is only a refinement of Acton's 'political nation', and a Soviet national a member of that political nation. The laws governing the coexistence of nations in the Soviet 'political nation' guarantee the real freedom of each nation and every individual under the universal authority of socialism. And my hypothetical Soviet spokesman might end his (slightly circuitous) dissertation by underlining once again his agreement with Acton: 'The greatest adversary of the rights of nationality [nationalism] is the modern theory of nationality. By making the State and the nation commensurate with each other ... it reduces practically to a subject condition all other nationalities that may be within the boundary ... [thus] the inferior races are exterminated, or reduced to servitude, or outlawed ...'

Let me stress that this is the kind of thing my hypothetical Soviet leader would be saying to a *non-Marxist Western audience*. Back in Moscow he would, of course, fall back on the standard Leninist-Stalinist formula that Soviet rule is 'national in form, socialist in content', and explain that the absorption of ethnic groups and small languages in larger nations and widely spoken languages had already been performed for the socialist state by the uniformising tendencies of capitalist mass production and capitalist mass markets.

Seton-Watson You have made a very good case for your Soviet spokesman. However, I'm afraid my reply to the quotations from Acton would be simply that they are bad history. Shocking thing to say of Acton, I admit, but it would take too long to make my case, and it is a bit irrelevant to our argument. I personally have more respect for the arguments which Soviet spokesmen actually do use.

One is the argument that the nations of the Soviet Union, and of Eastern Europe, are 'socialist nations', being led by persons who are children of workers and peasants, unlike the 'bourgeois nations' from which the nationalist movements of the past proceeded. Now this is true. The regimes under which these nations live are indeed manned by persons of such social origin. Yet the national consciousness of the socialist Polish, Hungarian and Uzbek nations seems to produce exactly the same attitude to their Russian overlords as was produced in their predecessors, the bourgeois nations. They show absolutely no sign of regarding the Soviet empire as a unit of higher civilisation than their own national culture.

The second argument by Soviet spokesmen which I take seriously is the argument that since 1917 the peoples of the Soviet Union have made immense economic and educational progress—in short, that the Soviet regime has done them good by giving them factories and schools. Now this too is absolutely true. Where the Soviet spokesmen go wrong is in assuming that these great improvements have made them grateful to their kind Soviet Russian imperial masters. The truth is that the Uzbek's reaction to the improvements is to ascribe it all to his people's hard work and other virtues, and to insist that the progress would have been much greater if the Russians had not been sitting on the Uzbeks' necks. This is probably unjust, but it is how they see it, just as the Indians saw their own progress under British rule. I see no reason to believe that the Soviet empire is exempt from one of the great laws of history—one of the *zakonomernosti*, as the Russians like to call them—the Law of Colonial Ingratitude.

As for Stalin's well-known formula which you quoted, I think that it can be easily amended in order to give us the truth in a nutshell: the Soviet Union is a state socialist in form, imperialist in content.

Lessons for Africans

Urban You have said that our knowledge of what happens after the disintegration of large empires is much deeper today than it was at the time of the dissolution of the Habsburg Monarchy. May I suggest that we pursue this theme a little further, bearing in mind that charges of prejudice and worse are waiting to be hurled at us by eagle-eyed historians at the slightest suspicion of a limping analogy.

Seton-Watson The parallels one can draw between what happened after the break-up of the Austrian Monarchy and the dissolution of the British, French, Dutch and Portuguese empires are many, and although I agree with you that analogies can be misleading, we are, as I will try to show, on sufficiently safe ground here to pursue some of them. One set of parallels concerns the question of the successor states; another is the internal development of the mother countries themselves after the collapse of these empires—of metropolitan Austria, Britain and France.

The central feature of post-Austro-Hungarian Central Europe was the endless and bitter quarrels between all the successor states. Not all of these were really nation-states because most of them had large national minorities, but they were national in the sense that one group of nationalists was effectively in charge of each state. And, as we know, these groups of nationalists were at daggers drawn with each other and their feuds gave Hitler his opportunity.

Something very similar is to be seen in Africa today. There are differences, of course, the main one being that, although every successor state in Africa contains among its citizens a multitude of tribes and languages, and although it is quite possible that these different tribes will become nuclei for future national consciousness and eventually of nationalism and national separatism from, say, Zaire or Angola, their development has as yet not reached the point where this is certain to happen. But there are exceptions. The most striking one is Somalia where the Somalis' movement for unity reminds one strikingly of the movement for the unity of all Rumanians and all Serbs before 1914: there are Somalis under Ethiopian rule and others under Kenyan rule, and the independent state of Somalia intends in one way or another to get all these Somalis united and annex the corresponding territories. Conversely, in Ethiopia the policy of the late Emperor Haile Selassie was essentially the same as that of Hungary under Dualism: for Magyarisation read Amharisation—Amharic being the language of the dominant people in Ethiopia. It would appear that the attempt to force Amharic culture on the non-Amharic Ethiopians is still prevalent in the chaos which we see in Ethiopia today.

Another type of post-Austrian situation prevails in Nigeria. Nigeria, too, has a great variety of tribes and languages. Some of these, the Yorubas, Ibos and Hausa-Fulani, are both more numerous and culturally more highly developed than the rest, so that one may reasonably describe them as nations rather than tribes. A few years ago the inter-tribal conflicts in Nigeria led to civil war which claimed some two million lives and ended in the victory of the central government. This won the applause of both the British and American governments. Why?

Anglo-American approval was symptomatic of the great difficulty we have in thinking away from our own national experiences and mustering sufficient intuition to understand an historically unfamiliar situation. In Britain, public opinion was shaped and led by a powerful lobby of ex-colonial administrators who looked upon a united Nigeria of some 50 million people (today nearly 80 million) as the proudest creation of the British empire in Africa. It was a country they had conjured up at the beginning of the century, a country to which they had given a federal constitution and which they had happily guided to independence. Nigeria was a success story—Nigerian unity in accordance with all the rules of nature.

The Americans approved of the suppression of Biafra and the forcible assertion of Nigerian unity for different reasons. Their overriding image of statehood goes back to their Civil War which makes them look upon secession as something inherently wicked. They perceived Ojukwu, the Ibo leader of secessionist Biafra, as a kind of black Jefferson Davis who had to be put down because he threatened the integrity of the Union. Thus both British and American hostility to an independent Biafra was based on prejudices deeply anchored in their national psyche. Now that the federal government has won, the general assumption in the English-speaking world, and especially in America, is that Nigerian unity has been upheld, the new government is generous towards the defeated, and the problems of Nigeria are happily resolved. Of course, the comparison with the 1865 American experience is absurd because the white Americans in North and South were the same people, despite their great temporary differences, whereas the Ibos, Hausas and Yorubas are completely different from each other. The fact that the war was won says nothing of the future, and it seems to me all too likely that the centrifugal force of minority dissensions will eventually reassert itself, and Nigeria will become another Austria-Hungary.

Urban Is there any sign that the sobering history of European nationalism has made an impression in Africa—that the Africans will heed the lessons of our own fratricidal wars? In one of Herzen's writings there is a highly optimistic maxim which may be worth testing against the African experience: 'Human development is chronological unfairness because late-comers are able to profit from the labours of their predecessors without paying the price.' Are they?

Seton-Watson I hope Herzen will be proved right by events, but there is as yet no sign of it. The picture which the African educated class has of the troubles sown by European nationalism is distorted because, in so far as the educated African has learnt any European history, he has learnt it through English, French and Portuguese eyes—which is as good as not having learnt it at all. Think of the amount of Central European history an English or Belgian secondary school child is asked to assimilate, and you realise that the Africans' knowledge can be, at best, extremely superficial and naive. To most of them the Central European world is completely unknown.

This does not, however, prevent black African nationalist politicians (the late Nkrumah was one good example) from warning against the horrors of the 'Balkanisation' of Africa. They seem to be thinking that the African nations represent some superior civilisation which must not be dragged down to the level of those dreadful Balkan states—Bulgaria, Serbia and the rest. All one can say is that if the Africans manage their affairs half as well as Bulgaria or Serbia did, they will have done extremely well. Their problems with discordant language groups turning into nations are just beginning. It seems to me, therefore, that the kind of ideas Otto Bauer and Karl Renner put forward in the Austrian Monarchy might be usefully put to work in Africa. When cultural and tribal groups haven't yet reached the stage of militant national consciousness, it might be possible—with high-quality statesmanship and with a lot of luck—to satisfy them with the type of cultural autonomy that Bauer and Renner foresaw, and to reconcile them to the central government.

Urban To be fair to the Africans, it seems to me that expecting them to imbibe the lessons of Habsburg history would be asking them to make a kind of cultural jump that no nation, not even the Japanese with their exceptional gift for the cultural *tour de force*, has yet managed to make. The Central European nations themselves can hardly be said to have put their past safely behind them—Rumanian/Hungarian, Czech/Slovak, Serb/Croat feelings persist. How much more difficult would it be for uneducated African tribesmen to assimilate the lessons of an entirely alien civilisation! The Africans might understand us a little better if we referred them to the genocidal activities of nomadic Pechenegs, Uigurs and Onogurs on the steppes of eighth-century Eastern Europe; but sophisticated schemes of Central European socialists of the stamp of Bauer and Renner?

Seton-Watson Of course one must have one's doubts. However, there are some sophisticated people among African leaders, both politicians and intellectuals, who are quite capable of understanding the essence of the problem. I am not suggesting that they should apply Bauer's or Renner's ideas to their situations, but that they should study the Bauer and Renner approach, and work out their solutions for themselves. It would be better than accepting Soviet domination—inclusion in a new Soviet African empire policed by Cubans—or relapsing into warring *Kleinstaaterei*.

Urban Nationalism is a broad term—it has worn different ideological clothing at different times and in different places. You have yourself repeatedly written of the contrast between the liberal democratic content of nationalism in the early and mid-nineteenth century, and the nationalism that began to afflict Europe at the turn of the century, and eventually cost the world two bloodbaths and the collapse of European power and self-confidence. On the face of it, the African wars of national liberation are in the 1848 tradition, for they claim to combine the struggle against foreign hegemony with the democratic transformation of society. Is that your reading of the current phase of African nationalism?

Seton-Watson No, it isn't, but to answer that question more fully we must first take a quick look at the main stages of nationalism. The impression which your last words gave was that nationalism up to about 1848 was 'good', and after that was 'bad'. But it was more complicated than that. In the first period of the nineteenth century the dominating idea of the national movement was liberalism, more particularly the idea, and almost the ideology, of individual liberty. Until about 1870 the nationalist leaders strongly believed that the liberty of the individual citizen and the liberty of the nation must go together. This was nineteenth-century liberal nationalism, and we may think of Garibaldi as an obvious figurehead of the period. Then came the involvement of the masses in the political process, the franchise was extended, socialism became an important force and the oligarchical liberal state gradually gave way to mass democracy. Nationalist leaders now felt that they had to concentrate their concerns on the fate of the masses and paid less and less attention to the freedom of the individual.

In the period between the two world wars nationalism took two principal forms. In Europe, where Fascism and Nazism seemed for a long time to be politically set for victory, nationalists tended to be Fascists. In the colonies in Asia and Africa nationalisms were essentially anti-British and anti-French movements. Their leaders, as for example Nasser, Sadat and the young Egyptian officer class, looked to Germany and Italy for salvation. This was also true of a section of the Indian Congress Party, and still more true of the South East Asian nationalists, whose hopes were pinned on Japan, the ally of the Fascist powers in Asia.

After the defeat of Fascism and the victory of the Soviet Union, colonial nationalism spread from the Muslim and Asian world south of the Sahara. But now, in post-war nationalist eyes, the enemy of the colonial powers, and therefore the friend and protector of Afro-Asian nationalism, was not the defeated Fascist states, but the victorious Soviet Union: nationalists began to spout little-understood Marxist slogans, and their movement was gradually painted in Marxist or, to be more precise, pseudo-Marxist colours.

One might therefore describe the four stages of nationalism as: pseudo-liberal; pseudo-mass-democratic; pseudo-Fascist and pseudo-Communist.

If we look at nationalism in the world today we see the Soviet Union training Arab and African guerillas, supplying arms and cadres both to various guerilla movements and to states which have achieved independence. The African leaders in turn mouth Marxist slogans about African 'socialism'—something which the more sophisticated Soviet Marxists view with well-deserved derision but exploit to the hilt, for they are realists and Leninists enough to know that nationalism in its anti-Western phase is tailor-made for their purposes.

If we look at the nationalist movements themselves, it is more and more difficult to tell where Fascist nationalism ends and Communist nationalism begins. Both use the same murderous methods as were characteristic of European Fascism in the 1920s and 1930s—for example, of the Iron Guard in Rumania and the Arrow Cross in Hungary. The similarity of the appeal by both Fascists and Communists to the most primitive instincts of the population under demagogic slogans of social revolution and racial supremacy is unmistakable. True, the Africans haven't got Jews—but members of the Chinese diaspora, Greek and Lebanese traders are pressed into service as substitutes: behind their ideological garment of Marxist 'socialism', the nationalist movements in the Middle East and Africa reveal themselves more and more visibly as Fascist movements.

Urban How would the Polish and Hungarian upheavals of 1956 and the Czechoslovak events of 1968 figure in your tabulation?

Seton-Watson They are almost exactly the opposite. When nations rise against the world's one remaining colonialism, the Soviet empire, they revert back to a nineteenth-century type of liberal nationalism with a Garibaldian flavour. This was true of Hungary in 1956 and Czechoslovakia in 1968—both were conscious imitations of 1848. This need not really surprise us. Basic political liberty, which people lacked and longed for under Metternich's police system before 1848, was precisely what was missing and what was desired under Rakosi and Novotny—admittedly, two much harder masters than Metternich. One might, with a little oversimplification, draw the conclusion that when you are fighting a retreating Western parliamentary regime, you tend to adopt a half-Fascist, half-Communist idiom; when you are fighting a totalitarian regime, you adopt a liberal idiom.

Was there, then, you may ask, no nationalism involved in 1956 and 1968? Are the Russians wrong in claiming that there was? Originally, the movements in Hungary and Czechoslovakia had been movements of the 1848 type—movements for constitutional rights, individual liberty and social justice. Both, however, were turned into movements of national resistance by Soviet behaviour. When the Soviets intervened with armed force, a mass explosion of national feeling followed, with the Russian invader as its natural target. But neither the Hungarian nor the Czechoslovak revolution *started* as a nationalist movement. They were socialist movements, impregnated with liberal values, perverted by Soviet imperialism and Soviet ineptitude into struggles for national liberation.

Urban Your distinction between national revolutions that adopt a Fascist/Communist idiom and those that adopt a liberal idiom is persuasive—but is it saying very much? Does it go beyond the truism: 'democracy breeds tyranny; tyranny breeds democracy', with our knowledge of the problem hardly advanced beyond the conclusion that history does indeed move in circles?

Seton-Watson Well, I suppose Aristotle would recognise these phenomena fairly quickly if he could come back from the Elysian Fields for a refresher course. Even so, I think it is worth our while to say all this—to show that nationalism *does* fit these patterns, that it is not uniquely good or uniquely bad. These things need saying, because today they are not understood, not even by highly learned Western intellectuals who ought to know better, not to mention busy Western politicians. And apart from that, I cannot accept the statement that 'democracy breeds tyranny' without a great deal of qualification which would take us far outside our subject.

Post-imperial Austria and post-imperial Britain

Urban You've said that your second parallel between post-imperial Austria and post-imperial Western Europe concerns similarities in the internal development of the mother-countries.

Seton-Watson Yes—the predicaments of the British after losing their empire and of the Austrians after losing theirs have certain points of resemblance—both differing from the French.

When Austria was reduced to a homogeneous German-speaking republic the politically conscious segments of Austrian society were gradually gripped by an identity-crisis. Who are we?—they asked—what do we stand for? These questions emerged because the Austrian empire had been a dynasty, not a nation—nobody had ever claimed that there was an Austrian nation—and as there was no simple answer on hand, the Austrians were pulled in different directions. There was the pull of the Danube basin with its old and still powerful historical associations, and there was the pull of German culture and the demand for unification with Germany, which had been refused by the Entente powers in 1919. A third and much less serious pull came from Italy with Mussolini's ambition to turn Austria into a kind of honorary protectorate—an absurd ambition which had no long-term prospect of success.

The Austrians were eventually swallowed up by the Third Reich, went through the horrors of Hitlerism and war—some became enthusiastic Nazis, others didn't—and they all suffered what Germany suffered. They were lucky to be able to emerge from the holocaust as a separate state from which, in 1955, occupation by the four powers was miraculously removed and, for more than twenty years now, the Austrians have had an independent, sovereign and neutral state with a record of admirable internal stability and prosperity. Their power as the centre of an empire has long since gone; their sense of mission in Europe has gone—they have become a small, comfortable, commercially and industrially efficient people who appear to be happy as they are. But think of what they had to go through before they got there!

Now after the collapse of the empire, the British were torn in a rather similar way: 'Who are we?' I am not saying that people were pacing up and down Oxford Street with an anxious look on their faces asking themselves exactly that question (the British have too little feel for metaphysics and metahistory for that), but this was the sort of uncertainty they had at the back of their minds. When Dean Acheson put it into words: 'Great Britain has lost an empire and has not yet found a role'—there was uproar in England; but, of course, Acheson had hit the nail squarely on the head.

The British, like the Austrians, were pulled in three directions. There was the European mainland with which they were intimately associated in their foreign policy, through the sacrifices made in wars of every kind, and through their culture. Secondly, there was the English-speaking world—the US, Canada, Australia, New Zealand—with which they had no common territorial boundaries; and, thirdly, the Commonwealth—a rather absurd idea when you consider that Britain's links with former colonies such as Tanzania and Ghana were supposed to solve the British people's identity crisis.

Where do the British stand on all this today? We still don't really know. Speaking for myself, I consider myself a European, but I am also aware of my links with America, Canada, Australia, New Zealand and English-speaking South Africa. I have grown up aware of these countries since early childhood; I have lived for a time in all of them except New Zealand; I have friends and relatives in all of them. I cannot cut myself in two as de Gaulle demanded of us, and say that I am only a European or only a citizen *à part entière* of the English-speaking world.

Britain is now part of the European Community, but this is only the first step in answering our problem. The EEC is a latter-day Carolingian empire, consisting of the same lands as the empire of Charlemagne, but moulded this time by Charles de Gaulle. It is admirable as far as it goes. But to identify this Carolingian empire with Europe is absurd. So our crisis of identity is unresolved. Mercifully we are not faced, as the Austrians were, with the alternative of a Third Reich threatening to absorb us as its kinsmen. One may of course talk of the perils of a sort of cultural recolonisation by the United States through the less admirable features of American civilisation. But this is just a journalists' *boutade*: there is no real parallel.

Urban Do you think the post-imperial French are gripped by a similar identity crisis?

Seton-Watson No, the French don't question their identity: they are *French*. Of course the French went through as terrible an experience as the Austrians had done: they were conquered and trodden on, and when they emerged from the war they fought a couple of long and painful wars trying to keep their colonies—something the British, whether from wisdom or from indifference, never did. And yet, at the end of it all, French identity was unscathed. Why? Because for the average Frenchman the fact that France lost an empire was never very important. The French were never, so to speak, *part* of their empire—they were *French*. France had various accretions round the world, there was the *mission civilisatrice* to spread culture among the culturally less fortunate (and this view still exists to some extent); but whether or not the French had an empire was not a significant fact of French life. On the other hand the belief in the superiority of French culture over all others was deeply rooted among all classes of the French nation.

For the British the empire mattered to a much larger part of the population, including persons in all classes, even if only to a minority all told. The chief reason, I think, was that the empire included large territories inhabited by people of British stock and speaking the English language. The French did not fill large parts of the world with French people. The one exception was New France, nowadays known as the Quebec province of Canada, which the King of France made no attempt to take back from the British when he had the chance in 1782, after the war of the American Revolution. In the nineteenth century the French were the only great European nation which did not send a mass of emigrants abroad. The French stayed behind in France, the centre of the world, the only truly civilised country. Now, heaven knows, the French were often bitterly divided by ideological, political and social cleavages of every kind, and dreadful things may happen in the coming years if the conflict between Left and Right becomes acute. But for all these Frenchmen, whether of the Left or Right, their cultural and national identity has always been clear: they had no doubt in their minds that they were French. This was not so with the Austrians, and it is not so with the British.

Urban You said Austria was not a nation—is Britain?

Seton-Watson Here again we have a parallel of sorts. I have been using the word 'British' with some hesitation—for what does British mean? British is a term denoting citizenship—as Austrian was—but it is not a national term. There was a British empire, there is a British Crown, and a British army, and a British democracy, but there is no 'British' nation; there never has been. There have long been an English nation, a Scottish nation, an Irish nation and a Welsh nation, but not a British nation. (The Americans invariably get this wrong when they refer to Britain as a nation. Indeed they use 'nation' every time we would refer to 'country'.)

Among the nations making up Britain there is no doubt that the Welsh, the Irish, and the Scotch have retained their identity, and indeed their nationalism has in recent years become much sharper as a result of various economic misfortunes which, as small, nationally conscious communities living at the geographical periphery, they have inevitably—though often unjustly—attributed to the central government in London.

But the case of the English is different. I said the English have been a nation. I'm not so sure that they are any more. The English nation appears to have lost the sense of its national identity, which worries me. I can say this without bias for I have not a drop of English blood in my veins: I am Scottish on one side, Irish on the other, and I have lived and worked in England for most of my life. If anybody has a right to call himself British, I have. I do not want the English to abdicate—I want Britain to remain a force for civilisation and decency in the world, as it has been for so long. Therefore I wish the English were more aware of their Englishness than they are.

How do we account for this decay of national consciousness in the English? The English make me think of a type of rock structure which, if you hit it with a hammer, splits into vertical sections. Under the hammer blows of the last thirty years English society has split into vertical strata—each strictly separate from its neighbour, none wanting to have any knowledge of or responsibility for the others. This is not our old friend the Marxist class struggle, which represents a horizontal stratification. That of course also exists, but what I am talking about is a militant and vicious sectionalism which is all but destroying the unity of the English nation. In this matter Austria does not provide a parallel because the Austrians, as we saw, have never thought of themselves as a nation.

Urban Let me add two longish observations to this decline of Englishness in the English. The first puts an even more pessimistic interpretation on it than your own, and may be crudely summarised in the proposition that this creeping loss of national consciousness is only one aspect of the decline of the English as a competitive industrial nation—and perhaps as a nation.

This is a large topic in its own right, so let me simply quote a few figures. The average Briton (of whom the English make up some 90 per cent) produces half what his opposite number produces in America and Japan, and just over half of what the Dutch and German workers produce. For example, in Britain a steel worker produces 62 tons per man per year—against 158 tons in Italy, 161 tons in Germany, 247 tons in the US and 340 tons in Japan. An employee of Pan American Airlines handles three times the traffic of an employee of British Airways. One Dutch man-hour equals two British man-hours. British Leyland realises annual sales of $12,000 per worker while Volkswagen and Volvo achieve twice as much. Britain's share of the world tonnage of shipbuilding has fallen from 38 per cent in 1950 to 4 per cent in 1976. Her share of world trade in the same period has shrunk from over 20 per cent to about 4 per cent, and her share of the supply of the world's manufactured goods from 30 per cent to 8 per cent. In a recent study of productivity in the nine EEC countries, Britain came last in 34 out of 36 industrial groups examined. As a consequence of all this, per capita real income in Britain is about half of that in Western Europe, and it cannot be otherwise when you consider that in 1976 the British Gross Domestic Product was 215 billion dollars for a population of 56 million against Western Germany's GDP of 453 billion (population 62 million) and Sweden's 73 billion for a population of 8 million.

Now if we look at the record of other ex-colonial powers for comparison—the French, the Dutch or the Belgians—we find not only that these countries have failed to show similar signs of a post-imperial decline, but that their industrial and export performance has, in the same period, moved dramatically ahead, so that Britain's extraordinarily poor performance is without parallel.

This problem has been widely analysed, not least and almost masochistically by the British themselves, and I do not presume to have a pat answer where so many others have failed. I would, however, tentatively offer the Toynbee-esque explanation that the English have run their course in history and lost the spirit to do anything particularly well as a nation (individual performance is, of course, another matter).

This loss of motivation expresses itself in most English collective attitudes and activities, the decline of English national consciousness being only one of them. Others include qualities where the English used to excel but excel no longer: thrift, punctuality, pride in work and workmanship, corporate and individual responsibility, service—the list is almost endless.

More depressing still, according to a *New Society* survey of April 1977, British people have become strangely unambitious. 'Very few sincerely want to be rich. Most people in Britain neither want nor expect a great deal more money. Even if they could get it, the vast majority do not seem prepared to work harder for it. . . . There appears to be a new phenomenon: a revolution of *falling* expectations.' And, endorsing what you have said about the differences between low English and robust Scottish national consciousness, the survey found that *only* the Scottish respondents were highly and almost uniformly optimistic about the future.

My second (and much shorter) observation concerns the enormous contrast between England's easy-going current attitude to her Englishness and the proud nationalism of Cromwellian and Miltonian England. Reformation England was nationalistic England *par excellence*, and nationalistic England conceived of herself as the vanguard of the human race—a new Israel. One may recall Cromwell's famous boast: the English were 'a people that have had a stamp upon them from God; God having . . . summed up all our former honour and glory in the things that are of glory to nations, in an epitomy ...' Or this expression of national conceit: 'The only parallel of God's dealing with us that I know of in the world [is] Israel's bringing out of Egypt through a wilderness.' I do not want to ask you the natural question: 'how did this come out of that?'—for it would divert us from our principal theme, but it is perhaps as well to paint in the contrast and remember the days of English Messianism.

Seton-Watson On your first point, I can't contribute anything original to the economic analysis, which you quite rightly call masochistic. I would only admit that the economic decline must apply to the Scots and Welsh no less than to the English. As for your Toynbee-esque theory, I won't buy it yet. Certainly the existing political and economic leadership seems unable to get results out of the British, but whether this means more than that certain political institutions are obsolete, certain channels of communication blocked—whether it means that the English nation as such has lost the will to survive, I as a Scot with Irish blood beg leave to doubt.

On your second point: it is right to remind ourselves that there was a time when the English not only had a very strong national consciousness, but were the most nationalistic people in Europe, including some of the worst things we understand by that word. In the days of the great Queen Elizabeth I, whose minister, Walsingham, was a kind of sixteenth-century Himmler, and whose bandits raiding Spanish ships terrorised the seas, England was an aggressive, lawless, hyper-nationalistic state. But now the English seem to have lost their national identity. Of course, I don't want the English to go round the world saying the sort of thing of themselves you have quoted from Cromwell, but there is room in English life for a little more self-confidence and national consciousness.

It is symptomatic of what I've been saying how little the English can understand the motivation of nationalism even when it stirs in their own bailiwick. Think of the recent debate on 'devolution', especially as it affects Scotland. I have no doubt that the English officials who have done the negotiating with the Scots are enlightened, liberal-minded people who want to meet Scottish demands as best they can. But they simply cannot understand what these extraordinary people, the Scots, are talking about: a Scottish 'nation'? Nationalism? Their horizons are limited to bureaucratic gobbledygook and they use meaningless words like 'devolution'. They work out enlightened bureaucratic schemes, but miss the essence of the picture because they cannot grasp that Scotland isn't just an *area* which needs decentralisation of government, but that the Scots are a *nation* in the full historical and cultural sense of the word. Why can't they understand Scottish nationalism? Because the Scots have retained their national identity while the English have not retained *theirs*.

Urban Coming back to our parallels between post-imperial Austria and post-imperial Britain—does the unmanageability of Britain in the 1970s strike you as analogous with the polarisation of Austria in the early 1930s, leading up to civil war in 1934?

Seton-Watson There was in both cases a deterioration in the climate of opinion and a breakdown of tolerance. But the circumstances in which they arose were different.

The collapse of the Austrian empire coincided with defeat in war. The Austrian people came out of the war in 1919 in miserable economic conditions and with a sense of great bitterness. In Britain the abandonment of empire, the giving of independence to India and then to a number of other states took place at a time when there was no such bitterness. On the contrary, there was a euphoria of military victory and optimism about the future. There was a feeling that Britain was becoming a model democracy, leading the world with its enlightened policies. Both our new social services and our peaceful withdrawal from the empire were regarded as examples. Never defeated and humiliated in war, the British could not imagine how defeat could come their way through a different route.

It wasn't really until the mid-1960s that the British began to realise that they had, in fact, lost the war—that they had been defeated politically—and with this realisation the embitterment began. It has now lasted about as long as it did in Austria between 1919 and the civil war in 1934. The last few years have seen an extraordinary growth of social resentments and violent rhetoric. Neither is justified by facts, because the majority of the British are tolerant people who accept their neighbours as citizens and want to live together with them in a lawful manner. Nevertheless the climate of hatred and the number of those who peddle hatred—whether it is race hatred from the National Front, class hatred from the left wing of the Labour Party or from various extremist socialist sects—has been growing with alarming rapidity.

It has often been said by students of Austrian history that in the 1930s the Austrians *talked* themselves into civil war. And there is some truth in that observation: the Austrian socialists were by no means bloodthirsty revolutionaries—they were moderate, intelligent and humane people who set to work to make Vienna a city fit for workers to live in and had admirable achievements to their credit. But some of their leaders, Otto Bauer and others, indulged in wild revolutionary rhetoric. This was met by an opposing wild rhetoric on the Right. Between them, the orators of Right and Left injected a climate of hatred into Austrian public affairs. From then on the process of hatred and counter-hatred escalated until the two sides got themselves into a position where minor incidents led to civil war.

Something like that seems to be happening in Britain today. I don't think we shall have a civil war in the near future, but the deterioration in our public climate is unmistakable and it has, as I say, something to do with the realisation that Britain was, after all, defeated in war. I think it also has something to do (I am not sure what the connection is) with the loss of English national consciousness. It is arguable that the loss of national consciousness is more characteristic of politicians, bureaucratic mandarins and business leaders than of the English people themselves, who have not really lost what used to be called their patriotism. It is indeed arguable that the successes of that odious organisation, the National Front, may be due not only to their anti-black racism but to the fact that they talk about the English nation when the other politicians never mention it. There are, mind you, no very obvious reasons for the deterioration in class relations because there is far less social injustice in Britain today than there has ever been, so that the growth of class hatred is not justified by social or economic facts. Yet class hatred, much of it deliberately worked up by a number of Labour politicians, is a fact of our political life, and it is sadly true to say that the demagogy of class hatred is much more widespread in Britain than in any comparable country. There is no sign of it in the US where unemployment is much higher than it is in Britain, nor does one see much of it in the Federal Republic of Germany.

Urban Britain is said to be a freer society than either America or Germany but less democratic. I think this is true. For a trivial example: I remember playing tennis with cleaning women at the University of Southern California and celebrating *Fasching* with office messengers in Germany. I can remember no such thing during my twelve years of service with the BBC, nor did anyone think that a BBC commissionaire (porter) could or would wish to get anywhere near a tennis court.

Seton-Watson One peculiarity of Britain is the coexistence of many different subcultures. Different groups of people live different lives. Why shouldn't they? They have different tastes and don't mix with each other. Why should they? But the idea that this constitutes class oppression and should give rise to class hatred is now more and more widespread, though it seems sheer nonsense to me. There *are* differences, but these are being exploited by demagogues and inflated to a condition of class hatred, and here the British case may very well run parallel with the bitterness of Austrian society in the 1930s.

Urban Did the loss of the empire really have as unsettling an effect on the ordinary Briton as you have suggested? What the man in the Lancashire cotton mill knew from his own experience was that his personal lot struck *rock bottom* when the empire was at its *greatest*, and that his life got better and better as the empire *disintegrated* (all very confusing for Leninists). The ideology of empire always struck me as an upper-class affair, peculiar to perhaps 100,000 men who ran the show and enjoyed the privileges.

Seton-Watson Yes, you are right, there was an upper-class ideology of that sort—which, incidentally, was utterly rejected by a large part of my own generation of 'public school' or 'Oxbridge' people in the last years before the Second World War. But I think the empire meant more than that to a much larger number of people. There *was* a belief, which filtered down to the mass of the population, that Britain is the strongest country in the world, that foreigners are inferior and so on. This national pride, mixed with a lot of unpleasant xenophobia, was widespread and was responsible for the ordinary Briton's belief during the war that Britain was going to win even if she was facing grave odds after Dunkirk.

This feeling of greatness and undefeatability seems to have disappeared, though I'm afraid the xenophobia is still there. Indeed the British now suffer from an inhibition that there is *no* game they can win. This is not, of course, entirely due to the loss of the empire—it is probably still more a consequence of economic troubles, some of which of course are linked to some extent with the dissolution of the empire. What the man in the street knows about all this is a vague feeling that the British have become *scapegoats*; they are the people whom everyone can insult, who never answer back in the United Nations, who can be kicked and spat on by 'wogs'. In this crude and slightly unsavoury manner the consciousness of the loss of power and empire has penetrated the British people as a whole.

Urban Wouldn't you say that this feeling, which undoubtedly exists, has become an *idée fixe* which is quite unjustified? If one of the marks of the influence of empires is the cultural 'imperialism' they leave behind, then in one sense the British have little to complain about, but in another perhaps rather more. That the language, the law and much of the culture of the US, Canada, New Zealand and Australia is essentially English, and that India, Pakistan and other former British colonies bear the imprint of British institutions and in many cases cherish British traditions of liberty and parliamentary democracy, is nothing to be ashamed of.

At the same time the British political class, having played head-prefect in the empire for two hundred years, also distinguished itself by a mixture of cultural philistinism and arrogance. Your Oxford-educated District Officer in India, while impeccably fair in the administration of justice, never thought that Indians could or should be assimilated into British culture. Indeed, his own contact with culture was more likely to have been at the level of the university boat races than of opening books. Hasn't the British people's current mood of surly alienation something to do with the loss, not so much of British power, as of prestige in the world?

Let me note very briefly that upper-class British cultural philistinism has always been in marked contrast to French, German and even Russian attitudes to culture as a national asset and a source of prestige. The French have long made a practice of elevating the best brains in their cultural elite to high offices of state and sending them abroad as ambassadors. Paul Claudel, Jacques Maritain and André Malraux come to mind as outstanding examples. The British, who have never been short of universally respected scholars, writers and scientists, seldom make ambassadors of them.

Seton-Watson Yes, you have touched a very important point here. But let me first put in a word for the Indian Civil Service. It was from its ranks that some of the greatest Oriental scholars emerged, who taught the Indians themselves a good deal about their own culture. Most ICS officials knew one or several of the Indian languages. My own grandfather, on my mother's side, was quite a promising scholar as an Indian Civil Servant in Bengal, but he died in his thirties. My great-grandfather, as an Indian army officer, wrote one of the first grammars of Sindi. He too died in his thirties! I don't think they, or most of their colleagues, despised Indian culture. The fault of the British political class was not that they despised other nations' cultures, but that they made no effort to spread their own. That is where they differed from the French. The French were pioneers of keeping alive the mirage of being a great power while in fact having lost the substance. Remember that after 1815 France ceased to be a great power either militarily or economically. Nevertheless it remained such in French eyes, and was accepted as such in the world, right up to 1940. One of the main reasons for this was the success of French cultural diplomacy—the great network of French cultural institutes all over Europe and beyond, and the encouragement to learn French and to enter the French cultural world. This is in striking contrast with the English who never did anything of the sort. In the meantime the English language—whether the British or the American variant—has replaced French as the main language of international communication, and the gates to a sweeping dissemination of English culture are, theoretically at least, wide open. But neither the British government nor the British political class has made the slightest effort to derive any benefit from this cultural windfall. Whenever there is a budgetary cut in Britain—and can you remember a time when there wasn't?—the first to be axed are the overseas services of the BBC, which is a great agency for English culture, and the British Council. The French realise what a wonderful asset their culture is to them—the English don't. This is another example of the evaporation of national consciousness and of plain English ineptitude. When you recall that during the war, and for some years after the war, British prestige was sky-high in Europe and indeed throughout the world, the philistinism and short-sightedness of our political class strike one as devastating.

Urban My impression is that the failure of the English to act as the French do is not so much a matter of ineptitude as of an insular cultural solipsism: how can a foreigner understand anything as English as the Brontë sisters? Why should we introduce him to the feel of life in a Yorkshire vicarage? If this is true, there is perhaps hope yet for English national consciousness and even nationalism.

Seton-Watson Undoubtedly there is an element of insularity involved: if the foreigner makes the effort to come to England to learn from the English, they will be glad to see him. But they will not go out of their way to tell him anything. I would have thought this was a deadly way of pursuing cultural diplomacy. But I'm afraid we have to be still more pessimistic. The British political class up to the generation of Attlee and Cripps did not wish to spread British culture, but they respected it and even encouraged it within Britain itself. Not so the political class of 1978. If one looks at their treatment of universities and of writers, and the attitude of trade unions to freedom of the press, one can hardly avoid the conclusion that they positively hate their own nation's culture and wish to destroy it.

Thinking is to their minds a socially divisive luxury which must be suppressed. Today it is a matter not of passive cultural policy but of active neo-barbarism.

Marx and the Soviet Union

Urban There is a passage in your latest book (*Nations and States*) which appears to invest the idea of nation with a sense of inevitability: 'Nations cannot escape their history, and individuals cannot opt out of their nations'. There are two questions here: is your statement fully attested by facts, and, if we regard it as an historian's moral judgement, should we approve of it?

You no doubt have your evidence in response to my first point, so let me expand a little on the second. Your articulation reminds me—wrongly perhaps—of Hegel's famous maxim: *Die Weltgeschichte ist das Weltgericht* (world history is the world court of justice). With the vengeful consistency of the Old Testament, the sins of the fathers shall be visited upon the sons—neither nations nor individuals can escape a fate which they have not chosen and for which they are not responsible. This is an un-Christian view (though Calvinist theologians might tell us that it accords well enough with the doctrine of predestination), for it restricts the redemptive power of Christ's sacrifice to those nations and individuals whom a mysterious fate has elected to be virtuous. It is also an unhelpful view because it appears to underline some unspecified but stubborn continuity in the lives of nations, and thus to condone the vicious circle of national hatreds and counter-hatreds.

The wrongs committed in the name of this doctrine have been great and numerous. Let me, however, restrict myself to some of the evidence in our own time. It is commonly asserted that the Soviet system is not a Communist system at all but rather a latter-day expression of some slavishness and love of tyranny inherent in the Russian soul itself; it has taken the Catholic Church 2,000 years and the extermination of 6 million Jews under Hitler to declare that the Jews are not collectively responsible for the Crucifixion of Christ; we expect Germans, who were yet unborn when

Hitler ruled Germany, to answer for the crimes of their fathers; we ascribe the murderous thuggery in Northern Ireland to dark forces peculiar to the Irish psyche in much the same way as Irish Catholics and Protestants themselves heap charges of collective guilt on one another for things that happened three hundred years ago.

My question, then, is: how can nations and individuals ever make a fresh start if they cannot jump clear of the shadow of their forefathers' activities—imputed, imagined or real? And if the historian's task is—as it inevitably is—to be the interpreter as well as the chronicler of human affairs, should he not try to isolate the weakest element in this vice-like grip of the past over the present and show us the point where nations *can* escape their history and individuals *can* opt out of their nations?

Seton-Watson This is a difficult problem. I did not, of course, mean to say that nations are legatees of the deeds of their forebears to the end of time and should be held responsible for them. Your point about the Jews and the Catholic Church is a good one—the concept of the collective guilt of the Jews for the Crucifixion of Christ has always been absurd. By the same token the notion that all Germans are wicked people because of Hitler is equally absurd. All I meant to say in the sentence you quoted was that the historical past of a nation is a fact of which all nations must be aware. We cannot, of course, expect individual men and women to be history professors and spend their time harmonising their activities with what the history *they* have received tells them about their past. But we must be prepared for the often disturbing experience that an uninvited past, for which we are in no way responsible, nevertheless impinges on our personal and collective fortunes with the force of Greek tragedy.

To stick to Germany as an example: the German past is made up of a number of formative elements. The paintings of Dürer, the music of Bach, the achievements of Frederick Barbarossa and the semi-barbarian culture which Tacitus found beyond the Rhine when he wrote his *Germania* have all gone to shape German culture. Hitler is only one element in that picture. Let us remember that in the mid-nineteenth century (that is, not very long ago) the image which the rest of the world had of the Germans was that of a pleasant, hopelessly inefficient, mild lot of people with whom one could spend hours talking philosophy and drinking good wine.

Certainly the Germans were no threat to anyone because they were not organised and did not have a unitary state—whereas the people who *had* a powerful state, great armies, and were the terror of the world were the French!—

Urban —one is reminded of Balzac's memorable description of Monsieur Hermann, a German business man (in *The Red Purse*): 'a stout, good-natured German, a man of taste and learning, above all a pipe-smoker who had a broad, handsome German face, with a square, open forehead embellished by a few meagre strands of blond hair. He was typical of the children of that pure and noble Germany, so rich in honourable characters, whose peaceful way of life has never faltered even after seven invasions.'

Seton-Watson This was the world's picture of the German character right up to German unification. Well, our image of Germany has changed in the last hundred years, but the point to remember is that different aspects of national tradition become important at different times in national life. The Germans today are not a bit like the Germans of the Third Reich—nevertheless, Hitler *was* there, and no German can say that Nazism just did not happen.

There are highly discreditable elements in every nation's past—the Scots were, right up to the seventeenth century, a barbarous, savage and murderous race who committed the most appalling crimes against one another as well as their enemies. The creation of the modern French nation by the conquest of the French South from the thirteenth century onwards was one of the most brutal chains of events in recorded history. The armies of the kings of Northern France used methods in comparison with which Bismarck's wars were a governess's teaparty. Yet it would be quite wrong to infer, and nobody does infer, that Scots, or Germans, or Frenchmen are history's natural barbarians or that they possess any other unalterable characteristic—good, bad, or indifferent.

We are, all of us, involuntary legatees of our national

past, and we must be conscious of our national past—but we are not *slaves* to our national past.

Urban You are saying that every nation's past contains a variety of traditions. We lift from it whatever responds best to the requirements of our present condition: there is a Germany of the Teutonic Knights, a Germany of Kant, a Germany of Beethoven, one of Streicher, and so forth. This is a very acceptable view, for it makes it possible, theoretically at least, for every nation that *has* such a reservoir of traditions to conduct its affairs in a civilised, tolerant and libertarian manner. The problem arises with a country like Russia which has in its national repertoire very few and only feeble items of a liberal provenance, while its repertoire of despotism and autocracy is almost identical with Russian history itself. If we accept your view that nations cannot jump clear of the shadow cast by their past, then we must surely take an extremely dim view of what the Soviet Union has in store for the world as well as for its own population.

Seton-Watson I do take a dim view—but perhaps, for the sake of balance, I ought to say a word on the opposite side of the argument before proceeding to say *why* I take such a dim view. There is in the Russian tradition, in Russian Orthodoxy, an important element which speaks of human liberty, of the equality of every soul in the sight of God and therefore deserving respect. In so far as Solzhenitsyn stresses that, he is doing a service. His is, of course, an extremist position, but we must remember that he is writing against a kind of ogre model of the Russian character, and it is right that he should try to restore the balance by drawing on the positive elements, as he sees them, in the Russian past. Even if one does not agree with him, he has a great piece of truth on his side, and the sad thing is that this argument to and fro cannot be publicly conducted inside the Soviet Union.

Urban The essence of Solzhenitsyn's case is that the terrible things that happened in the last sixty years to the Russian people, and to other nations at the hands of the Russian people, are entirely due to an alien ideology—Marxism-Leninism—and not to any inherent shortcomings in the Russian character. The case I have tried to summarise starts from the contrary premise. *Is* the Soviet system more Communist than Russian, or more Russian than Communist?

Seton-Watson It is a bit of both, but, in the final analysis, the incubus of Russianism predominates. One can argue that a residual Marxism-Leninism has been subsumed into a new version of Russian Messianism, or, conversely, that slogans taken from the Russian past and Russian Messianism have been harnessed and subsumed into Marxism-Leninism. I would not deny that Marxism-Leninism has greatly added to the perversion and savagery of the despotism that has ruled Russia since 1917, but I cannot subscribe to the notion that, if it wasn't for Marxism-Leninism, the Russians would be a civilised and happy people among themselves and excellent neighbours. Lots of evidence points the other way.

Urban But isn't there some truth in the view, widespread among the Russian intelligentsia, that Russia has rendered the rest of mankind a unique service by being the first to have suffered the full force of Communism and exposed its fateful inadequacies? This contemporary version of Russian Messianism, the image of a long-suffering people passing through the purifying fire of Communism and doing penance for an uncomprehending West, is a recurrent theme in Solzhenitsyn and figures prominently in Vladimir Maximov's magnificent *The Seven Days of Creation*. It goes side by side with an older and even more far-fetched claim that their long ordeal has made the Russian people the world's natural Christians—keepers of the conscience of the civilised world against materialism and Western degeneracy.

Seton-Watson I don't hold that view. God protect us from the Russians—wherever an acre of land is occupied by Russian soldiers the grass withers.

Let us be fair, though: all of us owe a debt to the Russian soldiers who fought on our side in the last war and did more than anyone else to destroy Hitler. Early in the nineteenth century all of us were in the debt of the Russian armies because they defeated Napoleon.

But what happened after these Russian victories? In 1815 the Russian soldiers went back to become serfs again—in 1945 they went home to become the industrial serfs of Stalin. The liberation of Europe, in which they played so important a part, did not entail their own liberation. This inability of the Russian people to break out of their enslavement even when they have spent millions of lives and years of suffering to defeat another enslavement strikes me as extraordinary. It helps to explain the amoeba-like growth of a small nucleus around the city of Moscow in the fourteenth century into an empire which engulfed more and more territory and spread serfdom and tyranny wherever it went.

Personally I feel the Russian people deserve better than that, but there is a piece of electric wire missing from their political and psychological mechanism—something to connect their admirable private virtues and brilliant intellectual capacity to analyse their situation, with the will to change it. This gap between laying bare the disease from which you suffer and your ability to do something about it seems to me to be different in kind from anything one experiences elsewhere in Europe. And this is why I take a dim view of what Russia may have in store for the rest of the world.

God knows, we have nothing to teach the Russian writers and intellectuals about their own condition. They have thought and written about it with a depth and imagination none of us in the West can match. And undoubtedly Solzhenitsyn, Maximov, Sinyavsky and the other well-known writers and thinkers are only the tip of the iceberg—there must be thousands more who think and write like them but are unknown to us. The tragedy is that they *cannot* make themselves heard.

Urban I often wonder whether this inability of the Russian intelligentsia to assert itself in practical ways is simply an expression of an Oblomov type of sluggishness and ineffectuality, or whether it is a sign of some subconscious wish to *invite* suffering because only the state of being wronged by the world creates the conditions under which the Russian soul can flourish. Solzhenitsyn's refusal to leave Russia always struck me as highly natural—he *needs* his Gulags. How can the electric wire surrounding his home in Vermont compensate for the real thing?

Seton-Watson Maybe so. It is easier for us to go on admiring these fine perversions of the Russian psyche *from a distance*, than to be fair to the Russians when they are sitting on our necks!

Solzhenitsyn's insistence on remaining in Russia doesn't strike me as strange either, but not for the reasons you have given. For any writer to be torn away from the land in which his language is being spoken, and is growing and changing as all languages grow and change, is always a ghastly blow.

Urban We have been saying hard things about Russian nationalism and the growth of the Russian empire. It may be as well to remind ourselves that one of the sternest critics of Russian expansionism was Karl Marx himself. He perceived Pan-Slavism as we perceive Communism—as a vehicle for the spread of Moscow's universal tyranny. Writing in *The New York Tribune* on 12 April 1853, Marx observed:

> It would appear that the natural frontier of Russia runs from Dantzic, or perhaps Stettin, to Trieste. And as sure as conquest follows conquest, and annexation follows annexation, so sure would the conquest of Turkey by Russia be only the prelude for the annexation of Hungary, Prussia, Galicia, and for the ultimate realization of the Slavonic empire which certain panslavistic philosophers have dreamed of.

And to leave us in no doubt about the nature of the disease from which he was anxious to protect Europe, Marx added in 1856: 'The bloody mire of Mongolian slavery, not the rude glory of the Norman epoch, forms the cradle of Muscovy, and modern Russia is but a metamorphosis of Muscovy.'

Would you say that Marx, if he looked at the Soviet empire today, would be a Eurocommunist?

Seton-Watson Marx had a tremendous hostility to all things Russian. He would never give the Russian government the benefit of the doubt. If *I* were writing about the scene in Russia at the time when Marx was, I would be very much kinder to Moscow than Marx managed to be. Marx was repelled by the treatment of Jews in Russia (although his own attitude to the Jewish question was highly ambivalent); he had Polish friends and great sympathy for Poland, and, of course, he shared the view of the European

Left of his time that Russia was the most monstrous dictatorship of his day which must be destroyed.

Today, Marx might well be a Eurocommunist, and perhaps he would be no Communist at all. If he were allowed to make a trip around the Soviet empire for a few months and see what has been done there in his name he would come back horrified. He would, if he thought the Soviet system was worth redeeming, apply his theory to the analysis of the Soviet system, and I am sure that an analysis of Soviet society done *by Marx himself* would be something worth having! Nothing that contemporary Marxists have written about the Soviet empire, not even the work of that heroic German heretic Rudolf Bahro, whom I would call the Martin Luther of Communism, could equal the devastating strictures of a critique of 'existing socialism' by Marx himself.

Urban You said Marx never gave the Russian government the benefit of the doubt. I think he and Engels went further than that—they never gave the Russian *nation* and the Russian *character* the benefit of the doubt either. Time and again Marx warned, in really most un-Marxist, and indeed anti-Marxist, fashion that Russian politics are guided by a 'traditional identity', that 'they bear the stamp of the quotation from known pages of [Russian] history', and so on.

In other words, whatever he may have said in his theoretical writings, in his utterances as a journalist and commentator on contemporary history, Marx acted very much in consonance with your observation: 'Nations cannot escape their history, and individuals cannot opt out of their nations.' This involved him and Engels in the arrogant dismissal of Croats and Bulgars as 'well-nigh nomadic barbarians'; of South Slavs as 'national refuse'; of Rumanians and Transylvanian Saxons as 'decayed nations, entirely lacking in active historical forces'; of Slovaks as 'lethargic in character', 'never had a history'; and even of Czechs as 'wielders of the pen', 'continuously in the tow of the German Reich'.

Seton-Watson We must be fair to Marx—it is true enough that his and Engels's contemptuous dismissal of the Slavic nations (the Poles were the only exception) was honeycombed with prejudice. But their reason for doing so was their concern to promote the cause of revolution, using as their weapon the nationalism of those Central European nations which were (as they thought) advanced enough to make revolutions—Poles, Austrian Germans and Hungarians. In so far as Slovaks, Rumanians, Croats and Czechs presented obstacles to Hungarian and Polish national ambitions, they appeared to Marx and Engels to be reactionary forces and therefore not deserving to survive. 'The chief mission of all the other great and small nationalities and peoples,' Engels wrote of the Slovaks, Rumanians, Serbs, Ruthenians and Croats, 'is to perish in the universal revolutionary storm.' But these are arguments not from history, as you suggest, but from ignorance of history.

Where does all this leave us? Marx and Engels got the character of the emerging Slavic (and Rumanian) nations substantially wrong—partly because they were ignorant, partly because they had an axe to grind. Their analysis of Russian history and of the Russian national character was more profound, and to the extent that Marx recognised the vicious continuity of Russian expansionism from Sviatislav, the yet pagan Grand Duke of Russia in the eighth century, to Nicholas I in the nineteenth century (both having threatened Constantinople), he deserves our respect, especially as this recognition was in doubtful harmony with his theory of history.

A look at Soviet-Russian imperialism in 1978 would convince Marx and Engels that the continuity in Russian history is unbroken; only the power of the *Soviet*-Russian empire to spread 'Mongolian slavery' is infinitely greater than anything they had reason to fear in their own time.

Urban History has its ironies—on 18 June 1848 Engels wrote an eloquent article on 'The Prague Rising', and on 13 January 1849 another on 'The Magyar Struggle'—

Seton-Watson Yes—if Marx and Engels were alive today they could bring those articles up to date and appeal to the world's proletariat to rise against the reactionary dictatorship of Moscow.

Notes on Contributors

Manuel Azcárate is the International Secretary of the Central Committee of the Spanish Communist Party and the editor of the Party theoretical journal *Nuestra Bandera*.

Jacob D. Beam was US Ambassador to Poland (1957–61), Czechoslovakia (1966–9) and the Soviet Union (1969–73). He is the author of *Multiple Exposure*.

Eduard Goldstücker was President of the Czechoslovak Writers' Union in 1968 and Pro-Rector of Charles University (1966–8) as well as Head of the Department of Germanic Studies and Professor of German Literature. His earlier appointments included Deputy Ambassador to the UK, Ambassador to Israel, and Minister-designate to Sweden. He joined the Communist Party in 1933 and was imprisoned between 1951 and 1955.

Antonin J. Liehm is Professor of Comparative Literature at the University of Pennsylvania and a former political editor of the Prague journal *Literarni Listy*. He published *The Politics of Culture* (with an introduction by Jean Paul Sartre).

Vladimir Maximov was until 1967 the editor of the Soviet journal *October*. In 1973 he was expelled from the Soviet Writers' Union and in 1974 permitted to visit France and then deprived of Soviet citizenship. He is now the editor of *Kontinent*. His publications include *The Seven Days of Creation*, *The Quarantine* and *Farewell from Nowhere*.

Zdenek Mlynar was the Secretary of the Central Committee of the Czechoslovak Communist Party in 1968 and a member of the Czech delegation which signed the 1968 Moscow Protocols. He published his memoirs under the title of *Nachtfrost*.

Claiborne Pell is US Senator for Rhode Island and a member of the Senate Foreign Relations Committee. He was an American Foreign Service officer in Prague and Bratislava between 1946 and 1948. He has published *Megalopolis Unbound* (with Harold L. Goodwin), *Challenge of the Seven Seas*, and *Power and Policy*.

Eugene V. Rostow is Professor of International Law at Yale University and Executive Chairman of the Committee on the Present Danger. He was Undersecretary of State in the Johnson Administration (1966–9) with special responsibility for political affairs. He has written *Planning for Freedom; The Sovereign Prerogative; Law, Power and the Pursuit of Peace* and *Peace in the Balance*.

Hugh Seton-Watson is Professor of Russian History, School of Slavonic and East European Studies, University of London. His publications include *The East European Revolution, Neither War nor Peace, The Russian Empire 1801–1917* and *Nations and States*.

Ota Sik was Director of the Economic Institute of the Czechoslovak Academy of Sciences and a member of the Central Committee of the Czechoslovak Communist Party. In 1968 he was a Deputy Prime Minister. He is now Professor of Economics at the University of St-Gallen.

G. R. Urban is a writer on contemporary history, a former Senior Research Associate of the University of Southern California and Research Fellow at Indiana University. He has written *Kinesis and Stasis* and *The Nineteen Days* and is the editor and co-author of *Can We Survive our Future?, Toynbee on Toynbee, Détente, Hazards of Learning* and *Eurocommunism*.

Index